Now Go
Forward

Now Go Forward

Reaching Out to Grow Your Congregation

J. DAVID ESHLEMAN

Herald Press

Scottdale, Pennsylvania
Waterloo, Ontario

Library of Congress Cataloging-in-Publication Data

Eshleman, J. David, 1936-
  Now go forward : reaching out to grow your congregation / J. David
Eshleman.
    p. cm.
  Includes bibliographical references (p.   ).
  ISBN 978-0-8361-9445-6 (pbk. : alk. paper)
  1. Church growth. 2. Capital Christian Fellowship (Lanham, Md.) I. Title.
  BV652.25.E84 2009
  254'.5–dc22

                                                              2008039904

NOW GO FORWARD
Copyright © 2009 by Herald Press, Scottdale, Pa. 15683
  Published simultaneously in Canada by Herald Press,
  Waterloo, Ont. N2L 6H7. All rights reserved
International Standard Book Number: 978-0-8361-9445-6
Library of Congress Catalog Card Number: 2008039904
Printed in the United States of America
Book design by Joshua Byler
Cover by Sans Serif

14 13 12 11 10 09   10 9 8 7 6 5 4 3 2 1

To order or request information please call 1-800-245-7894
or visit www.heraldpress.com.

*To my wife, Helen, without whose loving support
this book could not have been written.
Her faithfulness in standing by me and generosity with her gifts
of teaching, encouragement, and intercessory prayer
have greatly enhanced my ministry.*

Contents

Preface

One of the great mysteries of life is that God chooses us for his work. From my childhood, I had a desire to serve him. Why would he choose me? I was a stuttering, insecure kid from a sheltered home and a conservative Mennonite congregation in Lancaster County, Pennsylvania. But God is the hound of heaven, constantly calling, loving, persistently urging us to fulfill the great commission.

My favorite Bible verse is Ephesians 2:6: "And God raised us up with Christ and seated us with him in the heavenly realms in Christ Jesus." I cannot comprehend even a small percentage of its meaning. I am honored and blessed that God called me to work with him, but I will never comprehend his marvelous grace.

According to Ephesians 1:18-22, God raised Jesus to his position in the heavenly realms, which is a place above all the problems we could ever imagine. We are seated with God's Son, Jesus, in the seat of victory. Do you think of yourself in this way, as God's coworker?

A rather unusual aspect of my fifty years pastoring growing congregations is the variety of churches I have served. After three years a student pastor in seminary, I first served two traditional rural Mennonite congregations, one in Ohio and one in Illinois. Then I served ten years in an urban congregation, Northside Mennonite Church in Lima, Ohio. I jokingly tell people that's where I got my education. Lima at that time was an industrial city laden with social problems, and was frequently referred to as "Little Chicago."

Then the Lord called me to serve as church planter in Elyria,

Ohio, west of Cleveland. My next church plant was in North Port, Florida, near the Gulf Coast south of Sarasota. The first began with two families; the second with three families. My sixth and final pastorate was a revitalization project just east of Washington, D.C., at a small one-room family church known as Cottage City Mennonite Church. Within ten months of my arrival in 1994, we renamed it Capital Christian Fellowship. The church moved ten miles northeast to a college auditorium in Laurel, Maryland, and then into a twenty-six thousand square-foot facility in Lanham. I will touch on the story of this church throughout this book. Since 2007 I have been employed as a church consultant and on the ministry staff at Lancaster Mennonite Conference in conjunction with Eastern Mennonite Missions, and I have served as interim bishop in the conference.

My passion is serving the Lord by helping congregations that have plateaued or are in decline to reach their communities for Christ. The church growth movement influenced my pastoral ministry. In more recent years the terminology has changed from "church growth" to "church health," with a focus on being missional. Many today are unfairly critical of the church growth movement, characterizing it as focusing mainly on numbers. But by also being missional, the church growth movement puts an emphasis on God's people being missionaries, penetrating the community for Christ, rather than only focusing on bringing unchurched people inside the four walls of the church building.

Mission is not a separate department of the church; it is the driving force of the church. When we leave the building, we engage the culture with the love and passion of our Lord. Chad Hall writes: "A missional church lives out the church's three-dimensional calling: to be upwardly focused on God in worship that is passionate; to be inwardly focused on community among believers that is demonstrated in relationships of love and compassion; and to be outwardly focused on a world that does not yet know God."[1]

This is a healthy corrective. Before the term *missional* was in vogue, I worked intentionally with people in the community, in addition to making disciples in the gathered body of believers. In more recent years we related to postmodern youth as well.

In Acts 2:18-21, the Spirit was given to all believers. That was a tremendous breakthrough. Christians had an effect on the Roman Empire itself. In the third century, Satan came up with his ingenious plan to sidetrack the church with the development of the state church, introducing a barrier between clergy and laity and causing the church to be become weak and anemic. Then, with the invention of the printing press in the fifteenth century and the Protestant Reformation in the sixteenth, Christians were able to read the Bible for themselves. In the twentieth century, Christians woke up to the fact that the clergy could not do the ministry alone.

I believe that in the twenty-first century, we are in a new day. Many Christians are beginning to realize that to be missional, we need to live out the gospel and share the Good News. To be missional, we take responsibility not just for the internal life of the church but also for bringing God's kingdom to a needy world. That's a critical move in the right direction. We are never closer to God than when we are involved with his mission. Jesus was the greatest missionary, and as he was sent, so he sends us.

The emphasis of this book is not primarily the growth of your congregation or the church gathered; it is to make disciples who are set out to extend God's kingdom in our local community.

With this book, I hope to encourage discouraged congregations. I hope to shed light on why nearly 85 percent of churches in the United States are not growing. I hope to help churches that desire a turnaround from decline to growth so they can draw their communities to the kingdom.

I am a practitioner, not a theoretician. My prayer is for God to use these pages to encourage and motivate pastors, church leaders, and congregations in their desire to extend the reign of the Lord Jesus into their communities. May this effort help our churches turn from an inward to an outward focus. It will be a great day when Christians move from doing church work to doing the work of the church.

I am grateful to many people who assisted with this project. Our son, Chet Miller-Eshleman, who returned from mission work in Colombia and is now a church planter, gave many helpful insights and additions. Others assisted with revision and proofreading: Noah Kaye, Lewis and Helen Good, John and Alice Lapp, Nita Landis, Conrad Kanagy, and Eldon King. I thank my life group and Sunday school class from Lititz Mennonite Church for their helpful suggestions. I also thank the hundreds of diverse families, singles, and youth I have had the privilege of pastoring. Without these many years of pastoral ministry, this book could not have been written. Most of all I am greatly indebted to my wife, Helen, for her persistent prayer ministry for this work, her time and efforts in proofreading, her timely corrections, and for tolerating the many hours when I closed myself off in the study.

Thanks to Michael Degan, book editor for Herald Press, who did an outstanding job on my manuscript.

For the most part, the names of persons in the illustrations have been changed to protect their identity.

You'll find the material adapts well to Sunday school classes, leadership teams, small group study, or individual study. It speaks more directly to congregations from sixty to five hundred.

Jesus said, "I will build my church." Above all, I thank Jesus. I present this work to him as an offering to be used for his glory.

Dave Eshleman
February 2009

Introduction

I believe most Christians and their churches have bought into the lie that the world does not want to hear the Good News of Jesus Christ. As a result, they have lost their passion to share it, and so often keep their mouths shut.

When it comes to sharing the Good News, Christians in general are "neither cold nor hot" but lukewarm (see Revelation 3:15-16). Many people would rather have a root canal than share their faith with friends. No wonder most churches are declining.

The reality for thousands of churches is this: unless they discover the passion of God and move from lukewarm to hot, they will become extinct. Most churches have become irrelevant to younger generations and to their communities. Would the younger generation in our communities miss us if we closed our doors? Would anyone besides regular attendees miss the churches?

Our churches are focused on keeping the reached rather than reaching the lost. We are focused on keeping the ones we already have happy when we should be discipling them and sending them out into the harvest field. How often do you hear people even noticing that no one new is showing up?

At the core of my being, I believe the local church is the hope of the world. It not only addresses every need, but it leads people into God's way of living; by doing so, it transforms communities.

The future belongs not to the government, military, or even the Red Cross. The future belongs to Christ and to his church. Don't even bother to look elsewhere. As Bill Hybels says,

Its potential is unlimited. It comforts the grieving and heals the broken in the context of community. It builds bridges to seekers and offers truth to the confused. It provides resources for those in need and opens its arms to the forgotten, the downtrodden, and the disillusioned. It breaks the chains of addictions, frees the oppressed and offers belonging to the marginalized of this world. Whatever the capacity for human suffering, the church has a greater capacity for healing and wholeness.[1]

Impacting our communities for God's kingdom is God's will. It is God's work, but he has chosen you and me as his instruments. Paul writes,

I planted the seed, Apollos watered it, but God made it grow. So neither he who plants nor he who waters is anything, but only God, who makes things grow. The man who plants and the man who waters have one purpose, and each will be rewarded according to his own labor. For we are God's fellow workers; you are God's field, God's building. By the grace God has given me, I laid a foundation as an expert builder, and someone else is building on it. But each one should be careful how he builds. For no one can lay any foundation other than the one already laid, which is Jesus Christ. (1 Corinthians 3:6-10)

If we change our focus from navel-gazing to loving our unchurched neighbors with the compassion of our Lord, God can change our churches into vibrant, enthusiastic, articulate communities of faith. I invite you on a joyful search for God's direction in reaching our communities for Christ.

Dwelling in the Word

At the beginning of each chapter of this book, I have placed a brief section called Dwelling in the Word. If you are reading this book alone, I encourage you to read the suggested Scripture and meditate on your thoughts and questions.

If you are in a group setting, have someone read the suggested verses. Then have each participant find another person he or she does not know intimately. In two minutes or so, share with each other any thoughts or questions the Scripture brought to mind. Listen closely to each other. The leader may ask a few persons to share with the group what their partner shared with them.

This exercise can help us to become good listeners and to train us to hear what the Spirit is saying through our brothers or sisters. Too often problems in our churches are the result of poor communication. Using the Dwelling in the Word exercise forces us to verbalize what someone else said they heard from the Scripture, encouraging us to listen carefully to others. When we improve communication, we help people feel understood. This builds bridges, aiding love and unity to begin taking shape. This exercise may bring life from God's living Word to our sometimes lifeless meetings. Dwelling in the Word should be followed by a period of prayer.

I am indebted to Church Innovations of St. Paul, Minnesota, for introducing this approach to the study of Scripture.[2] So often we read a few verses at the beginning of our meetings and then lay the Bible aside. Dwelling in the Word is a sincere effort to bring the Word to bear on our context.

Following the Dwelling in the Word exercise, I include a brief testimony about someone who found new life in Christ in one of the churches I pastored. If I were to begin my ministry again, I would have people share their testimonies more frequently. Testimonies speak to both the unchurched as well as the churched. In as little as three to five minutes, people can tell what their lives were like before they met Jesus, how they met Jesus, and how God is working in their lives today.

1

The Mission Field is Here

Dwelling in the Word: Read Luke 10:1-12, 17-20.

Testimony

After my first pastoral visit with Jim, I wasn't sure I wanted him at our church. I don't ever recall feeling that way about another person. Jim's anger was so deep that it bordered on rage. His neighbors had accused him of sexual improprieties, and he was so focused on getting revenge for the accusations that he was contemplating murder. I wondered if I should call the police. I expected to open tomorrow's newspaper and read that he was in jail.

Amazingly, Jim came to church week after week. The change in him was gradual but quite obvious to me. He became a new creation in Christ. His hatred turned to love, and he surprised me with his gift of reaching out to persons in need of a loving touch. What a miracle! Thank you Jesus!

~

Pastoring a growing, ethnically diverse congregation takes lots of energy. After I turned sixty-five, various people began urging me to consider work as a church consultant. At the same time, I was asked to serve as bishop of our Washington/Baltimore District of Lancaster Mennonite Conference. To think of serving as a consultant and bishop seemed presumptuous. After praying and recognizing that my energy level is not what it was when I was younger, I approached our conference leadership about the possibility of serving as church consultant. They encouraged me to pursue this ministry. It wasn't more than a few months into this work that the Lord seemed to be nudging me to begin writing this book. While I know my primary gift is not writing, I was amazed at the daily guidance of the Holy Spirit.

This book is about congregational revitalization, and my experience at Capital Christian Fellowship (CCF) serves as a prime model of how it can work. But before I relate that experience, I believe it will be helpful to set forth some assumptions about how congregations become revitalized.

Helping a Church Reach Its Community

Christians approach church revitalization and the church's mission in the world quite differently. Some in the more conservative Mennonite tradition say, "We are to separate ourselves from the world, to be *the quiet in the land*. We must protect ourselves from the evil world. We must take our children out of the public schools and place them in Christian schools or home schools." Some even believe they should keep people busy at church so they don't have time for involvement in the secular world.

On the other hand, others say, "We must be the leaven, the light, and the salt of the world. We should come out of our salt shakers and penetrate the world. We should connect with the unchurched and share the Good News of Jesus Christ, bringing light and life to the darkness in our society and pushing back the evil."

We are in the world but not of the world. Jesus prayed, "Father, I don't ask you to take my followers out of the world, but keep them safe from the evil one" (John 17:15 CEV). Jesus also said, "Two men will be in the same field, but only one will be taken. The other will be left. Two women will be together grinding grain, but only one will be taken. The other will be left" (Matthew 24:40-41 CEV). These verses make it clear that the saved and the unsaved will be working side by side when he returns.

Assumptions about the Church and Its Mission

1. Jesus wants his church to be a missional church. If a church is not making an impact on the community, it needs to seek God's wisdom to understand what is keeping it from growing and being missional. God expects us to be both faithful and fruitful. Churches dare not settle into a survival mode; instead, they must be assertive in presenting the Good News in both word and deed as Jesus commands. Before plateaued and declining churches can become missional, they must recognize where they need help and be willing to receive that help. Many churches in growing communities are declining but claim to be healthy. Many haven't baptized a new adult believer for years. (See Matthew 25:31-46; Luke 5:33-39; John 15:8; Acts 2:47; Acts 8:4; Colossians 1:6; and 2 Peter 3:9.)

2. No one, not even God, will turn a church around if it is not open to change. Our culture is constantly changing. Many people will hold five different jobs in the fifteen years following graduation from high school or college. Twenty percent of our population moves each year. We are in a changing world, and the church needs to be open to change if it is to be effective.

3. Growth needs to be focused on the unchurched, not growth in people from other churches. Too often churches grow at the expense of other churches. Instead of shuffling sheep from one pen to another, let's find the lost sheep that are not in the fold of Christ and bring them into God's family (see Luke 15:4-7). It's more appropriate for worship leaders to welcome visitors from other churches and to send greetings to their home churches than to encourage those visitors to remain in the worship leader's church. This promotes church unity, which is of prime importance to our Lord (see John 17).

4. The missional church needs to focus outwardly and on the

future; it is vision-driven. Sometimes a driver needs to look in his or her rearview mirror, but most of the time the driver's eyes must be on the road ahead. Discover the needs of the people in your community, and then seek God's wisdom and strength to meet those needs. The average church gives more effort to programs for those already attending than to fulfilling their biblical mission. We can meet the needs of people in our communities with the Good News when the gospel is expressed in both word and deed; people of the world need to hear the gospel and see it in action (see Matthew 25:31-46; Luke 4:18-19; Acts 8:4; and Acts 10:38).

5. Jesus wants us to reach our neighbors at home, not just those abroad. Most church people are more excited about going on mission trips to other countries than witnessing to their neighbors a few miles away. Someone once said, "A missionary is not someone who crosses the seas; a missionary is someone who sees the cross." Mennonite denominations, like other Christian denominations, have been successful in foreign missions but have struggled here at home. Lancaster Mennonite Conference, for example, has approximately sixteen thousand members in the United States but a quarter of a million members abroad. Jesus said we are to witness first to Jerusalem—that is, at home (see Acts 1:8).

6. In our culture, our neighbors are often our peers at work or school as well as those who live near us. Most people spend far more time with co-workers than with their next-door neighbors. The longer we are Christians, the fewer friends we have who are not Christians. Even though we may work or study alongside non-Christians, we generally tend not to befriend them or pray regularly for them. This must change. We must take Christ into the workplace, the classroom, or wherever we go. If we aren't touching others with the gospel, we should wonder if Jesus is really alive in our hearts.

7. We are to invite men and women of all races, classes, ages, and cultures into the local church of Jesus Christ. Revelation 7:9 reminds us that people from every nation will be in heaven. Jesus taught us to pray for his kingdom to come on earth as it is in

heaven. It is not right that Sunday morning is still the most seg-regated hour of the week. (See also Matthew 28:18-20; Revelation 5:9; and Revelation 14:6.)

8. Jesus has given us authority to witness for him and to over-come the evil one: "As the Father has sent me, I am sending you" (John 20:21). It seems clear from this verse that God sends us under the same circumstances and with the same authority and resources as Jesus. God does not set any arbitrary limits to the church's use of divine resources. He has made available all that he is to a believing church, "one blessing after another" (John 1:16). As Paul Billheimer writes:

> God has given us the keys of the kingdom of heaven, but he does not compel us to use them. He waits. The rest is up to us, his church. In his triumph over Satan he has given us the needed weapons. How well we use them is our responsibility and may well determine our rank in the Bridehood.[1]

9. We need to grow disciples, not just programs. God does not bless programs; he blesses people. Many American Christians never intend to become disciples. They expect the church experience will improve them rather than change them. They come to church to receive grace and are unaware that they receive grace in order to extend grace (see Matthew 18:23-35). Discipleship requires a lot of time and work. Jesus began with people where they were and moved them to maturity, sending them into the world to extend God's reign (see John 17:18 and Ephesians 4:12-15).

10. God's mission isn't to make people more religious! His mission is much bigger than that. We are called to take the initia-tive in sharing the gospel. We are not to be passive or aggressive but assertive. We are not a vendor of religious services and goods; we are people sent on a mission. We need to see everyone as a potential child of God, a potential member of God's kingdom. The presence of a U-Haul in our neighborhood should excite us as an opportunity to invite the new neighbors to our church. We need to believe that God is already at work in the lives of every-

one to whom we witness. We work *with* God, not for God. The church doesn't exist primarily for us. We are the church, the body of Christ, and we exist for the world (see Luke 14:23; John 3:16; Acts 4:13, 29, 31; and 2 Peter 3:9).

11. It takes more than prayer and dedication to Jesus and the Word of God to make a church grow; it takes skill, sacrifice, and effort. Multitudes of churches have dedication, but they are not missional. We must learn to build intentional relationships with people who are "pre-Christian." One-on-one interaction has always been the most effective approach in reaching people for Jesus and extending God's reign. When Christians are experiencing God's transforming power in their own lives, they will embrace the one-on-one approach.

12. I reject remnant theology, which implies if you are faithful you will be small. Some Christians believe that any Christian ministry that is large is suspect. I find no indication in Scripture that small is better or big is inferior (see Acts 2:41; 4:4). If one person is worth more than the whole world, then numbers are important. Numbers represent people. Remember that Moses, who was more humble than anyone on earth, led two million people (see Numbers 12:3). Having said that, however, we should remember that we are commanded to make disciples, not just church members (see Matthew 28:18-20).

Assumptions Concerning Congregational Revitalization

Some claim that church revitalization necessarily begins with personal revitalization. Who can argue with that assumption? It's safe to say that a church can't experience new life unless its people have new life. If people are overflowing with rivers of living water (see John 7:37-39), doing greater works than Jesus did (see John 14:12), reigning with Christ in heavenly places (see Ephesians 2:6), and living in the reality of God's mighty power within, then they can accomplish infinitely more than they would ever dare to ask or imagine (see Ephesians 3:20). Our churches will be revived. But most Christians—myself included—don't live up to that level, so we also need to challenge the congregation. Personal revitalization and church revitalization go together.

From this starting point, I bring the following assumptions about discovering God's preferred future for a congregation.

1. Realism is necessary. Unless a congregation honestly faces its situation, it will eventually die (see 2 Corinthians 13:5; Galatians 1:6-9; and Revelation 2–3).

2. The congregation must have a biblical foundation, but it needs to be a bridge to the culture. The message must never change, but the methods used to deliver it must change so that a church can reach its community. When a congregation no longer reaches people, it is being unfaithful to Christ (see 1 Corinthians 9:19-27). Many times a church can do the same things it has always done but with small changes. Our society is increasingly pluralistic, and absolute truth is highly suspect. As we come to terms with this reality, we see that traditional religiosity too often becomes an enemy of the gospel.

3. Congregations must offer earnest prayer for the Holy Spirit's guidance and leading. Jesus was a man of prayer and is our model. If we learn to listen to the Lord, he will reveal the preferred future for our particular congregation. This future is unique for each local church. We can learn from other growing churches and ministries, but we need to realize every context is different and that each congregation has its unique mission.

4. A healthy congregation is committed to growing mature disciples, not merely making people comfortable. Healthy congregations also have a simple process for making disciples, a process visualized and understood not only by the leadership but by the members. Complexity is confusing; simplicity is better. Spiritual growth is intentional, not accidental or automatic. Mushrooms grow overnight, while oak trees take sixty years. Christian growth is caught more than taught. Discipleship takes time.

5. Congregations must learn to help each other. Often a struggling congregation is too proud to learn from a growing church just around the corner. We must humble ourselves and learn from

others, not to duplicate another church but to integrate aspects of their ministry that may work in our context. We can explore ways to partner with each other in reaching out to minister in our community. We can learn to work hand-in-hand with those with whom we don't see eye-to-eye. We may not agree in every detail of doctrine, but we can love each other and work together. Our bias needs to be in the direction of cooperation.

6. The pastor needs to provide the vision for the church. Working in conjunction with the leadership team, the pastor not only knows the way but shows the way. The leadership team needs to acquire a shared perspective with the pastor so everyone knows the vision and direction of the congregation.

Often, especially in small congregations, the real leaders of the congregation are not on the official leadership team. In this situation, the "official" leaders need to relate to the "unofficial" ones to be sure they are amenable to the vision. Otherwise the vision will fail.

The pastor models the vision, which needs to be implemented through teamwork. People are more aware of what the pastor does than what he or she says. Relationships and passion are more important than words in communicating a vision.

7. The leadership team must also be dedicated and passionate about the need for the congregation to be missional. In many churches the usual pattern is that the leadership team meets monthly. I contend that *this monthly pattern will not result in a missional church.* If the church is serious about being missional, the leaders will meet more frequently to pray and hear from God, as well as to develop strategies to carry out their mission into "Jerusalem" and beyond. Our culture is quite different than the culture described in Acts 2, which says of the early church, "Every day they continued to meet together" (Acts 2:46). But if they met daily, how often should we meet?

8. It is helpful when the leadership core lives in the community God has called them to reach. While there may be exceptions, our witness will be more effective if we live with the people we are

sent to reach. Jesus left heaven and lived among us. Someone has wisely said, "You will not mature until you allow the Lord to plant you somewhere." Wherever I have been planted as a pastor, Helen and I have called that place home.

9. Jesus blessed the children, but he worked with adults. There are situations in which children have brought the adults to Christ, but those situations are few. The typical congregation does better when it ministers to adults, who usually will turn and minister to their children.

10. The church is not so much a collection of individuals each finding self-fulfillment; rather, it is a community witnessing to the power and reign of Christ. Listening to one another will help us listen to God, and listening to God will help us listen to one another. As the church, we are the body of Christ; as Christ's body, we do his work.

11. We need to be people of faith, but faith is often spelled R-I-S-K. A congregation that does not change because "we never did it that way before" is a dying church.

12. Pray to find people who are open to God's peace (see Luke 10:6). Pray for the Lord to help you find the people who have influence in your community. Once they come to Christ, they will bring their families, friends, and peers to Christ, or at least try to (see Luke 8:38-39; John 4:39-42).

13. The New Testament churches were messy. The apostle Paul planted the church in Thessalonica in three weeks, but the people didn't become mature believers in three weeks. In all his letters, Paul instructed his readers to lay aside the sins of the flesh. When we bring new people into our fellowships, it adds to the messiness (see 2 Corinthians 12:20-21).

14. If we are to reach the community near our church building, a facility on par with or a notch above the average house is almost a must. A church plant can begin in a rented facility that is not attractive as long as energy, vision, and anticipation are so evident in the new congregation that it overrides appearances. There are signs that the house church movement may be reviving,

but until that blossoms, church plants need inviting facilities if they are to reach families in new housing developments.

15. I believe a church is not really planted until it has indigenous leadership. We have learned in foreign mission work that the church does not cultivate deep roots until indigenous leaders lead the church. We must apply the same principle to church plants in North America.

16. Don't neglect to empower the evangelists in your congregation. The Ethiopian church calls evangelists before they call pastors. We in the West can learn from them. Every person may not be gifted as an evangelist, but all believers are commanded to be witnesses.

17. Missional churches rely on their members to do evangelism, but they also allocate above-average amounts of money for missional activities. Missionaries often report that their greatest struggles are with each other; in the same vein, the greatest difficulties in missional churches may involve arguments over the church's budget. One cause of this may be the makeup of the leadership. If everyone on the leadership team has been in the congregation for more than three or four years, or if there are no young men or women on the team, the leadership structure of the congregation needs some new blood.

The High Cost of Revitalization

A congregation that wishes to reverse its decline needs to make a commitment greater than any in its corporate history. In 1994 I challenged the people of Cottage City Mennonite Church to a commitment greater than any they've made since accepting Christ or getting married. God blessed their commitment beyond their wildest imagination, as Scripture promises. "But the seed planted in the good earth represents those who hear the Word, embrace it, and produce a harvest beyond their wildest dreams" (Mark 4:20 Msg).

A congregation that wants to revitalize needs to make significant commitments in several areas:

1. Its vision must be external as well as internal. In a missional congregation, God's mission permeates everything. Worship, small groups, even social activities are all focused on training disciples who will then mentor and train others. There is no disparity between outreach and congregational life. All in the church see themselves as missionaries sent to where they live and work.

2. The staff will pay a price to see their church reach prebelievers and disciple others for Jesus. For most pastors, there will be a noticeable difference in their job description and schedule. The staff will need key lay volunteers.

3. Spiritual commitment will be needed especially in the areas of prayer, the spiritual disciplines, and dependence on the Holy Spirit. Too often the focus of prayer is for a church's latest building project rather than for those who don't know Jesus.

4. Time and energy is required for obedience to the great commission. To give priority to God's kingdom work, Jesus and his kingdom must be our life! "And he will give you all you need from day to day if you live for him and make the Kingdom of God your primary concern" (Matthew 6:33 NLT).

5. The budget speaks clearly about a church's vision. A congregation committed to revitalization needs to give a sizeable portion of its finances to meeting needs in the local community and international missions.

6. Our evangelism and our understanding of salvation need to move beyond conversion, as important as it is, to the making of disciples. Conversion is certainly the first step, but to grow vital churches we need to "make disciples," as Jesus commands (Matthew 28:19). We work to help new believers understand that a Christian follows Christ in daily life.

7. In a North American context, church facilities need to communicate that this congregation has a vision. An up-to-date church sign is important.

8. A traditional church name can be a stumbling block. A contemporary name may open the door to your neighborhood. Denominational names can often be limiting.

The changes from maintenance to missional will be so great that some longtime members may say, "It doesn't seem like our church anymore." Only God can turn a church from maintenance to one that is missional. He is a miracle-working God! Jesus loved the church so much that he died for it; the gates of hell will not overcome it. He is on our side. We are on his winning team. Hallelujah!

Capital Christian Fellowship

There are moments when God says, "It is time for transition." After nearly twelve years as lead pastor at CCF in Lanham, Maryland, God told me it was such a time. I was past retirement age, and the congregation had younger leadership in place. On our final Sunday, it was an overwhelming joy for me and Helen to stand before the more than four hundred people of many nationalities and denominational backgrounds. Helen had once considered serving in foreign missions. Now she was thanking God for bringing the international community to our door. The mission field was here!

A dozen years before, the congregation consisted of twenty-five adults and about a dozen younger people at what was then called Cottage City Mennonite Church. Its small church building was located one mile northeast of Washington, D.C., and had been founded in the 1920s. I prayed, sought counsel, and prayed some more before knowing this is where the Lord wanted us. I arrived as pastor in August 1994, after receiving the call to revitalize this highly committed yet declining church.

The congregation sent *Together*, an inspirational magazine that also seeks to attract new families to the church, to two thousand homes in the area. In the first issue after I arrived, I offered six options to readers and asked them to respond. The choices were: a Bible study on Wednesday evenings, a Bible study especially designed for the local Filipino community, a financial management course, marriage enrichment, or anger management. Finally, there was a place to indicate that the family wanted to receive a Thanksgiving basket, an existing tradition in the congregation. More than thirty indicated they wanted a Thanksgiving basket. None of the other choices were checked.

As we delivered the baskets to the families, many people were amenable and grateful. I made a serious effort to relate to many families and found that they respected Cottage City Mennonite Church. But they had no intention of coming. It was obvious to me there were cultural and racial differences, and I sensed a disconnect.

Later, over coffee, I asked different members of the church if they would invite any of their friends to attend church. Many said they would, but their actions and body language spoke otherwise. One leader in the congregation said he would invite his peers, but I was not convinced. Others said they would invite their Mennonite friends but likely not the others. With those kinds of responses, how could this congregation grow?

Growing CCF

One solution was to move to a new location. But would that be possible after nearly sixty years in the present building? Did it mean we were abandoning the local community? The church owned houses on either side of the church building. One of the houses was used for an after-school program and ministry to the children of the community. The other house was rented to a family active in both our church and in the community. What about them?

Over the years, I had observed dozens of congregations move from the inner city to the suburbs and grow into large prosperous congregations. I always felt that such a move was a cop-out and doubted that Jesus would move away from the needy people in the inner city to prosperous suburbia. But after many nights of prayer, and after confessing my judgmental spirit concerning other churches that made this move, the Lord seemed to say that we should seriously consider moving as an option.

So after four months at Cottage City Mennonite, I presented the elders with three options for the future of the church: (1) stay here and die, (2) stay here and become integral to the community, or (3) move to a new location. I had written a three-page paper outlining these options, and one influential person told me after reading it, "Don't let anyone see this." I ignored this advice and began visiting members in their homes to present and discuss the three options.

Looking back at those years, I marvel at the Holy Spirit's leading and answers to prayer. At my very first home visit, which I made on New Year's night in 1995, I outlined the option to move and waited nervously for a response. A college-aged young man immediately responded, "That's exactly what I've been telling my parents. We need to move to a new location." He'll never know how that encouraged me.

I had earlier received permission from the leadership team to participate in a discernment seminar through Eastern Mennonite Missions (EMM). I returned from it with renewed energy and hope. Later EMM agreed to provide us with a congregational subsidy so I could go from an 80 percent salary to full-time pay, with the understanding that a coach would walk with me. I met with the coach monthly for prayer, accountability concerning my personal life, and discussions about church vision and strategy, especially in the areas of worship, outreach, and small groups.

Another stipulation from the coach was that I have a team of intercessors. I have sent monthly prayer letters to this team ever since, and the team has grown from a dozen to about a hundred people and families. This coaching and the intercessors were vital to helping Cottage City Mennonite Church become a healthy missional congregation. Members and attendees are also sent frequent praises and prayer requests via email, a practice that has helped bind the congregation together in love and unity.

On April 1, 1995, the adults voted unanimously to move to a new location. We had no idea where that would be. As I searched for locations in the Washington, D.C., beltway area, I was amazed to discover many other church plants taking place in the region.

The Cedar Ridge congregation pastored by Brian McLaren, an

author who is considered a leader in the emergent church movement, had just moved out of the Capital College auditorium in
Laurel, Maryland. One of our members was a graduate of the college and contacted the school for us. The Lord opened this door,
and we moved there in June 1995. Imagine fifty or sixty people
meeting in a college auditorium that seats nearly three hundred
and fifty! But we held our grand opening the first Sunday of
October.

I was exceedingly blessed with a solid core of committed disciples to launch this revitalization effort. Lewis Good, the resident
overseer and former pastor, and many others were supportive, but
not all families were at first. One family who was a vital part of the
ministry said they would stay and help for a year to see how things
went. After a worship service at the old facility just before the
move, a woman had tears in her eyes as she approached Helen and
said, "My husband will never drive ten miles to church." She lived
just around the corner from the Cottage City church. "He only
comes here when our daughter is in a program. He will never come
now!" Helen replied, "I don't know your husband, but I know
God. I will pray. He will come. We have a great God." He came
the first Sunday, despite having to drive ten miles, and soon he
dedicated his life to the Lord. This family is actively serving in
many ways; they have found new life in Christ and are ministering
effectively to others.

Even though the new location was ten miles from the old one,
more people from Cottage City came that first Sunday than when
we were in their neighborhood. The good news is they stayed and
remained workers in the church. The vision was catching on. In
fact, everyone made the move from Cottage City except one older
man who attended periodically. What a miracle of God! Over the
next nine years the congregation grew from an average attendance
of forty-five to about two hundred. After we moved again, this
time to a brand-new facility in October 2004, our attendance
doubled to about four hundred.

Personal Contact: A Must

When I was twenty-one years old, I was blessed to be part of a church plant during my student pastorate in Mount Jackson, Virginia. As a young student pastor, I learned to reach people by relating to them on their turf. By visiting the unchurched in their homes, I built many lasting relationships. In nearly five decades as a pastor, I spent most Saturday afternoons making at least one contact with an unchurched family, and it was not uncommon for me to visit a half-dozen or more unchurched families. This has been one very important factor in seeing the congregations I've pastored grow. It is a joy to look back and see fruit from this effort. Jesus spent time with his disciples, but he often took them with him as he related to nonbelievers in the community. I wish I had made more effort in training others to do these visits. These visits were often to people known by members of the congregation.

Phone Ministry

One of the greatest discoveries of my life in the area of evangelism has been using the phone to make connections with people. In most urban areas, especially in large apartment complexes, a person using the door-to-door approach is not necessarily welcomed. I was frequently told, "The only people who knock on doors here are the bill collectors." How do we reach our urban unchurched neighbors? Some megachurches use TV. We did not have the funds for a TV ministry or other mass-media efforts. Nor did we have sufficient personnel or resources to provide many community services.

Many pastors have seen the advertisements in Christian magazines for companies that offer to sell names and addresses of people who just moved into the area. The companies obtain this information from court records as deeds are recorded. Frequently the phone numbers are not available at the closing of the sale of the property. For the most part I have worked only with those whose phone numbers were listed with the new addresses. The cost of the service is minimal. One company charges five dollars a month plus about thirty-five cents per name. The companies provide information based on zip codes you want to target. Because this urban area had more names than I could work, I only used those that had phone numbers along with the addresses.

Usually, I received the information on these new residents about three months after they moved in. By that time, most committed Christians had found a church home. So I was usually working with people who were not committed Christians. For several years, I made about six hundred phone calls per month inviting people to CCF.

My usual method of operation was like this: As I dialed the number, I prayed, and many times Helen bathed this time in prayer. One of her primary gifts is the gift of intercession, which helps to explain the effectiveness of my phone ministry. If a child answered I asked to speak with the name of the person on my list. I said the following in one breath, which is important because people tend to hang up on telemarketers: "Hello, I'm Pastor Dave from Capital Christian Fellowship on Greenbelt Road. If you have a church family that's WONDERFUL; if you don't have a church, would you give me permission to send a flier in the mail extending an invitation to worship some Sunday at Capital Christian?"

I did not say "this" Sunday because it was too easy for them to give an excuse why they couldn't come this Sunday. It was more difficult for them to find an excuse since I invited them to come "some" Sunday. About one in five would grant permission to send a flier.

If you choose to adopt this method of making contact, the flier needs to be attractive. I always addressed the envelope in longhand and used first-class postage. Most people will open first-class, hand-addressed mail.

The secret of the success of this method is persistence. If fact, if you are not willing to make follow-up calls, I'd question whether you should use this approach. I'd call back in a week or ten days and ask if they received the flier. I would ask to speak to the same person I talked to earlier. Most of the time, people remembered receiving the invitation. I would ask if they might consider worshipping some Sunday morning with us. At that point I usually was able to enter into meaningful dialogue.

People asked three questions more than any others. The first was: "How did you get my name?" I simply told them how I received their name and number as well as why I was calling—namely, to encourage them to discovery the joy of walking with Jesus and experiencing a loving and supportive church family.

The second frequently asked question was: "Are you a Spirit-filled church?" This naturally meant that they had some knowledge of church. I often responded by saying that it would help me to answer if I knew his or her church background. If they were from charismatic churches where the spiritual gifts were freely endorsed, I would assure them they would feel at home. If they were from backgrounds where the charismatic gifts were not practiced, I would likewise inform them that they would love our worship time. I informed them that we had a worship band and that people were free to say "Amen" or raise their hands in our services, but that they would be comfortable worshipping in whatever way they liked. Later, when our website started running, I would tell them to check us out on the internet, which many of them did.

The third frequent question was: "Are you affiliated with a denomination?" I simply said that we preach that Jesus is the way, the truth, and the life, and that we help people become disciples and servants of our Lord. Then I changed the subject by asking the person their denominational background. If they continued on this subject, I would tell that we were Mennonites, but not before I shared my philosophy of ministry concerning the centrality of Jesus Christ and what it meant to be his disciple.

Usually during the conversation, I was able to discern a need or concern the person was experiencing. This was a green light for me to pray for them. Most people in the United States believe in prayer, so it was usually safe to pray without being offensive. I didn't ask them if I could pray with them; I simply started to pray. For example, I'd say, "Heavenly Father, you know Sue's concern. . . ." Many were touched by that act of kindness; often I could tell by their voice that they had tears in their eyes. I prayed for almost anything you could imagine: ill persons, sick dogs, safety in travel, financial needs, restoration of broken relationships, strength to help others, wisdom for various problems such as how to free up their schedule for time to come to church.

If they did not come to church I called back once a month. I took notes so that when I called back, I would mention any prayer requests. I would say that I have been praying for them and ask how their trip was, or how the child who had been ill was doing. I was building a relationship over the phone. When they came to church they would frequently come in the door and ask, "Where is Pastor Dave? He has been calling me."

Evangelism is relationship. I had a congregation of people I had never seen or met except over the phone. If after six months they did not show up, I would call again and say, "I don't want to waste your time or mine. I am going to take you off my list, if that is okay. Or would you like me to continue calling?" It was surprising how many wanted me to keep calling.

Another encouraging aspect of the ministry was that some people who did not come to Capital Christian returned to their church because of the calls inviting them to worship. Still others who had a church often affirmed this approach and said they would share it with their pastor.

One practical challenge was figuring out the best time to call. During the week, I found it was best to call in the evening, between seven o'clock and quarter after nine, Late Saturday morning or Sunday afternoon and evening were also good times to make calls. Snow days and holidays were harvest days, when many people were home and often more willing to talk.

We reached scores of people through this method, and many who came to church in turn brought their friends. This encouraged the congregation to likewise invite their friends. It was also how we broke into the international community. Frequently I called not having any idea how to pronounce the person's name; often a heavily accented voice made it clear that the person was an immigrant. What a joy it was to use the phone as a tool to reach people for Jesus![2]

A New Name

A name change affects much more than the sign in front of the church or the letterhead on your stationery. For Capital Christian, it was a major step in revitalizing our identity and vision. While this is not the case in many communities, in the urban areas around Washington, D.C., the Mennonite name was a stumbling block to many people. Most people did not know who the Mennonites were, and this was especially true in the African-American community. Others associated Mennonites with the Amish. Some went on the internet, and what they found was not always helpful. It's also true that young people, for the most part, are not excited by denomination labels. So it is necessary to consider whether a church's name is a stumbling block or an open door.

Just before we moved to Capital College in 1995, we changed our name from Cottage City Mennonite Church to Capital Christian Fellowship. While this name change was difficult for some, most understood that our denominational name was an additional hurdle. We invited the congregation to suggest names and then voted among the top three suggestions.

Facility Search

In many urban settings, finding a suitable facility for worship can be a nightmare. We searched for three years. We checked out a nursing facility, shopping center buildings, an automotive sales building, other churches, and dozens of empty buildings. We found that it would have cost us more to renovate many of these places than it would cost to construct a new facility. We were fortunate that two architects, a husband-wife team, were members of the congregation. Their counsel was invaluable.

Lewis Good, our overseer, was also in real estate, and he spent countless hours searching for a building site. Finally, after much prayer by the congregation, he saw a plot he thought might work.

Unfortunately, it was not listed and was apparently not for sale. Lewis asked me to call the owner to see if she might be willing to sell the property. When I spoke to the owner, she said, "I have two contracts, one in front of me on the coffee table and the other on the kitchen table." One contract was from a large and well-known grocery store chain; the other was from a local developer.

The next day, Lewis and I met with the owner and asked her to not accept either offer for three days. We returned and gave her five thousand dollars more than the best offer, and we purchased the plot where we are today. This was nothing less than a miracle.

Because of all the bureaucracy, building restrictions, and regulations of the Washington, D.C., area, it was another three years before we moved into our new twenty-six thousand square-foot facility. Interestingly, the NFL schedule of the Washington Redskins was one of the many things that delayed the approval of our building permit. The Redskins stadium was about five miles away. We were required to conduct a traffic count during a normal Sunday morning service. When the Redskins played on Sunday afternoons, this affected when we could do the traffic count, which resulted in yet another delay.

Within three years of moving into the new facility in October 2004, the congregation has grown to four hundred. On special occasions, or holidays like Easter Sunday, there are more than five hundred people worshipping at the two Sunday morning services. Today there are four full-time pastors and a full-time administrative assistant. Throughout this time of growth, we kept reaching persons from many nationalities and backgrounds. In the succeeding chapters, you will learn more details of God's blessing as he builds his church.

There is no greater joy than seeing God carve out a multicultural congregation. My prayer is that the church will continue to reach across all socioeconomic and national barriers. To me, this model is a foretaste of heaven and a powerful witness to our often segregated communities. While CCF is far from perfect, it is God's instrument in bringing many to Christ and helping them mature in their walk of discipleship.

Congregational Cycles Diagram

The diagram below shows how congregations go through cycles. Starting on the bottom left of the diagram, we see that churches begin with vision and lots of energy. They implement lots of programs, and many people are willing to help. At their peak, the church runs smoothly with excitement and a clear sense of God's presence. But fatigue eventually begins to show, and people do not volunteer as they once did. Sunday school teachers become harder to find; evangelism and the church's vision lose their central focus. Next, people question the church's leadership and effectiveness, and one continues to hear or see signs of growing fatigue, lack of enthusiasm, disunity, and then death.

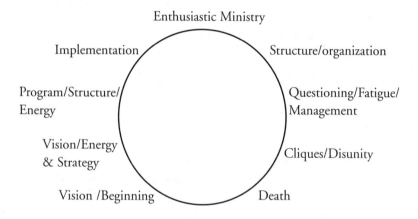

Where do you place your congregation on this diagram? If you are on the right side of the diagram, can the order be reversed? If so, what steps do you need to take to restore your church to a healthy maturity and enthusiastic ministry?

One study says that after a church is twenty years old, it will decline unless it introduces a new vision. If your church is twenty or more years old, can you look back and see when it was on various places on the diagram?

For Discussion

1. Do you agree with the assumptions and approaches to revitalization at the beginning of this chapter?

2. Do you find some of them objectionable? If so, which ones and why?

2

The First Thing:
A Passion for Souls

Dwelling in the Word: Read Matthew 28:18-20 and Acts 1:4-8 (see instructions at the beginning of chapter 1).

Testimony

As a little girl, Sue was terrified of her alcoholic father. Whenever he came home, she would hide in the closet. As an adult she gave her life to Christ, and her emotionally crippled life began to heal. It was not an easy road for Sue, but she is now a leader in one of our church plants. She is also reaching her family and friends for the Lord. Sue has made it the first thing in her life to reach people for Jesus. "Those who become Christians become new persons. They are not the same anymore, for the old life is gone. A new life has begun!" (2 Corinthians 5:17 NLT).

~

The success of Rick Warren's book *The Purpose Driven Life* indicates that people are looking for purpose and willing to study to discover it. God has given Christians and the church a clear purpose—a purpose I believe that most churches have lost. Why are nearly all denominations in the United States in decline?

Roughly half of all churches in the United States did not add one new person through conversion growth in 2000. It takes the combined efforts of eighty-five Christians working for one year to produce one convert. Worldwide it is a different story. Three thousand new churches open every week. In Africa and China, the church increases by twenty thousand or more per day, and in India by fifteen thousand. Christianity is growing at the rate of ninety thousand people a day.[1]

For every seminary student in Africa there are six hundred congregations. The church in South America is growing three times the rate that the population is increasing. One hundred years ago, the ratio of Christians to non-Christians in the world was one to twenty; today, it is one to nine.

It is no wonder Jesus instructed us to pray for workers. While this worldwide growth is wonderful, it in no way keeps up with world population growth. Neither does it always mean growth in sincere followers of Jesus.

North America has become the third largest mission field of the world. The unchurched population of the United States is the largest mission field in the English-speaking world and the fifth largest globally.[2] The statistics are sobering. "Since 1991, the adult population in the United States has grown by 15 percent," write Ed Stetzer and David Putman. "During that time, the number of adults who do not attend church has nearly doubled, rising from 39 million to 75 million—a 92 percent increase."[3] Gene Wood writes, "Nationwide we close seven more churches per day than we plant."[4] Eighty-five percent of churches in the United States have either plateaued or are declining.

Fields Ready for Harvest

We need to return to the first thing—a passion for souls—and keep it the first thing. But is it right that we send missionaries abroad when our churches are declining? Calling and equipping men and women to reach people in our communities and neigh- borhoods must be our first priority. Our mission field is not only overseas, it is also next door. In fact, the United States is receiving more missionaries than we are sending.

In 2006 Helen and I moved to Lancaster County, Pennsylvania, often perceived as a "Bible Belt" county. While church attendance is only one indicator in measuring kingdom impact, it is still surprising that even in Lancaster County, only about 30 percent of residents are in church on Sunday.

Is your county, town, or city doing better? Jesus told us that the harvest is ripe. "Do you think the work of harvesting will not begin until the summer ends four months from now? Look around you! Vast fields are ripening all around us and are ready now for the harvest" (John 4:35 NLT). When you are working beside your peers, pumping gas, shopping at the grocery store, or waving at the neighbors, you are constantly bumping into the harvest. Lord, open our eyes to see your harvest!

I see a relationship between the church in the United States and the church of Laodicea described in Revelation: "I know all the things you do, that you are neither hot nor cold. I wish you were one or the other! But since you are like lukewarm water, I will spit you out of my mouth! You say, 'I am rich. I have everything I want. I don't need a thing!' And you don't realize that you are wretched and miserable and poor and blind and naked" (Revelation 3:15-17 NLT).

In 2008, I worked with a church in an area where new housing was going up. Dozens of new families were moving into the immediate area. While I certainly cannot read the hearts of the people in the congregation, I did not detect a concern or hear a prayer for those people. No wonder our churches are not growing! So often the mission is even within walking distance of the church building, but we are lukewarm and seemingly unconcerned.

Revitalization of churches and the planting of new ones is a must if evangelical churches are to become missional. We must move from cold or lukewarm to hot, or our churches will be extinct before long. It is that serious—a matter of life and death! To see our churches experience new life will take much prayer and obedience to the Holy Spirit. Revitalization of plateaued and dying churches is a difficult and often painful journey; my wife Helen and I, however, have found it to be one of the most rewarding experiences of our lives.

Why Did Jesus Come?

Jesus' primary purpose in coming to earth was to reach the lost and bring in the kingdom of God. That is the purpose of his church. When Jesus gave his final commission, he said we would be witnesses in Jerusalem, Judea, Samaria, and then to the ends of the earth (see Acts 1:8). Is it appropriate to go to the ends of the earth and neglect our next-door neighbors? We need to pray much and seek God's answer for our plateaued or declining churches.

The statistics I cited above provide ample evidence to show that many people do not hold the great commission as the church's first priority. But do we have a passion for the purpose to which Jesus calls the church? Ed Silvoso writes:

> We must have a passion for the lost. I am not talking about having a keen interest in the salvation of sinners. No! I am talking about an all-consuming passion for the lost ones. I am not talking about subscribing to a program to evangelize people. No! I am talking about a lifestyle through which we devote every ounce of our energy to winning the lost. If you lack this kind of passion, do not be discouraged. This is not something with which we are born, not something that can be learned. It can neither be bought nor taught. It has to be imparted by the Holy Spirit. To receive this, we need to go to God in full repentance to plead for an impartation of His heartbeat for the lost. In 2 Peter 3:9, we read that God is patient toward us (the believers), not willing that any (of the unbelievers) should perish, but that all should come to repentance. This passage, along with 1 Timothy 2:4-6, states in unequivocal terms that God's will is for all men to be saved. Of course, this does not necessarily mean that all men will be saved.[5]

A clear and direct relationship exists between Jesus' mission and our mission. In Matthew 4:19, Jesus invites us to follow him and says that he will make us fishers of men. Are we willing to be molded and made into fishers of men? Jesus prayed to his Father, "As you sent me into the world, I am sending them into the world" (John 17:18 NLT). Later, after his resurrection, Jesus tells the disciples, "As the Father has sent me, so I send you" (John 20:21 NLT). Elsewhere in John's gospel, he says, "You did not choose me. I chose you and sent you out to produce fruit, the kind of fruit that will last" (John 15:16 CEV). God is a sending God. The word sent appears fifty-one times in John's gospel.

Jesus was conscious of being sent. Do we think about the fact that we are sent? Most of us have heard that we are called by God to serve, but God also sends us on a mission. Are we more concerned about our comfort than about being sent on Jesus' mission? Oswald Chambers comments on this theme:

> The controlling factor is not the needs of people, but the command of Jesus. The source of our inspiration in our service for God is behind us, not ahead of us. . . . The goal is to be true to Him—to carry out His plans.
>
> Personal attachment to the Lord Jesus and to His perspective is the one thing that must not be overlooked. In missionary work the great danger is that God's call will be replaced by the needs of the people, to the point that human sympathy for those needs will absolutely overwhelm the meaning of being sent by Jesus. The needs are so enormous and the conditions so difficult, that every power of the mind falters and fails. We tend to forget that the one great reason underneath all missionary work is not primarily the elevation of the people, their education, nor their needs, but first and foremost the command of Jesus Christ—"Go therefore and make disciples of all the nations" (Matthew 29:19).[6]

Jesus wants us to be in the world relating to people. He said to his Father, "My prayer is not that you take them out of the world but that you protect them from the evil one" (John 17:15). We *must* take our faith to the world.

In John 15:27 Jesus said, "You must also tell others about me because you have been with me from the beginning" (NLT). We too are with Jesus!

In a survey carried out by the Philo Trust, one thousand churches were asked the question, "In the last ten years, have you taught and equipped your church how to evangelize?" Only thirty-six churches—that is, 3.6 percent—answered yes.

The church is ultimately about three things: worship, well-being, and witness. The reality, however, is that the church spends at least 90 percent of its time on worship and well-being and only 10 percent on witness. This is a great imbalance that cannot be handled from the pulpit alone. Without a heart for evangelism and a passion for lost people, efforts at evangelistic preaching will not be effective.

Jesus Promises to Be with Us

In Luke 10, when Jesus sends the seventy-two disciples to preach and heal, they return with joy and report that even the demons submitted to them. Jesus responds with a powerful statement: "I have given you authority to trample on snakes and scorpions and to overcome all the power of the enemy; nothing will harm you" (Luke 10:19). This promise, similar to the great commission, reminds us Jesus will never leave us. We should have a passion to witness with confidence to our sinful culture. Jesus reminds us that our joy should come not so much in our authority and power to cast out demonic forces but from the fact that we are in God's family and are citizens of heaven.

If you know you have to go away, and you have a few last words with someone you love, you make your words count. You share what's most important. That's precisely what Jesus did for his disciples—for you and me—before he left this world. He gives us a critical mission:

> I have been given complete authority in heaven and on earth. Therefore, go and make disciples of all the nations, baptizing them in the name of the Father and the Son and the Holy

Spirit. Teach these new disciples to obey all the commands I
have given you. And be sure of this: I am with you always,
even to the end of the age. (Matthew 28:18-20 NLT)

As someone once rhetorically asked, "What is it about the
word go that we don't understand?" In the Greek, *go* is a participle
that might be better translated "as you go" or "as you are on your
way." The command is to make disciples as we move about in our
daily lives. Too often we pray and work for converts and neglect
making disciples. Jesus made disciples by walking with them, mentoring them, and modeling discipleship. That takes time and is
best done one-on-one and in small-group contexts.

Do we forget the end of the verse? Jesus promised to be with
us every day until he returns. Because he is with us as we go, we
can go in boldness and confidence even if we are lambs among
wolves (see Luke 10:3). We can baptize people into the kingdom,
then teach them to be disciples. That is our purpose. May it
become our passion!

In the United States, we have made many converts but few disciples. Converts too often are Christians in name only. Christianity
for so many is only an "add-on" among a dozen other activities.
Faith does not affect the daily lives of many Christians. Consequently, people see Christianity as having little or no relevance.
On the other hand, disciples influence society because they will not
compromise their faith. They walk their talk: they feed the hungry,
clothe the exposed, minister to the sick, and give loving care to the
needy (see Matthew 25:31-46). When this happens, the kingdom
of God has come!

Where to Begin

It's good to know something about religious heritage. For
Christians like me who connect with the Anabaptist faith tradition,
it can be surprising to learn that the great commission was quoted
more frequently by our sixteenth-century Anabaptist ancestors than
any other Bible text. Today, we have lost much of this passion. Our
church ancestors not only quoted these verses; they lived them and

spread the gospel throughout much of Europe and Asia. It cost many of them their lives. Thousands died for Christ. They were more than converts; they were disciples—the sent ones of Jesus! Pray for God to send an awakening to his church today.

Jesus' very last words before he ascended into heaven were: "But you will receive power when the Holy Spirit comes on you; and you will be my witnesses in Jerusalem, and in all Judea and Samaria, and to the ends of the earth" (Acts 1:8). We are Christ's witnesses. In the Greek, *witness* and *martyr* are the same word. This implies we must be willing to sacrifice and even die for Christ. When we tell what Jesus has done for us, we give witness to the power of the Holy Spirit working in us. We share the good news that makes a difference in our lives.

Where do we begin to share Jesus? Jesus says in Jerusalem. For us that means that we are to go across the street. The disciples had denied him in Jerusalem. Jesus tells them: go back to where you made your biggest mistake, back to where you blew it, back to where they know you, and share the Good News.

Transparency and vulnerability are materials the Holy Spirit uses to extend the kingdom. Jesus humbled himself and was vulnerable, and we are called to be humble and vulnerable as well. People are also drawn to integrity.

Churches in the United States have had success going to the ends of the earth, but what about our Jerusalem? When Jesus empowered the woman at the well, she went back to where they knew her. With her poor reputation, the whole village responded to her invitation to come and meet Jesus. When Jesus healed the man who lived among the tombs, the healed man begged to be allowed to follow Jesus. But Jesus said, "'Go home to your family and tell them how much the Lord has done for you, and how he has had mercy on you.' So the man went away and began to tell in the Decapolis how much Jesus had done for him. And all the people were amazed" (Mark 5:19-20). The people in the surrounding towns (the Decapolis means "ten cities") all knew this man who had been healed; he would be the most effective as a witness for Jesus, therefore, in that place. I wish Scripture would tell us how many church plants grew out of his witness.

When he met Jesus, Levi—that is, Matthew—invited his friends to a banquet. They knew his past life as a tax collector, but he was transparent and risked ridicule from those who knew him. Therefore, God used him in a mighty way. In Matthew 9:13, Jesus says, "I didn't come to invite good people to be my followers. I came to invite sinners" (CEV). We need to do the same.

People don't connect with a church; they connect with other people. Before they come to Jesus, they'll come to you. Jesus said, "Anyone who welcomes you is welcoming me" (Matthew 10:40 NLT) and, "He who listens to you listens to me; he who rejects you rejects me" (Luke 10:16).

All believers have a great responsibility: to draw others to Jesus. To help do this, people need to feel comfortable in our presence. People will be drawn to those who are vulnerable and transparent; if we hide our sin, people will catch on. Are people drawn to your passion? Can they see it, or do you keep that passion and joy hidden?

Jesus calls us to be responsible witnesses to those with whom we live, work, or go to school. Paul said that if he shared the gospel and people did not receive it, he is cleared of his responsibility (see Acts 18:6; also Ezekiel 33:6). Scripture implies that if we don't share the gospel, Jesus may hold us accountable on judgment day for our neighbors' lost state. May our passion for the lost become white hot!

Developing the Passion

Passion is the burning in our heart to please God and walk in obedience. It is loving God with all our hearts (see Mark 12:30). When Jesus wept over Jerusalem (see Luke 19:41), that was passion.

Passion for the lost has to be imparted by the Holy Spirit. We receive it when we draw near to God in full repentance and beg for an impartation of his heart for the lost.

God may develop passion in us by opening our eyes to the suffering in our communities. God may use us to meet some of those needs, although God may need to fine-tune our passion first. Moses, for example, saw his people in slavery and was compelled to bring justice, but in his zeal he killed a man. God had to help him control his passion before he could use that zeal to deliver his people.

In Matthew 6:33 Jesus says to seek first the kingdom of God and his righteousness. When we say *righteousness*, we often refer to relationship to God. But righteousness can also be translated justice, which has a broader meaning. Justice is more horizontal; to seek it means to have a passion for those who are hurting.

Most American pastors have never felt the joy of baptizing persons with no church background. If you are a pastor, you can learn from growing churches by visiting and studying them. Attend seminars, read books, and get a feel of what God can do and is doing to reach the unchurched. It is invigorating and exhilarating and may help to raise your faith level.

In *Back to Jerusalem*, Paul Hattaway relates how many house church leaders in China developed a passion as they traveled through southeast Asia, where Buddhism was strong. He "saw hundreds of temples, multitudes of lost souls worshipping idols, young boys proudly walking down the roads as trainee monks and a complete absence of gospel light everywhere we traveled."[7]

We may lack passion because we believe we have only a small debt to be forgiven (see Luke 7:36-50). Maybe we don't recognize who we really are, and so we don't see our need for grace. Some of us have known Jesus for many years, and the wonder of his love and grace may have diminished for us. We need to once again celebrate his grace and remember that we are all sinners, reconciled to God and to one another because Jesus has paid our huge debt.

Pray that God will give you passion for building his kingdom. Ask the Holy Spirit to soften your heart and move you to action. God will give you a burden as well as a vision to bring justice. This passion will line up with your gifting and your heart's desire. But nothing will happen if you don't take a prayerful approach and an active interest in making something happen. Friendships will not form with the unchurched unless you take some steps to become a friend. Take the initiative, take risks, and go out on a limb: that's where the fruit is.

The price of growth is to see ourselves as God sees us. But we must also humble ourselves. If it is obvious our present ways are not fruitful reaching people for Christ and extending his kingdom, then we have to change the way we do things.

I believe there is a direct relationship between prayer and passion. When Eastern Mennonite Missions asked representatives from the Council of International Anabaptist Ministries in Ethiopia why they took one day each week to pray and fast, they said they found when they stopped this practice, the church stopped growing. Their churches no longer planted daughter congregations. When they gave a day each week to prayer and fasting, however, the work was blessed by God. Lives were changed, churches were planted, and God's kingdom expanded.

Joe, a good friend of mine, had a passion to see people come to the Savior. He gave much of his time and energy to developing friendships. He visited, made phone calls, and befriended people. He brought them to church. When he died, I preached at his funeral. I asked those who attended how many came to Christ because of his testimony. Many hands went up. I give anyone opportunity to share how that happened. For nearly two hours one person after another shared how Joe had impacted his or her life. Needless to say, Joe had a passion for people. He is in heaven now enjoying his rewards.

Sally Morgenthaler writes:

> We need to understand that the "if we build it, they will come" mentality couldn't be farther from the Great Commission. We are told explicitly to go, not to marinate in our subcultures. Second, church shopping habits have changed. Until about 1995, a fair percentage of the unchurched seemed willing to darken our doors on a Sunday morning. Now, the percentage

of non-Christian, unchurched faith-shoppers has plummeted, which means the Sunday service is no longer the front door for seekers. The new front door is relationship—offsite connections that include sacrifice, service, and a whole bunch of time. This is where following Christ gets real."[8]

God will give us passion for the lost if we cry out to him in repentance and ask him to break our hard and stubborn hearts. But it's going to take passion, persistence, and a willingness to change our approach if we want to reach the postmodern people of our culture.

Passing the Passion to Others

When I look back over my fifty years as a pastor, I'm thankful for the time I spent with people who were unchurched and marginalized. I do wish, however, that I had made more of an effort to take members with me and equip them to relate to the unchurched. Our congregations need to become training institutes to share the Good News.

Paul needed to remind the Christians in Philippi to "Be humble, thinking of others as better than yourself. Don't think only about your own affairs, but be interested in others, too, and what they are doing" (Philippians 2:3-4 NLT). We too should be interested in others. As we grow and mature in discipleship and experience the fruit of the Spirit, we minister to others. A basic human need is significance. We experience significance as we serve others under the direction of the Holy Spirit.

At Capital Christian Fellowship, one of our core values reads: "We believe that unless people respond to Jesus Christ in repentance and faith they will be lost. If they place their trust in Christ, they will serve him for eternity." Do you believe this? Even many church people question whether nonbelievers will be lost. They say that a loving God would not send people to hell. That's true; a loving God does not send anyone to hell. Rather, we send ourselves when we reject God's plan of deliverance. Jesus provides the way to God and even now is preparing a fantastic future for us (see John 14:6, Romans 5:8, and 1 John 4:9-10). God is just toward both the saved and those who have not yet come to faith. Our job is to love and invite people into the kingdom—or if necessary, to compel them into his kingdom, as Luke 14:23 advises.

While we are to be passionate about reaching people for Jesus, we are still called to imitate Jesus' calmness and gentleness. In Matthew 11:29 he says, "I am gentle and humble." In 2 Corinthians 10:1, Paul writes, "Now I, Paul, plead with you. I plead with the gentleness and kindness that Christ himself would use" (NLT). In Philippians 1:8, he exhorts the saints with "the tender compassion of Christ Jesus" (NLT).

John A. Lapp once noted: "Jesus was not overwhelmed with the urgency of the cause. His primary concern was nurturing his followers in godliness. Jesus never appears to be anxious about numbers. His concern was the quality of discipleship."[9] This perspective gives us a healthy balance.

While Jesus frequently rose at daybreak to pray (see Luke 4:42), or prayed all night (see Luke 6:12-13), and often told his plans ahead of time (see Luke 2:49; 4:43, 9:22, 13:43; 14:18, John 4:4; 9:4), he nonetheless remained peaceful and calm in his demeanor.

God wants us to rest and relax in his love. As we become sensitive to the Spirit, he will move us. When he wants us to show love by helping another person or by verbally sharing God's love, the Spirit may even cause a fire to burn in our hearts. As we earnestly pray and walk in obedience, he will open and close doors so his kingdom can advance through our efforts.

Quality or Quantity?

I find the following story helpful in trying to understand the balance between quality and quantity of people. A family goes camping. Their two children get lost. The parents search and search in growing desperation. They find one of the children, and then a "friend" makes a ridiculous suggestion to the parents: "This is a quality child. Just forget about his brother." The parents say, "No way!"

Jesus died so no one need be lost. Numbers are important because numbers represent people. A good shepherd not only feeds the sheep; he counts the sheep. If there is joy in heaven over one sinner who repents, then someone is keeping track. It's true that numbers cannot be the vision; rather, they are the product of the vision. We are called to the mission of reaching and discipling people, all people, for his kingdom (see John 17:18 and 20:21).

In *Road Signs for the Journey*, Conrad Kanagy cites three sobering findings from his 2006 survey of Mennonite Church USA members: (1) only 2 percent of members are new believers; (2) only 30 percent of members are under the age of forty-five; and (3) women members are giving birth to an average of 1.4 children.[10]

For Mennonite Church USA, these findings mean that unless we reach our unchurched neighbors, we will become extinct. It is that serious! When we stand before Jesus he will ask us if we have been faithful. His commission is clear, and we will be judged accordingly (see Matthew 25:31-45; 28:18-20; Romans 2:6; and 2 Corinthians 5:10).

While witnessing and evangelizing are important, we also need to consider what it is about our churches that might be keeping people away.

We Like Our Small Church

Pastors who have a passion for the great commission sometimes hear members of their congregations tell them, "I like our church size the way it is." The pastor needs to boldly but politely ask these members to discern their priorities. Which is more important: their own comfort, or the fact that staying the same size means that their neighbors will spend eternity separated from our Lord? Jesus described that separation in rather depressing terms, to say the least. Growing a church is about reducing the population of hell and filling up heaven. People's destiny is far more important than our comfort in church fellowship. When the church has plateaued in a community in which new housing is going up or into which new families are moving, there is something seriously wrong!

Michael Fletcher speaks to the small church dilemma. What makes a small church successful, he writes, is what will eventually halt its growth. Everyone in the small church knows everyone else. This creates a tight community, composed largely of the kind of people "we like"—people who are "like us." This makes fellowship close and builds a family-type atmosphere. Without realizing it, small churches intuitively resist growth; continued growth threatens the closeness they so enjoy. After a certain number of relationships, a person just doesn't have room for more. Folks cannot remember everybody, and the underlying guilt that says we *should* know everybody produces an awkwardness that actually pushes others away. Those who are "in" are in, and those who are "out" are not likely to break in without a tremendous amount of tenacity. Small churches fear that growing might destroy the family they have become.[11]

"Pastors should recognize that 5 percent of church folks are by nature dissatisfied. They grew up in church traditions or in family structures that nurtured continuous complaining. For these people, fixing things never fixes things; they are not happy unless they are unhappy. Death, taxes, and that irritable 5 percent come with the territory in church leadership."[12]

Why We Don't Share Our Faith

When we are excited about our own salvation, we can't help but share the Good News. In doing so, we confirm our salvation (see Romans 10:9-10). But still many of us hesitate to share the gospel. Why?

In my years as a pastor, I've observed several reasons why we hesitate to share the good news:

(1) *We are lukewarm.* The rivers of living water are not flowing from us as they should be (see John 7:38). Are we abiding in

Christ and allowing his life to flow through us? Are we drinking daily from the fountain of life? If we are passionate about our mission and filled with God's Spirit, the Spirit will open our eyes to see opportunities to share God's love with the thirsty people around us. If I am not energized by what Jesus has done for me, how can I share my faith? If my relationship to Jesus is boring, it will bore my friends.

Maybe we forget the incredible significance of Jesus' forgiveness. As believers, we have royal blood flowing through our veins (see Colossians 1:13). Maybe we forget who we are in Christ? We are "the chosen ones of God, chosen for the high calling of priestly work, chosen to be a holy people, God's instruments to do his work and speak out for him, to tell others of the night-and-day difference he made for you—from nothing to something, from rejected to accepted" (1 Peter 2:10 Msg).

(2) *We don't know anyone not already connected to the church.* It's true that the longer we are Christians, the fewer unchurched people we know. But there is an abundance of unchurched people in every community, and as believers we are called to build relationships with those souls.

(3) *The hellfire "turn or burn" approach has turned us off.* I have been with people who are obnoxious in their attempt to witness, and they have embarrassed me. Scripture is clear that we are to witness gently: "Always be prepared to give an answer to everyone who asks you to give a reason for the hope that you have. But do this with gentleness and respect, keeping a clear conscience" (1 Peter 3:15-16). Just because some people use inappropriate and obnoxious approaches to reaching the unchurched does not mean that we should neglect to share the Good News. (See chapter 11).

(4) *We are not sure that a God of love would send our nice neighbors to hell.* God does not send anyone to hell. He gives us a choice. Many Americans don't think about heaven or hell because their present life is so comfortable. Too often pastors say little about having to face God. Paul writes, "For we must all stand before Christ to be judged. We will each receive what we deserve. . . . It is because

we know this solemn fear of the Lord that we work so hard to per-suade others" (2 Corinthians 5:10-11 NLT). The King James Version uses the term "terror" of the Lord. Let's join Paul in work-ing hard to persuade others, knowing that we will all face our Lord, who is not only a God of love but also a just judge. I take comfort in the fact that our loving Father will do what is right (see Genesis 18:25).

A pastor went to a bar to relate to the unchurched. In the midst of witnessing, the pastor made a statement about the reality of heaven and hell. A boisterous guy declared, "You don't believe that." "Why not?" replied the pastor. "Well, if you believed in hell, you would have been here long before this to warn us about it." Do we believe in the immediacy of our Lord's return?

C. T. Studd, founder of Worldwide Evangelization Crusade, once read the following, written by an atheist:

> If I firmly believed . . . that the knowledge and practice of reli-gion in this life influenced my destiny in another, then religion would mean to me everything. I would cast away earthly enjoyments as dross, earthly cares as follies, and earthly thoughts and feelings as vanity. Religion would be my first waking thought and my last image before sleep sank me into unconsciousness. . . . I would esteem one soul gained for heav-en worth a life of suffering. Earthly consequences would never stay my hand, or seal my lips. Earth, its joys and its grief, would occupy no moment of my thoughts. I would strive to look upon eternity alone, and on the immortal souls around me, soon to be everlastingly happy or everlastingly miserable. I would go forth to the world and preach to it in season and out of season, and my text would be: "What shall it profit a man if he gains the whole world and lose his own soul?"[13]

(5) *We are uncomfortable with bringing people into the church.* This one is perhaps the most important of all. Many church members, fearful of embarrassment, don't even think of inviting their unchurched friends. Perhaps the church is not welcoming, and the members may not want to risk losing face by inviting a

friend. But when our churches overflow with the genuine love of Jesus and the fruit of the Holy Spirit, we will automatically invite our lost friends to church.

Once a Christian gentleman in his sixties, a person I respect highly, asked me how my work of coaching churches is going. In the midst of our conversation he said he talks to many people about Jesus, but he would not bring them to his Mennonite church. He would encourage them to go to other churches, perhaps an independent church where, in his eyes, there was less tradition and more flexibility. He just recently left the Mennonite church.

These conversations are painful, but instead of defending ourselves we must look at why this is so. I think it's because we expect people to be like us before they come, and so we know intuitively that strangers will not be comfortable. After all, would you be comfortable at a mosque or a Buddhist temple if you've never been to one before? This is a huge issue for most older congregations.

Only 18 percent of Christians in Mennonite churches try to convert others to faith in Christ, and only 13 percent invite non-Christians to attend services or activities at their church.[14] Why are so few inviting people to church? Might it be because they fear the visitors will not hear the gospel message? Do we have an intuition they will not feel at home in our church?

Church services need to be relevant and understandable to the unchurched. It's been said, "To be irrelevant is to be irreverent." If we continue to use methods that do not welcome the unchurched, we are being unfaithful to our Lord. If my church experience is a dull duty, why would I want to invite someone to join me? (We will explore this theme in chapters 9 and 10.)

(6) *Satan does not want us to witness.* I believe the forces of hell are ordered into action when people freely testify. Several years ago a schoolteacher accepted Christ. She was a dynamic, vivacious extrovert growing in her faith. She came into my study and asked, "Why is it that I can be in the teachers' lounge and talk about everything

under the sun, but when it comes to sharing my faith I am tongue-tied?" I believe Satan works overtime to intimidate us so we will keep our mouths shut.

There are times, of course, when the Holy Spirit wants us to be quiet and just live our faith. St. Francis of Assisi famously said, "By all means, proclaim the gospel, and if necessary, use words." We need to learn to discern between Satan's voice and the Holy Spirit's voice. If Jesus would not have explained to us verbally who he was, we would still be in the dark concerning God's plan of salvation. There is a need for both word and deed.

(7) *Intellectualism and materialism undermine the urgency of sharing our faith.* There is a huge difference between godly wisdom and secular humanistic intellectualism. Paul writes: "While knowledge may make us feel important" (1 Corinthians 8:1 NLT), feeling important or proud will not help our witness. Rather, as the end of the verse says, it is love that builds up and strengthens the church. As cultural intellectualism and materialism infiltrate our churches, the less evangelistic they become. But this influence can be overcome with a hunger and thirst for God's wisdom. The apostle Paul, a highly educated man, and Luke the evangelist, a physician by trade, clearly overcame this hurdle.

(8) *Pride will keep us from sharing the Good News.* I grew up in a home in which 1 Corinthians 10:12 was often quoted: "So, if you think you are standing firm, be careful that you don't fall!" Proverbs 16:18, "Pride goes before destruction, and haughtiness before a fall" (NLT), was also often repeated. I was taught these Scripture passages to discourage pride. But sometimes those verses hindered me from stepping up to the plate and giving a clear witness. As I was praying recently, the Lord seemed to say, "Dave, I'm tired of you asking not to be proud—speak out for me." Immediately I felt a need to check the concordance to see how often the words "bold" and "humble" appear in the New Testament. I was surprised to learn that Christians are told to be bold nearly twice as often as they are told to be humble. Saint Francis of Assisi's statement concerning our need to witness and if necessary use words is appropriate,

but we need to speak boldly too. If Jesus hadn't communicated boldly, we would still be lost.

As I noted earlier, I think the fifth reason above is often the greatest obstacle in sharing the Good News. Many congregations are friendly, but unless the congregation can move from being *friendly* to *making friends* with new people, it cannot function as Jesus commands in the great commission. If someone accepts Jesus without being connected to a church body, it is like a baby being born in a hospital but left on the street to fend for itself; the result is death. I have seen this happen far too often to new believers.

Winning people to Christ means conflict will likely occur at your church. Gene Wood writes, "When a significant number of new members arrive in a short period of time (probably anything greater than 15 percent of the total attendance), the potential for conflict is inevitable." He continues:

> As long as these new members are content to simply sit, perform menial tasks and give, things will likely go along peaceable. But this is neither biblical, nor desirable. When the newcomers begin to offer suggestions as to how the church might be more effective in bearing fruit, the old-timers are offended. Even more significantly, when new members are placed into positions of leadership or given regular places on the platform, conflict is assured.[15]

Change is difficult for most of us. But the alternative of not growing is usually a slow death. It's appropriate to ask whether our comfort, our preferences, and our traditions have become more important than our love for the unchurched.

Salvation is a Miracle

Do we believe we can reach people without God's power? I appreciate Paul Hattaway's challenge:

> I have come to understand that it is completely impossible for even a single lost person in the world to become a Christian

unless a great miracle takes place. . . . They cannot be argued into the kingdom of God because their problem is not an intellectual one. Nor is there any point in trying to change their outward behavior if they do not have the inward spiritual life that only Jesus can give. The Bible clearly says that every person outside of Christ is spiritually dead, and a battle needs to be waged for his or her soul. People living outside the grace of Jesus Christ are trapped by the devil, "who has taken them captive to do his will" (2 Timothy 2:26).

The demonic forces that hold souls captive are far more powerful than we are, in our own strength. There is not the slightest possibility that we can lead anyone to the foot of the cross unless Jesus himself becomes involved. Only his power can save a sinner. The good news is that we can be completely sure that Jesus will help us to reach the lost for him, for the word of God says, "He is patient with you, not wanting anyone to perish, but everyone to come to repentance" (2 Peter 3:9).[16]

The miracle of salvation occurs when we come to the end of ourselves. The miracle of a revitalized church occurs only when the church comes to the end of itself. When the church thinks it is doing quite well even though it is not reaching the unchurched, there is little hope for God to bring a fresh wind of the Spirit to renew that congregation. If we feel we are doing okay, we will not be crying out in repentance for God's restoring grace and mercy. Miracles happen when we cry out to God with clean hands and a pure heart.

Emphasize the Kingdom of God

Jesus emphasized the kingdom of God, which is broader than church or denomination. The church is a channel for God's kingdom. Kingdom language emphasizes the reign of God and of Christ. The gospels talk about the kingdom of God or of heaven 125 times. Church is mentioned only three times, all by Matthew. Even after the resurrection Jesus spoke to the disciples about the kingdom of God. "During the forty days after his crucifixion, he appeared to the apostles from time to time and proved to them in many ways that he was actually alive. On these occasions he talked to them about the Kingdom of God" (Acts 1:3 NLT). Instead of talking about building his church, Jesus spoke of the kingdom. And while this changes in the letters of the New Testament, kingdom language still dominates.

Our culture looks at Jesus as a great man but often ignores or even despises the church. So there is an advantage of using kingdom language in our North American culture, where Christianity is usually a mile wide but an inch deep. Kingdom language accentuates Jesus' kingship, rulership, and authority over our lives. We give our allegiance to him (see Galatians 2:20).

We seem to be moving toward a post-denominational age. I seldom use denominational language. As I noted earlier, nearly all denominations are in decline. Young adults show little appreciation for denominations. In my church plants in Ohio and Florida, and in the revitalization experience in Maryland, any publication that was controversial or negative about the Mennonite church I threw in the "round file." The many new Christians in these congregations did not need to hear about our controversies and bickering. There is enough negative news in the world. Why display the disunity and controversy in the church? They'll experience it soon enough.

I am not ashamed of being a Mennonite, but it can be an extra hurdle for people to jump. They sometimes think, "I have to become a Mennonite before I can become a Christian." Their image of Mennonites frequently is one of an exclusive and closed group. While we have many blessings we can point to, I am embarrassed when Mennonites are held up as a model because of our inconsistencies. In *Back to Jerusalem*, Paul Hattaway writes, "Denominational pride is one of the easiest ways the devil can deceive us."[17]

Like many Christian groups, Mennonites have much to learn but also much to offer. We need to learn how to make disciples.

With the increased reality of many tens of millions living outside of the kingdom of Christ, we need to learn how to plant new churches and revitalize existing ones, including large churches. We can learn from all streams of Christian faith.

On the other hand, I pray that we will have open doors to share with others many of our strengths, including the importance of interpreting the Bible through the lens of Jesus Christ. Our aim is to hold forth a theology that is Christ-centered, taking seriously not only Jesus' atoning work on the cross but also his teachings, including his call to take up our cross in daily practice.

In everything it is necessary to ask, "What would Jesus do?" The ability to link word and deed has *radical* implications for the church as it relates to our world. The New Testament call to non-violence, peacemaking, and reconciliation is greatly needed in our world today. I thank the Lord that people seem open to hearing this witness. Many of our congregations, especially in the urban areas, are linking social action and salvation in very healthy ways.

For Discussion

1. Looking at Christianity in North America, discuss whether God is dismantling, setting aside, or even destroying the present church so a new healthy church can emerge. Are we like the church in Laodicea (Revelation 3:14-22)? Unless we repent of our lukewarm condition he will destroy us. Jeremiah says, "My people ... have forsaken me, the spring of living water, and have dug their own cisterns, broken cisterns that cannot hold water" (Jeremiah 2:13). Do the unchurched see springs of living water flowing from us? Have we built religious systems that have become lifeless? Are we simply following our traditions and neglecting Jesus?

2. Do you agree that our first duty—the first thing—is to reach the lost and extend the reign of Christ? Have we lost our passion to bring in the kingdom of God? If so, how can we regain that passion?

3. What is God's passion? Is it taking care of our sin problem,

or is it loving the sinner? God's love compelled him to take care of our sin problem. Can we love the sinner for who he or she is, and let God take care of the sin problem?

4. Do you agree that unless we recapture our passion for reaching our unchurched neighbors, many of our congregations will dwindle and die?

5. How can those in middle-class North America be faithful? Some even wonder if the affluence of the middle class permits us to be faithful to our Lord. Discuss.

3

The Other First Thing:
The Great Commandment

Dwelling in the Word: Read Deuteronomy 6:4-9 and Mark 12:28-34. It may be helpful to compare your Bible translation with The Message.

Testimony

Margie was married to a stern career military officer. He seemed to be sincere in his commitment to Jesus, but he lived a double life. He was active in church and assisted with many church activities, but he maintained a different side as well; finally his double life caught up with him. His infatuation with another woman and nights spent out on the town broke the hearts of his wife and children.

After a long and painful divorce, the loving care of several sisters in the congregation and the prayers of God's people, Margie was healed. She is now ministering to other divorced women. Her pain and tears were transformed by God and she now brings healing to others.

> He comforts us in all our troubles so that we can comfort others. When others are troubled, we will be able to give them the same comfort God has given us. You can be sure that the

more we suffer for Christ, the more God will shower us with his comfort through Christ. So when we are weighed down with troubles, it is for your benefit and salvation! For when God comforts us, it is so that we, in turn can be an encouragement to you. Then you can patiently endure the same things we suffer. (2 Corinthians 1:4-6 NLT)

~

Jesus summed up the Old Testament—what he would call the Law—in these words: "'Love the Lord your God with all your heart and with all your soul and with all your mind.' This is the first and greatest commandment. And the second is like it: 'Love your neighbor as yourself.' All the Law and the Prophets hang on these two commandments" (Matthew 22:37-40).

Love is the most important commandment. Rick Warren writes: "Loving unbelievers the way Jesus did is the most overlooked key to growing a church. Without this passion for the lost, we will be unwilling to make sacrifices necessary to reach them. The command to love is the most repeated command in the New Testament, appearing at least 55 times."[1]

In this chapter I want to focus on the importance of the great commandment. The number one need in our communities is love. People go to bars to find it. They spend all their money on drugs, gambling, sports, pornography, and material things to find it. Some join gangs or cults in a search for love and acceptance. Why? Because persons in the cults and gangs show an interest in them and invite them into their group. The human need to be loved and accepted is evident. Being *friendly* takes little effort; being a *friend* is costly.

Loving your Neighbor

Many churches today fail to reach their communities because they lack the capacity for love. The church at Ephesus lost its first love: "But I have this complaint against you. You don't love me or each other as you did at first!" (Revelation 2:4 NLT). This church was orthodox. They would not tolerate sin. They had a full schedule of activities and good deeds, and they defended the faith. But their light was dim. They were not bearing witness to Jesus Christ in their community.

Today's churches need to ask the Holy Spirit to restore to us the joy of our salvation and to anoint us with a passion for Jesus and for our lost friends. We have not presented a holistic approach to love. Too often we give only part of the definition. Our culture understands love primarily as an emotion. As Christians we don't "fall in" or "out of" love. We strive not to let ourselves be controlled by our fickle emotions or impulses. We describe biblical love as a decision and a commitment. Love is action. Jesus showed his love by going to the cross.

Of course, true love includes strong feelings and emotions. Look at what Paul says in Philippians 1:7-8: "It is right for me to feel this way about all of you, since I have you in my heart; for whether I am in chains or defending and confirming the gospel, all of you share in God's grace with me. God can testify how I long for all of you with the affection of Christ Jesus." One can see Paul's heart for the churches he has planted.

So while love is an action, it is a feeling too. The Pharisees had lots of commitment, but Jesus condemned them: "Yes, how terrible it will be for you teachers of the law and you Pharisees. For you cross land and sea to make one convert, and then you turn him into twice the son of hell as you yourselves are" (Matthew 23:15 NLT). Again Jesus says, "These people honor me with their lips, but their hearts are far away" (Matthew 15:8 NLT). They didn't feel anything. Jesus didn't condemn the Pharisees for not doing the right things as much as he condemned them because their hearts were not in their actions. A heartless love is not what God wants. God wants people who love from the heart. The Pharisees had commitment but lacked love.

For example, a husband can be committed out of duty to do what is right, but a wife longs for more than commitment. God likewise longs for more than commitment and wants our hearts. People too, if we are to disciple them, want our hearts.

If we are fully committed to someone but lack love for them in our hearts, they will know. They need to know that we are savoring each moment. You can usually tell when you walk into a church service if the warmth of heart love is present or absent.

A heartless love does not satisfy anyone. People can tell if your love is from the heart. No one wants to be someone's project. We don't love people to just get them into our church. We need to love them from our hearts. Indeed, if we don't love people, nothing else matters.

When I've asked new Christians what attracted them to Capital Christian Fellowship, I've seldom—if ever—heard anyone say: "It's because of your beautiful building," or "It's because of your Anabaptist theology," or "It's your full calendar of activities," or "I see the commitment of your members." Instead, the most common response was, "I felt an incredible spirit of love toward me that drew me in."

At CCF our love is focused toward guests, not just toward each other. Often people would say to me as they entered the building: "What is it about this place? I felt God as I walked toward the building." My heart leaped with joyful praise to God. Only he can create that depth of love.

Loving Only Ourselves

Many churches may have great fellowship, but they are dying because their love is focused inwardly. The fellowship in these churches has become so tight that newcomers are unable to break in. They don't attract unbelievers because they don't love unbelievers. They are like potted flowers: they're bound so tightly together they can't grow. They can't let the beautiful aroma of Christ spread (see 2 Corinthians 2:14, 5:17-21).

All of us, including me, need to repent because we often don't love those who are different than us. We are like Simon the Pharisee in Luke 7. He saw the woman who anointed Jesus as sinful, while Jesus saw her heart and forgave her. Simon didn't need new eyes; he needed a new heart.

Loving others just to love them is being a good neighbor. We don't need to love them to make them Christians. We, of course, want them to become Christians, but that is not why we love them. God wants us to relax in his love. As we are sensitive to the Spirit, he will nudge us, even compel us, when we are to share God's love (2 Corinthians 5:11-21).

In *Blue Like Jazz*, Donald Miller describes how God changed him from negative fundamentalism and loathing of other people to a new person. He writes:

> I was set free. I was free to love. I didn't have to discipline anybody, I didn't have to judge anybody, I could treat everybody as though they were my best friend.
>
> When I am talking to somebody there are always two conversations going on. The first is on the surface; it is about politics or music or whatever it is our mouths are saying. The other is beneath the surface, on the level of the heart, and my heart is either communicating that I like the person I am talking to or I don't. God wants both conversations to be true. That is, we are supposed to speak truth in love. If both conversations are not true, God is not involved in the exchange, we are on our own, and on our own, we will lead people astray. The Bible says that if you talk to somebody with your mouth, and your heart does not love them, that you are like a person standing there smashing two cymbals together. You are only annoying everybody around you. I think that is very beautiful and true.[2]

We must be careful to reach across to people, not down to them. Jesus left heaven to reach across to us. I believe one reason we may feel more comfortable ministering to persons who have little of this world's goods is because we find it easy to reach down. But try placing yourselves in their shoes; no one likes to be in the inferior position. Love flows across, not down.

It is unlikely that any church that reaches out to its community week after week in Christlike love would not be growing. In the natural world, if a plant does not reproduce itself, it will die. The same is true of our churches.

Make Love Practical

When we think in terms of loving the unchurched, we must think in practical as well as emotional terms. Loving an unchurched person means we become their friend. We call them, we spend time with them, we seek them out. We laugh with them, we hurt when they hurt, we rejoice when they have joy, we learn from them, and they learn from us. Love is not often dramatic but is usually composed of ordinary stuff (see Romans 12:9-15).

Let's go to the cross of Jesus and be crucified again. Let's die daily and say to God, "If you could love someone like me, surely I can love someone like him or her." At its core, loving someone is a spiritual issue.

Many of us in the church say we love others. We give regularly to foreign missions, and we support local projects in our communities. While that's important, giving time to build relationships is more important.

Why do we see so little fruit in many of our churches? Missionaries who have been successful abroad often come home to pastor churches that seem to plateau. Is this because we have a less receptive culture in North America? Perhaps. Dan Kimball in *The Emerging Church* thinks so. He reports that missionary Lesslie Newbigin found that ministry in England was much harder than anything in India. The cold contempt for the gospel is harder to face than opposition. The difference was that people in India were hearing the gospel for the first time. England had become a post-Christian nation, and North America is closely following England, particularly with emerging generations. Kimball goes on to say:

> As we approach ministry to the emerging culture—a post-Christian mission field—we need to use the same approach we would employ entering a foreign culture. We cannot go on seeing ourselves simply as pastors and teachers; we need

to see ourselves as a new kind of missionary. And we must train people in our churches to do the same. We must dream missionary dreams. We must bleed missionary blood. We must pray missionary prayers.

Sad to say, the generations being born and raised in American today don't know who God is or what he has done, or what the Bible says about him or who the true Jesus is. We have to start all over again in a nation once characterized by a Christian belief structure.[3]

The Mennonite church tradition to which I belong experienced an inspiring birth during the Anabaptist movement of the early sixteenth century. In time, however, the churches were persecuted and went underground. To avoid persecution, they soon became "the quiet in the land" and did not speak to others about their beliefs.[4] This compromise of faith became a stronghold that has been passed down to the present generation. The good news is that by confessing the sins of our ancestors and claiming the forgiveness offered in the shed blood of our Lord, we can break this stronghold (see 1 John 1:9). We can cry out to God to break the bondage that has fallen upon many of our congregations.

Might the declining membership in Mennonite churches be the result of the image of Mennonites that people in the community hold? They may see us as a closed community and associate us with the more conservative and plain-clothed groups. Some people may even associate us with the Amish, a group they respect but have no intention of joining.

Or might the unchurched avoid Mennonites because we have lost the joy of the first thing—passion for the lost?

Love Bridges Cultural Barriers

Even casual observation shows that the population in America continues to diversify. This is true even in small towns and rural areas that were predominantly all white or African-American. People of different cultures are a blessing. International persons will help us be more flexible. They have wonderful gifts and talents that will enrich our congregations if we learn to appreciate their cultural expressions.

Many international Christians have a deep faith that has grown out of persecution and hardship. They have much to teach us if we are willing to learn. During my Eastern Mennonite Seminary days, my roommate was from Ethiopia. What a blessing he was to me. He taught me a new level of prayer. He would get on his knees beside his bed and pray a long time. In my work as overseer of the Ethiopian Evangelical Church of Baltimore, I've seen members come to church and kneel in prayer for twenty minutes or more before the service. Periodically the congregation calls for several days of prayer and fasting. These believers give me a deeper appreciation and model for prayer and sharing.

One of the greatest blessings and strengths of CCF has been the many nationalities represented in its membership. We affirm and empower them to minister in the congregation. Of course, tensions arise at times. The international families and singles were frustrated when I was clock-conscious as I gave the morning message. If I preached longer than usual it was difficult for the teacher in the children's department to keep the children's attention. The international people said, "Preach the word, and don't look at the clock." I responded, "Will you take care of our many children while I preach overtime?" Many said, "Bring the children into the auditorium with the parents." Tension was fairly high over this issue. Yet we continued to love each other and accept differing opinions.

Accommodating Other Cultures

As we moved to our new facility in October 2004, we continued to grow. Our style of worship became freer due to the rapid growth of an immigrant population. Some people entered worship and knelt at their seat or came to the altar and prayed. Spontaneous expressions to God, uplifted hands in worship, clapping hands, and the swaying bodies of little children and adults were common as we worshipped the Lord in song. This added a vibrancy and warmth to our worship of God.

As a leader I needed to validate and even encourage this vibrancy. The international people who knelt either at their seats or who came to the altar while the worship team led in worship were introducing practices different from what others were used to. If the international people detected that their actions were not appreciated, they often would not return. Their different expressions need to be affirmed; otherwise they may feel uncomfortable or judged.

Leaders have the privilege of expressing affirmation and appreciation for these innovations. Affirm the freedom to worship the Lord in this way. If the congregation needs to be educated to accept different cultural expressions of worship, leaders should do this publicly. The pastor or another leader might say, "I see some of you entering the service while the worship team is leading us in our worship. You kneel at your seat or you come to the altar. That's great. I hope more of you can begin to do this. It helps create an atmosphere of reverence and sincere worship. Thank you for leading the way and teaching us these new expressions of reverence in our worship."

Many of our international people did not come to the service on time. Rather than make a big issue of this or questioning their commitment, we accepted their behavior without condemnation. Cultural practices are difficult to change, and we need to be patient with people. In turn, many of them wondered where everyone went twenty minutes after the service! Many were accustomed to fellowshipping for at least an hour or more afterwards. Our culture required considerable change and adjustment on their part as well.

While I reluctantly accepted that many of our international people did not come to worship on time, I began the worship service on time. I began the leadership team meetings on time. If people were late they missed the first part of the team meetings. The longer people are in North American culture, the more they tend to become clock-watchers. Many times I'm sure I was a slave to the clock. We all know that relationships need to take priority. May the Lord give us wisdom to discern what is best in those situations.

We encouraged people to come in their native dress, especially on our annual International Sunday. On this day our auditorium was like a flower garden. The variety of color and dress was beautiful. On a recent International Sunday there were more than five hundred people from thirty-seven nations present as our members invited their friends and neighbors. It's a highlight of the church year.

The worship on International Sunday is followed by a meal with food representing many nations. When we have carry-in meals we encouraged everyone to bring food representative of their culture. Everyone has a culture to express, not just immigrants. Many exuberantly expressed thanks for the variety of dishes. Everyone felt loved and appreciated, especially our international brothers and sisters. It was one way we could honor them.

Another small way to help persons of different national backgrounds feel at home is to place their flag along with other flags. At CCF we keep the flags in the auditorium year around. The variety of flags also speaks to the fact that God's kingdom is for all nations of the world. God blesses the entire world, not just the United States. Having the U.S. flag without flags representing other nations in front of the auditorium is difficult for me to reconcile with Jesus being Lord of people from all nations. His kingdom has no national boundaries. It was always a joy to see people's faces light up when they spotted their flag in our worship auditorium. It created an atmosphere of releasing God's love for their culture and also a freedom for them to talk about their families and friends "back home," many of whom were living in very difficult situations. While only symbols, the flags became powerful bridges of Christian love.

Racial Challenges

The pastoral team at CCF consists of four pastors and an administrative assistant. Three of the five are persons of color. Even when our congregation was small and I was the only pastor, I insisted that at least one person of color be on the platform in some position every Sunday. I was criticized by some of my leaders for this intentional inclusion; they called it manipulation. Some felt that rather than intentionally including a black person up front every Sunday, I should let those with obvious gifts lead, even if they were white. My response was that if I were to attend a church where African-Americans were in the majority, and week after week everyone on the platform was black, I would question if they were prejudiced.

We had people from various nations who were obviously talented, especially in areas of singing, leading worship, and prayer. A group from Nigeria taught us some of their songs. Some gave rich testimonies of God's leading. These were positive experiences. We prayed for their relatives and friends to be released from prison and persecution. We prayed for victims of Hurricane Katrina who had moved with relatives into our area. Today they are part of our church community too.

All Cultures Are a Blessing

When we open our hearts and minds to hear what God is saying through those from cultures outside North America, our worship, our fellowship, and our Bible studies are greatly enriched. At first we may feel uncomfortable, but realizing God loves other interpretations of Scripture and expressions of worship just as much as ours enhances church life and worship. The congregation becomes a foretaste of Revelation 7:9-10:

> There before me was a great multitude that no one could count, from *every nation, tribe, people and language*, standing before the throne and in front of the Lamb. They were wearing white robes and were holding palm branches in their hands. And they cried out in a loud voice: "Salvation belongs to our God, who sits on the throne, and to the Lamb." (Italics added.)

Perhaps your congregation, like many others, is much less diverse than surrounding neighborhoods. How do you begin to reach other ethnic groups? Take the initiative to approach international persons and invite them to worship with you. Some are Christians with dramatic testimonies, and others may have Christian background. Invite them to share their testimony. Some can play an instrument and sing. If you feel this may not be acceptable for your Sunday morning service, have them come Saturday evening or to a neutral place like a park or fire hall. Encourage them to bring their friends. Provide food following the service. Instead of teaching them, let them teach you. Remember, people don't listen unless they have been heard.

If I were the lead pastor today I don't think I would do things any differently in terms of relating to people from different cultures. Love is the key to being missional. At CCF we never had a conference on race relations, yet we coached and encouraged our people to see each person and to love them for Jesus. God does something special with multicultural mission teams and worship services.

Roadblocks to Genuine Love

We can point to several factors that prevent us from showing love to the unchurched.

1. *Material things.* Jesus said, "No one can serve two masters. Either he will hate the one and love the other, or he will be devoted to the one and despise the other. You cannot serve both God and Money" (Matthew 6:24).

I am relating to a Spanish-speaking pastor who, after much prayer and thought, placed a seventy-thousand-dollar mortgage on his home so their congregation could purchase a worship facility. What sacrifice! His faith challenges me. I see a relationship between his example of commitment and the rapid growth of our Spanish-language churches. According to George Barna, U.S. Christians spend roughly twice as much money on entertainment as they donate to their church.[5]

I have frequently challenged my congregation by asking: "Do you spend more money at the restaurant for Sunday dinner than you give in the offering plate?"

2. *Poor use of time.* Researcher Conrad Kanagy informs us that members of Mennonite Church USA watch 2.4 hours of television per day and are on the Internet 1.3 hours per day. Meanwhile, only 8 percent of us attend church more than once a week.[6] While attending church more than once a week may not be the best indicator of our discipleship, I think we can at least raise the question of our commitment in light of these statistics concerning how we use our time.

3. *Family relationships.* Jesus said, "Anyone who loves his father or mother more than me is not worthy of me; anyone who loves his son or daughter more than me is not worthy of me" (Matthew 10:37). Our worst enemies can be those of our own household. If instead of a high-salaried job, one of our children chooses to accept a lower-paying position in which they have more opportunities to serve and witness, do we encourage them or discourage them? Do we think, "I wish they would go into business, purchase a nice house, and settle down like other professionals? Why aren't they saving their money for college for their children or saving for their retirement?" Sometimes family members resent it when other family members chose a different church affiliation or congregation. Minor doctrinal differences can also separate us from one another.

4. *Sin.* In Colossians, Paul writes:

> Put to death, therefore, whatever belongs to your earthly nature: sexual immorality, impurity, lust, evil desires and greed, which is idolatry. Because of these, the wrath of God is coming. You used to walk in these ways, in the life you once lived. But now you must rid yourselves of all such things as these: anger, rage, malice, slander, and filthy language from your lips. Do not lie to each other, since you have taken off your old self with its practices and have put on the new self, which is being renewed in knowledge in the image of its Creator. Here there is no Greek or Jew, circumcised or uncircumcised, barbarian, Scythian, slave or free, but Christ is all, and is in all.

> Therefore, as God's chosen people, holy and dearly loved,
> clothe yourselves with compassion, kindness, humility, gen-
> tleness and patience. (Colossians 3:5-12)

The sins of evil desires, sexual immorality, impurity, lust, and greed can destroy the church. The sins of speech listed in verse 8 can break relationships. In contrast, in verse 12, Paul sets forth relationship-builders: compassion, kindness, humility, patience, gentleness, and forgiveness.

Jesus operated both from the heart and the mind. We must learn to not be afraid to express warmth, love, and compassion along with the clear scriptural teaching of truth to guide our conduct. May the Lord help us live in that balance.

Unfriendly Churches

When I moved to North Port, Florida, to plant a church, our assignment the first couple months was to visit churches in the community on Sunday morning. It is astounding how unfriendly many churches are to first-time visitors. Being an extrovert, I placed myself in the middle of the foyer with dozens of people around me before and after church. I was often ignored, as if I were invisible.

I remember reading in a magazine of a traveling salesman who visited nearly two hundred churches; besides the ushers and pastors, only three people ever welcomed him! All churches say they are friendly. They are friendly, but only if you are in the inner circle.

Sensing this dynamic at work in one of his congregations, our son, Chet, a missionary and church planter, respectfully challenged the older leaders and members of the church he was attending, who insisted the strongest characteristic of the church was love. He surveyed many of the newer members and regular attendees. While they affirmed many aspects of church life, they rated love expressing itself in actions the lowest. Practical expressions of love and hospitality were somehow bypassing them. This new awareness helped provoke many positive changes, and the church's numerical growth was one positive result.

Practical Ways to Express Love

All people are beautiful and special. They are so special that Jesus died for them. Practice making people feel special, and what you give to others will return to you. Here are a few suggestions:

1. *See first-timers as guests of God, not as strangers.* See them through the eyes of Jesus. (I like to use the term first-timers rather than visitors. First-timers implies they will be back.) Never use the word "strangers."

2. *Smile at everyone and offer your hand.* Can you smile when you don't feel like it? Is that hypocritical? When Paul was in prison he wrote, "Always be full of joy in the Lord. I say it again— rejoice!" (Philippians 4:4 NLT). Proverbs 15:30 says, "A cheerful look brings joy to the heart." Later we read, "If you are cheerful, you feel good; if you are sad, you hurt all over" (Proverbs 17:22 CEV). It takes fewer muscles to smile than it does to frown. Smile whether you feel like it or not!

3. *Look people in the eye.* Eye contact expresses intimacy. It communicates, "I see you. You are important."

4. *Take the initiative to reach out.* In an article called "What the Church Visitor Saw," John Longhurst writes: "We took our seats surrounded by people who ignored us as they greeted each other and engaged in animated conversations. We felt like we had wandered into somebody's family reunion."[7] How would you feel at someone else's family reunion? Remember first impressions are very important.

5. *Learn people's names.* Our culture is on a first-name basis. First introduce yourself by telling them your name. When they give their name, repeat it in the conversation to help you remember it. This exercise may seem a bit artificial at first, but it will become natural to you, and you'll be glad you learned it.

6. *Touching is important.* Scripture indicates that "Jesus spent more time touching people and talking to them than in any other action."[8] Jesus touched the lepers he healed. CCF is a hugging church. I'm convinced there is a relationship between touch and

communicating Christian love. Touch communicates caring. The early churches needed to be reminded of the need to greet one another warmly (see Romans 16:16). An embrace expresses caring.

7. *Don't walk past others without noticing them.* In every part of the church building, greet people with a smile and a "good to see you" as you pass them. Some will say this is asking too much. Go out of your way to be friendly. Before or after church, recognize people even if you need to briefly interrupt your conversation with a longtime friend to do so. This may be very difficult for introverts. But it is a must for pastors. This behavior creates a positive, warm atmosphere that may encourage first-timers to return to your congregation.

8. *Include a time in services for worshippers to greet each other.* Appropriate expressions like "So glad you are here," or "Good to see you this morning," or "Wow! I like your hearty handshake" are welcoming. Worship leaders should be careful not to instruct people to say "I love you," or some endearing term; to some this would be awkward and inappropriate. If a single young man turned around and said, "I love you" to a single young woman, she may or may not appreciate it!

9. *Compliment.* Sincere compliments are always relationship-builders. The apostle Paul was a master at this. Even to the carnal Corinthian church he wrote, "I always thank God for you because of his grace given you in Christ Jesus" (1 Corinthians 1:4). In Proverbs we read, "Kind words are like honey—they cheer you up and make you feel strong" (16:24 CEV).

Someone said, "There are three things people need, encouragement, encouragement, encouragement, and if that doesn't work, try encouragement!" Compliment new persons on their willingness to come and check us out, their choice of clothes, their hearty handshake, their smile, or just say, "So glad you are here," or "Good to see you." Remember: it's not easy to go to a church for the very first time, especially for the unchurched.

When complimenting children, I like to focus on features such as a smile, or nicely combed hair rather than compliments for their impressive or fashionable clothing. Our culture has already encouraged fashion to an extreme. If there is an age spread with the person of the opposite sex, it may be acceptable to state how nice they look, but it is best for men and women in our culture not to compliment the opposite sex on appearance because of the temptation of reading too much into those statements.

When the worship leader or pastor gets up to speak, it is appropriate to enthusiastically thank the worship team, the soloist, those who read Scripture or gave a testimony. This helps to model a culture of thanks throughout the congregation.

10. *Ask questions.* Jesus asked more than a hundred and fifty questions in the gospels. He did not ask because he didn't know the answer. Asking questions shows you are interested. People don't hear until they are heard. Talk about their interests. Ask *what*, *where*, and *who* questions. Try to stay away from *why* questions, which tend to make people defensive. You might ask where they live, their type of employment, hobbies, or recreational interests. Most people like to talk, so a statement like: "That's very interesting; tell me more" is usually appropriate. If children are with them, greet the children, and talk to them. That's a winner every time. Stooping down to the eye level of the child will help the child to feel comfortable with you.

11. *Don't identify others in the congregation by their family name or denominational heritage.* This isolates first-timers. In the Mennonite church, where families have sometimes been members for generations, we must remind people not to play the "Mennonite game," in which we try to learn how people are related to each other. It is more welcoming to identify first-timers by their work or a geographical location. For example, you might say, "I'll remember you as the person on George Street. I go past George Street every day to work."

12. *Offer to take first-timers or guests with you to your Sunday school class.* Tell them where the restrooms are located. Take the children to their classroom and introduce them to their teachers. Show them around the church building.

If appropriate, turn the conversation to spiritual things in any number of ways. As you are in dialogue, they may share a concern. You can respond by offering to pray about that concern. Learn to pray short prayers on the spot. Growing churches have an atmosphere in which it is appropriate to pray at anytime. Remember that 97 percent of people in the United States say they believe in prayer. It's hard to go wrong in praying for people. Prayers of loving concern help to build relationships.

13. *Invite first-timers and new attendees to a social function.* Begin to see them as your friends. Err on the side of being assertive. As I shared earlier, one in three people in our society say they have no close friends, so become a friend. Remember that this will likely involve sacrifice and a change in schedule on your part.

14. *Be conscious of new people who are sitting or standing alone.* New persons should never have to sit alone. Take the initiative to go to them without delay. As a pastor, my eyes were trained to look for new people. If they were alone I would ask one of my elders or members to please go and sit with them or dialogue with them.

15. *Be sensitive in your reaction to the mistakes of others.* It was my first Sunday in a Sunday school class. The teacher was writing on the board and misspelled a word. Everyone laughed. I felt embarrassed for the teacher. Was I being supersensitive? To laugh at misspelled words or at others' mistakes is seldom, if ever, appropriate.

16. *Listening is usually a very effective way to show love.* God gave us two ears and one mouth. Might that indicate that we need to listen twice as much as we talk?

The Most Effective Gesture

One of the most impressive gestures we can extend to first-time visitors is for people with no official position to take the initiative and welcome them. When people are filled with the love of the Holy Spirit, there is a loving atmosphere in the congregation, and this will happen spontaneously. Many will naturally use their spiritual gift of hospitality.

At CCF, the congregation applauds as first-time visitors raise their hands so the ushers can give them a simple gift. First-timers feel affirmed and welcomed. Applause in our culture sends the signal that we like what we are hearing.

As your congregation exercises the gift of hospitality, God will draw people to your church. Jesus told us to let our light shine so people can see our good deeds. In this context, we express our good deeds with hospitality.

Generally speaking, the older a church is, the harder it is to create a warm and spiritually vibrant atmosphere. People know each other so well that they see other's hypocrisy and inconsistencies. The devil will whisper to you, "Remember Johnny stole some money when he was a kid. We cannot trust him." Or, "Remember Sarah did not follow through on what she promised you." Or, "George talks too much; I won't listen to him." Paul reminds us that love "keeps no record of wrongs." Mature Christians forgive, look past things, and give compliments. God's grace will enable us to do this with genuine love.

What Is the First Thing?

Earlier we asked whether the first thing is the great commission (Matthew 28:18-20) or the great commandment (Matthew 22:37-40). The New Testament letters addressed to the churches show that their love was not perfect. But the gospel went forth in spite of their imperfect love. I believe the church must be mission-driven. That is the first thing. The way we carry out our mission is with love. The way we express our mission and purpose is by loving God and loving others.

Love is the key to being missional. While there is no magical factor for church growth, the key to growth is love in action— God's love reaching out to people of all nations.

Tradition has it that when the apostle John was dying, people gathered around his bed and asked what is most important in life. He said, "My children, love one another!" Pause once again and ask Jesus: Lord, teach me to love!

Questions for Discussion

1. When you walk into the auditorium of your church, do you like to experience quiet reverence or do you like to see people relating to each other, talking and laughing? What do you think is the atmosphere in most growing churches?

2. Why do many find it difficult to be friendly?

3. Why do we find it hard to love those of a different culture, economic status, or religion?

4. Do you find it hard to make new friends? Have you made new friends in the past three months? The past year?

5. Can we learn to love people simply because Jesus loves them and not for what we will gain from their friendship?

6. In your congregation, identify issues that make it difficult to love unchurched people from your community.

4

We are Wounded Healers

Dwelling in the Word: Read Matthew 18:23-35.

Testimony

Sally was born out of wedlock and was a great embarrassment to her parents. For the first thirteen years of her life, whenever family members came to visit, she was locked in the closet until the visitors left! She did not know most of her relatives until she was well into her adult life. Needless to say, Sally had many problems. But God in his graciousness has transformed her into a trophy of grace. Today, thanks to a supportive and accepting church, Sally ministers effectively to many children and adults. Oh, the depth of the richness of the mercy and grace of our Lord!

～

Until we are healed by Jesus, we will not be channels of love to others. This chapter focuses on the quality of life Jesus desires for us so we can bring healing to the wounded we meet every day both in the church and in our world.

Sally, described in the testimony above, battled with feelings of not being wanted or accepted. Others battle with jealousy of siblings or abuse by parents or relatives. At some point in their life, nearly everyone battles with feelings of being unwanted or unaccepted. When we feel this way, we have difficulty accepting the heavenly Father's love. As we relate to people, we need to pray to discern what hurts they are carrying. Have they forgiven their parents or others they may feel rejected them? Are they carrying grudges toward those who have not lived up to their expectations? Only through forgiving can we experience a life of freedom and healing. When we forgive, we are able to minister to others the joy and freedom found in forgiveness.

In Matthew 18:23-35, the king's servant owes him an amount that might be considered as large as ten million dollars. The point is that it is an impossible sum to repay in a world where wages are only a few cents a day. So the servant begs for more time. The king does not grant the request; instead, he forgives the debt of the servant. The forgiven servant, not really realizing he is forgiven, sees a fellow servant who owes him twenty dollars and can't pay. But the forgiven servant throws this debtor in jail.

The ratio of the two debts is five hundred thousand to one. A worker could not even earn a dollar a day. But at a dollar a day, it would take more than twenty-seven thousand years to pay this huge debt. The forgiven servant did not comprehend what the king did for him. He was blind.

Receiving Forgiveness

Many of us also do not comprehend what Jesus did for us. Our debt to God is so great that it can never be paid. The good news is that it *has* been paid! I don't fully grasp God's gift of his payment of my debt. Many Christians don't understand that Jesus paid for and forgave their debt.

Failure to receive forgiveness results in emotional problems. In *Healing for Damaged Emotions*, David Seamans writes that we have emotional problems for two reasons: (1) failure to receive forgiveness, and (2) failure to give forgiveness.[1] In the Matthew story, the forgiven servant never hears the king's words. He asks for patience and extension of time to pay his debt; in his pride and stupidity, he thinks he can pay back ten million dollars if only he is given enough time.

But the king didn't extend the note; he tore it up! The servant can't believe the wonderful news. He can't receive it or enjoy the fact that his debt has been paid. In his mind, he remains a debtor and thinks that he has simply been given more time to work, skimp, and save until finally the debt can be paid. Because he doesn't realize the debt has been cancelled, the guilt, resentment, and anxiety of the imagined all-consuming debt continues to eat away at him. He thinks it still imperative to collect debts from others. Do we do the same?

We hear about grace and say we believe in grace, but we tend to live in debt. Too often grace is only in our head. Grace has not worked its way into our hearts; therefore it is not transferred into our interpersonal relationships. Grace can never be repaid. Too often we live as though we can repay our debt, which puts us on a treadmill of performance, achievement, and striving to get rid of guilt. We may read an extra chapter in the Bible, extend our prayer time, and end up going to church out of obligation. We exhaust ourselves in good works. No wonder we have lost our joy! We substitute activity for intimacy with God. We try to exchange intimacy with God for service. Like Martha, we must hear Jesus tell us, "Mary has chosen what is better, and it will not be taken away from her" (Luke 10:42).

In Matthew 6:12, Jesus taught us to pray: "Forgive us our sins, just as we have forgiven those who have sinned against us" (NLT). He says in verses 14 and 15, "If you forgive those who sin against you, your heavenly Father will forgive you. But if you refuse to forgive others, your Father will not forgive your sins." When we fail to accept and receive God's grace and forgiveness, we also fail to give unconditional love, forgiveness, and grace to other people.

Jesus came to forgive and reconcile. Talk about being missional is a waste of time if there are past hurts in our lives that are not forgiven. Those hurts are a roadblock to our health and the health of the church. Many churches are crippled and sick because people have not forgiven family members who have hurt them. Hurt people often hurt others. Often they have not forgiven God for difficulties they believe God has allowed to come into their life. God helps us to come to the cross and receive healing, knowing Jesus has already paid our debt.

God's Grace for Our Own Sin

Not only do we need grace to forgive others, we need grace to forgive ourselves when we yield to temptation. I hate watching commercials, especially after I have seen them a couple times, so I often change channels frequently. In fact, I am an expert with the TV remote; I can watch three ball games simultaneously. When I'm channel surfing, I'm sometimes tempted to stop when the women are attractive or scantily clad. If I yield to that temptation, I lust, feel cheapened, guilty, and unworthy. I need God's forgiveness. I'm not addicted to pornography, but I am human. I am a new creation in Christ, but my old sinful nature is still there, which means I am tempted. Everyone has fallen. That's why we need grace. The good news is: Jesus Christ gives each one of us grace and power to live in obedience. If my mother were living, she would add these appropriate words of Paul: "Let him that thinketh he standeth take heed lest he fall" (1 Corinthians 10:12 KJV).

Elita Barnhart, a hospital chaplain in Malawi, Africa, writes in an unpublished paper:

> I often tell patients and people who talk about how they struggle with guilt and condemnation that what pleases God more than anything else, what delights God the most, is our willingness to receive His love and forgiveness. This is what He died for us to do! Strangely, I find this the hardest for us, it seems too good to be true, too free. We want to "feel" more deserving, which can lead to legalism and a religious judging spirit. God's specific and particular love for us is a revelation that we need to grasp and be willing as an act of faith to receive more boldly. This I believe is what blesses God, not false humility that remains in the place of, "I am nothing but

God is everything." This is true, but we must receive God's love enough not to remain in that position but to boldly claim as a sacrifice of praise to God "I am nothing, He is everything and because he is so great He can do even greater works through me!" This is what He died for us to get, and leads to more "fullness of God" in us, and I believe we all desperately need deeper revelations of God's particular dynamic love for us to be sustained in ministry. It is also this love relationship that those we serve most desperately need to experience. I am ever mindful of this understanding of the love of God as I minister, and it shapes my interactions daily.[2]

Thanking God: A Sign of Our Healing

Until you can thank God for the lessons of your past hurts, or at least recognize God's presence in the traumatic experiences, you are not really healed. If you are not healed, it's very difficult for the grace and love of Jesus to flow through you to others, especially to new people who walk through the doors of your church.

Those who do enter come with baggage and hurts. Let's be honest: all our churches are messy because humans are part of them. No one is perfect. "All our righteous acts are like filthy rags" (Isaiah 64:6). Was the New Testament church messy? Every letter was written to correct some sin or some problem in the church.

Paul could have spent chapter after chapter telling us in detail of all his hurts, but he simply mentions them as illustrations of God's grace. He persecuted the church but later became the church's greatest missionary and the writer of at least a dozen books in our New Testament. He was a forgiven person, and he was free to forgive others. Peter promised he would never deny Jesus. Peter failed, but then became the rock on which the church was built. Peter was a man of many sins, but he did not dwell on them. Instead he wrote, "Most important of all, continue to show deep love for each other, for love covers a multitude of sins" (1 Peter 4:8 NLT). He concludes his first letter, "My purpose in writing is to encourage you and assure you that the grace of God is with you no matter what happens" (1 Peter 5:12 NLT). Peter's sins were forgiven. He was a healed man.

Scripture calls us to "grow in the grace and knowledge of our Lord and Savior Jesus Christ" (2 Peter 3:18). David went from an adulterer and murderer to a man after God's own heart. Aaron carved a golden calf for the people to worship. What a hideous sin! But to his surprise, God chose him as the first-ever high priest. These men were forgiven. They accepted God's forgiveness and forgave themselves. We must do the same. We are not under condemnation (see Romans 8:1). Jesus said to the woman caught in adultery, "Neither do I condemn you. . . . Go and leave your life of sin" (John 8:11). Remember why Jesus was sent to us: "God did not send his Son into the world to condemn the world, but to save the world through him" (John 3:17).

Letting Jesus Heal You

People came to Jesus because he was gentle, humble, and at peace with himself. He was a secure person you could trust. You cannot be like Jesus until you let him take your hurts.

Many of our hurts occurred during our formative years when we were more vulnerable. Go back to your past in your mind and remember times of hurt. Take Jesus with you. Imagine the loving arms of Jesus around you as you relive the pain. He is there, suffering the pain with you. If you are living in pain presently, remember he is in that pain. Trust him, and accept his love and grace. Feel his comfort and thank him for his forgiveness. You are free!

When I was a child, I stuttered and was laughed at in school. In my first years as a pastor, I think I prayed more for the ability to speak than for the right words to say. Jesus took my hurts and over time brought healing. How wonderful it is to be free of the hurt.

Perhaps, like many people, you were hurt at church. Someone once said the church is the only organization that shoots its wounded. Wounded people tend to wound others; abused people so often end up abusing others. So it is vital that you seek healing.

At a camp one weekend in 2007, I led a congregation through four sessions on becoming a missional church. When we finished, the pastor came to me and shared something he apparently was too embarrassed to say before the sessions began. "There are people in this church who will not talk with each other," he said. "They sit on different sides of the church auditorium." They need to heed the apostle Paul's words: "You must make allowance for each other's faults and forgive the person who offends you. Remember, the Lord forgave you, so you must forgive others" (Colossians 3:13 NLT). This church can go through fifty sessions on how to be a missional congregation, but it will not see results until people learn to forgive and love each other. Those who come into this divisive atmosphere stand a great chance of being contaminated with the same disease already in the body.

Do you carry grudges or repeat the same hurtful story over and over? That's a clear sign that the hurt has not been forgiven. Do you carry hurts from your childhood? Did parents, siblings, or others physically, emotionally, sexually abuse you or laugh at you?

Purging this pain is a process; you are not set free all at once. But intentionally giving over the trauma to Christ can start you on the path to freedom. Take Jesus with you to the spot where you were hurt. Picture him as he absorbs the pain. See him put his arms of love around you. Thank him for taking the pain.

Lies, anger, envy, jealousy, and pride need to be confessed. Unless these things are brought to the cross and put under the cleansing and healing blood of Jesus, you will not be the channel of love to other hurting persons that Jesus wants you to be. (See 2 Corinthians 1:4-6; 1 John 1:9.)

I repeat: picture Jesus with you in your pain. See him taking that hurt, that pain, and let him put his healing arms around you; hear him say, "I will help you to forgive. I saw your hurt. I was there and suffered with you. I paid for that hurt and pain." Not only will you experience new life, but you will feel a new freedom to love that you didn't know was possible. Don't spend your energy hiding those secrets. Someone once wisely said that we are as sick as our secrets.

Only when you get your secrets under the blood of Jesus can you reach out with the depth of love and grace from your heart so that other people can feel love and acceptance from you. Become transparent, free, and open. That's what Jesus meant when he said, "So if the Son sets you free, you will be free indeed" (John 8:36). *The Message* Bible says, "You are free through and through." Doesn't that sound like good news?

Bring It to the Cross

I have found the following exercise helpful for our church and encourage you to try it. Place a wooden cross in the front of the church along with hammers and nails. Have people write their hurts on paper. Then invite them to come to the front and nail those hurts to the cross. If you are in a traditional congregation in which people are frozen to their seats, perhaps the pastor could lead the way. Or coach your leadership team ahead of time so they come forward immediately as an example for the congregation to follow. Pray for wisdom to break through the icy barriers among your people.

For some, even this exercise will not cause them to feel forgiven. They will need an additional step. Sharing with Jesus may not be enough. Some hurts are only healed when they are shared with another person. As one little boy once said, "I need Jesus with flesh on." Share your hurts with at least one other person you trust, a person who becomes a priest for you. James writes, "Confess your sins to each other and pray for each other so that you may be healed" (James 5:16 NLT). When we experience love and forgiveness from another human being, we are better able to emotionally feel God's forgiveness.

It was difficult for me to forgive the leaders of my childhood church who taught that instrumental music was inferior to a cappella singing and that wearing plain clothes—such as a "straight cut" coat rather than a sport coat or lapel coat—was more spiritual. I more easily forgave the man across the street who divorced his wife and ran off with another woman. I suppose this was because my church experience was more personal.

The good news is that God's grace is there for us to receive. If you have hurts that have not been forgiven, Jesus wants to free you. It's possible to be a good Christian, go to church, read your Bible, sing the songs, but never let Jesus heal you. Don't live that shallow, empty life. Come to him and be healed. Become a fountain of grace. You will find that you can bear with one another, confront one another in love, encourage and warn one another. There will be a new level of living, a new level of joy and peace, and a new level of relationship. Picture a church full of people living in God's wonderful grace!

In his commentary on Luke, William Barclay defines *agape* love as "an active feeling of benevolence toward the other person; it means that no matter what that person does to us we will never allow ourselves to desire anything but his highest good and we will deliberately and of set purpose go out of our way to be good and kind to him."[3] Only God's grace can enable us to live on that level. People of grace want to see others experience the marvelous, freeing wholeness they experience in Jesus.

If we want people to be healed, we need to be vulnerable and transparent. When we experience forgiveness, we find it easier to be transparent. We are secure enough to not need to hide our sins and our weaknesses. When we can be open about our weaknesses, it will help others to do the same.

I once heard of a psychiatrist who wants to help clients become open so they can begin the healing process. He begins by revealing to his client something personal about himself, a secret that could damage his career if the client broke the confidence. This frees the client to talk.[4]

A Word of Caution

Sometimes people as well as congregations spend hours digging up old hurts. While it is necessary to bring them to our attention for healing, once they are healed it is counterproductive to keep them in front of ourselves or in front of the congregation. I have seen congregations hang out their dirty wash; old hurts were posted for months for everyone to see. Paul says in Philippians 3:13 to forget the past and focus on what lies ahead. Are you and your congregation future-focused?

Too often American Christianity is "me" centered. It's all about me. It will continue to be all about me until we see what Jesus did for us. When we see anew what Jesus did for us, we begin to focus on others and our mission. We lack power to be salt and light as long as the focus is on our needs. Realize, in faith, Jesus has already met those needs. Having had our needs met, the focus now needs to be on building God's kingdom. It is all about him. At CCF, the congregation sometimes repeats in unison until it echoes off the walls: "It's not about me. It's not about you. It's all about HIM!"

Jesus said, "And when I am lifted up from the earth, I will draw everyone to myself" (John 12:32 NLT). Paul said he concentrated only on Jesus Christ and his death on the cross (see 1 Corinthians 2:2). Concentrate on Jesus. Thank him daily for what he has done for you. Jesus paid your debt; now go forward gladly freeing others.

Why Christians are Often Quiet about Faith

We often don't share our faith because we do not realize the incredible significance of Jesus forgiving our debt. If I am not ener-gized by what Jesus has done for me and by the new life he offers, how can I share my faith? If my relationship to Jesus is a bore and my church experiences dull, I'm not likely to invite someone to church.

If you are running on empty, you probably can't give to others. So how do you keep refreshed? Pray that God's Word may become as precious as it was to David. When we feed on the Word of God, we will have something to offer. When we forgive others for the hurt in our lives, God's grace enables us to move on in victory.

For Discussion

1. Have you personally forgiven those who have mistreated you or overlooked your efforts?

2. When you were falsely accused and took someone else's punishment, did you forgive the accuser?

3. Are there individuals or relationships in your congregation that need reconciliation? What is keeping you from making the first step in working to bring healing?

5

Knowing Our Context

Dwelling in the Word: Read Acts 11:1-18.

Testimony
John was brought up in a home where his father and mother were constantly fighting. One night when he was thirteen, his father threw him out of the house in the rain with nothing but the clothes on his back. He was told never to come back. After many years and much love showered by an elderly Christian couple, John is growing in his Christian life. John has forgiven his parents, and the family that had ostracized him is showing clear signs of acceptance. Much healing has taken place, but more is needed. John brings a sense of stability to an otherwise unstable family. He is a positive witness to them as well as many others.

〜

In this chapter, I focus on understanding the context of our church. The painful reality is that many churches in our communities are declining. We are not replacing church members who die. In Mennonite Church USA, for example, couples are averaging 1.4 children each.[1] Many of our children will not stay in the community. Those who do stay are frequently not loyal to the denomination in which they were raised.

Denominational labels are not popular in our culture. Most congregations affiliated with a denomination are declining. The obvious response to this is to say that declining congregations must turn around or eventually die. After much prayer, a pastor and the leadership of the church must bring this painful reality to the congregation: grow or die.

As I noted in chapter 2, the mission of the church is to see people transferred from the kingdom of darkness to the kingdom of our Lord. But to do this, we need to reach out to the unchurched. What does that involve?

In Acts 10 and 11, Peter had a vision of a sheet coming down from heaven. In the sheet were "all sorts of small animals, wild animals, reptiles, and birds. And I heard a voice say, 'Get up, Peter; kill and eat them'" (Acts 11:6-7 NLT). Eating these animals, reptiles, and birds was forbidden by Jewish law, and Peter's first reaction was repulsion. Perhaps he gagged or felt like throwing up when he saw those forbidden animals and birds; he certainly couldn't imagine eating them. Peter was not easily persuaded, and the sheet was let down three times.

Sometimes when we work with the unchurched, we too may feel like gagging. Our problem is that there are not enough gagging Christians. We are afraid to enter the world and culture of pre-believers. Peter was outside his comfort zone. Likewise, we must venture outside our comfort zones to reach others for our Lord.

If our declining congregations are to reach their communities, we need to do some gagging. Pray for God to raise up people who are willing to be gaggers.

Approaching Revitalization

In order to grow, congregations need to move from seeing the church as something for themselves to seeing it as the instrument of God's mission. Our priority should be the spiritual need of those in our unchurched communities. We must refine our worship services and church activities to respond to those needs. Also we must unlearn habits, behaviors, and practices that are not appreciated by prebelievers. Having set forth this premise, my approach to church revitalization and growth contains the following elements and steps:

1. *Pray for wisdom and courage.* Prayer is the tool the Lord uses to develop both a vision and a passion for doing God's will. Prayer is the life breath of the church; it brings God into the picture. Apart from him we fail. The prayer focus for many Christians needs to be for the Lord to give us a love for the people in our community. We will reach only those we have the capacity to love. We will never reach our communities if we do not love people.

2. *Dwell in the Word and focus on developing strategy for reaching your community.* God's Word is our authoritative guide for the foundation, direction, and mission of the church. We must love the Word. King David is our model: "My soul is consumed with longing for your laws at all times" (Psalm 119:20). "Oh, how I love your law! I meditate on it all day long" (verse 97). "I have more insight than all my teachers, for I meditate on your statutes" (verse 99). Does your congregation love the Word and seek to obey it? Someone once said that the Word and prayer are like two sticks of dynamite: put together they will display God power in a mighty way.

3. *Listen for the Holy Spirit's direction.* We must coach our people to be more confident in their relationship with Jesus and God. That's the vertical dimension. Horizontally we must consult with other church leaders and mature Christians in our church family. It's my conviction that if we seek the Lord, he will speak to us through his Spirit, through the Word, through others, and through what we see with our own eyes. Jesus did nothing without consulting the Father (see John 5:30). How much more do we need to hear from our Father? The challenge is to take time to listen. Only as we learn to listen to the Father can we really hear our brothers and sisters.

4. *Implement.* After we understand the steps needed to reach our communities, we need the wisdom and courage to implement

those steps. That is not a quick exercise. It may take many months, sometimes years.

Greg Groeschel lists six steps that can lead toward revitalization of one's life as well as one's church: passion for God's presence, a deep craving to reach the lost, sincere integrity, Spirit-filled faith, down-to-earth humility, and brokenness, that is, recognizing our own sinfulness.[2]

Internal Factors

In older congregations, revitalization will be more difficult. If the median tenure of your members is more than twelve years, growth will be arduous. The longer people have been together, the more difficult it is to break into their patterns of church life. If the leaders of the congregation have longer tenure in church than the average for members, it is a signal that new people are not being absorbed into leadership. Attendance and offering trends are also important. If the trends are negative, it will be more difficult to turn things around.

The pastor needs to have a passion for ministering to the ninety-and-nine and also to the lost sheep. He or she must be a person of vision and faith. The faith of the church is never really larger than the vision of the pastor. If members have a larger vision than the pastor, their faith will be stymied. The congregation as a whole will not rise above the leader's maturity.

Some congregations are lukewarm. Some are not born again. They don't really know God or his Son Jesus; they only know about him (see John 17:3).

External Factors

Demographics aren't everything, but they cannot be ignored. Central Illinois seemed to me a vast plain of corn and beans. One could drive a mile without passing a house or barn. The church that I pastored there was the only congregation that did not grow during my forty-eight years of pastoral ministry. As you can imagine, these were difficult years for me. The young people all went away to college. After college all of them moved to other communities except for one young man, who returned to his parent's farm. The farms were becoming larger as the population declined. Many members were in their 70s, 80s, and 90s. One time I had four funerals in eight days, all for members of the congregation. While we reached a few community people, it was not enough to offset those who died or who moved away. I was anxious to move to a place with lots of people.

My conference minister challenged me to receive my satisfaction and fulfillment from nurturing the members. I was not able to find my fulfillment there. I was anxious to be in a context where I had more people to work with than I could contact.

Demographic studies can help us discover needs in our community. Demographics show us population numbers, ages, genders, size of families, number of married couples, number of singles, number of singles with children, races, average income, religions, education levels, political affiliations, and occupations of residents. Some data may show the percentage of people receiving a newspaper or listening to local radio and television stations. The findings from these facts can be of great help in determining the needs of the community.

But walking and talking give a greater understanding. Going door-to-door may still be acceptable in most communities. If your community consists of apartment complexes with "no soliciting" signs, however, consider talking to the owners to obtain permission for a door-to-door survey.

Many churches have used Rick Warren's survey questions.[3] He suggests greeting community residents by saying something like: "Hi, I'm Joe Smith. I'm taking an opinion poll of our community. I'm not here to sell anything. There are no right or wrong answers to these five questions, and it will only take two minutes: What do you think is the greatest need in your community?"

This question is basically to get the interviewee to open up and feel comfortable. Then ask, "Are you actively attending a church?"

Be careful not to ask, "Are you a member of a church?" Many

people may be members but haven't been to church for years. If they indicate they are active in church, go to the next person or the next home. We want to find out the needs of unbelievers, not believers.

If you continue, though, the next question would be "Why do you think most people don't attend church?" If you ask, "Why don't you attend church?" they may likely respond that it's none of your business. There is a good possibility that when the person answers that question, you will know why they don't attend church.

Then ask "If you were looking for a church to attend, what kind of things would you look for?" This is a crucial question, so listen carefully to the answer.

The final question is, "What advice can you give to a church leader who really wants to be helpful to people?"

I have found that many will say they are too busy to come to church. Ask them, "If there was a convenient time, would you consider coming to church?" You might ask if Saturday evening or a weeknight would be more workable.

Discover Your Target

A survey will help you decide on a target audience and some community needs. Then you can discern the strengths of your congregation and match them to the community's needs. We can't meet all the needs, but even a small church can meet some. Chapter 11 focuses on how spiritual gifts can be used for the various needs of the community.

What if your church strengths do not match the community needs? Rick Warren speaks to this situation in *The Purpose-Driven Church*.

> Often communities change, but the makeup of a church doesn't. . . . Don't try to be something you're not. If your church is primarily made up of elderly folks, decide to become an effective ministry to senior citizens. Don't try to become a baby-buster congregation. Don't worry about what you can't do. Keep doing what you're strong at; just do

it better. Chances are that there is a pocket of people in your community that only your church can reach.

Reinventing the congregation occurs when you intentionally change the makeup of your church in order to match a new target. You completely replace all the old programs, structures, and worship styles with new ones.

I want to be very clear: I do not advise this reinvention. It is a painful process and may take many years. People will leave the church due to the inevitable conflicts. If you lead this process, you will probably be vilified as Satan incarnate. I have seen this done successfully, but not without an enormous amount of persistence and willingness to absorb criticism. It takes a very loving, patient, and gifted pastor to lead a church in reinventing itself.

Don't even consider this option in a church with over one hundred attendees unless God tells you to. However, if you are in a church of fifty people or less, this may be a viable option for you. One advantage for the small church is that it can be completely transformed by having just a few families leave and a few new families join. But the bigger a church is, the less likely you'll be able to do this.[4]

Warren helps us face reality. It reminds us that, as Jesus put it, we don't "pour new wine into old wineskins" (Matthew 9:17). So what are our options?

Options to Consider

While the following list is certainly not exhaustive, it offers some options for plateaued or declining congregations.

1. *Stay here and die in X number of years.* People in the community are likely of a different culture than church people. Church people often have different values, interests, and lifestyles than unchurched members of the community. The church members are sometimes a subculture within the larger culture. We can be friendly but find it almost impossible to be a friend to the unchurched.

Established churches usually have a core of people who can meet the budget and keep the church operating. Often this self-sufficiency results in complacency. The church lacks the faith to believe community people can be discipled and can become church workers and leaders. I love the question: Is your next pastor saved yet? Do we have the faith to believe our next pastor will be raised up from our community? Often established churches don't even think in those terms.

2. *Stay here and focus our energy on reaching the local community, keeping our current style of worship and program.* Most people want their church to grow, but they are not willing to change. Many are content to splash around in the shallow waters of sameness. With a concerted effort of evangelistic zeal, this approach could reach a few folks in the community, but growth would be difficult and very slow. New persons, if they do come, will often leave after several months because there is no real bonding. In this approach we are essentially saying to the unchurched community people: "You must become like us by appreciating our music, our culture, our style of worship, and our lifestyle." This church is saying, "Our doors are open, and you are welcome to become like us. You need to adopt our culture, our values, our music, our way of operating, and then you can become one of us. We are not going to change."

For ten years during the 1970s and 1980s, I served as chairperson of the evangelism commission of the Ohio Conference of the Mennonite Church. One experience was a real eye-opener. I drove eighty miles every month for eight months to pull together a core group to begin a church plant. We then called a church planter who did a great job for sixteen months. Some changes occurred, and he felt he needed to move for the sake of his family. When the church planter left, the congregation was averaging about seventy-five attendees, with more than one hundred on Easter. (In the meantime, Helen and I moved to Florida to plant our second church.)

Within eight weeks of the arrival of the new pastor, the congregation dissolved! Why? The new pastor was a wonderful man of God, but he did not understand the culture of his newer urban believers. He thought he could bring his style of worship with him. To plant churches and make disciples, we must understand the culture of the people we work with and their style of worship. Church planters should be like the "men of Issachar, who understood the times and knew what Israel should do" (1 Chronicles 12:32; see also 1 Corinthians 9:19-27). We must operate like missionaries, with an understanding of the times and the culture of the people we are sent to reach.

3. *Stay here and become indigenous to the culture.* In this approach, we become friends to those in the immediate community. This approach usually demands a paradigm shift that is very difficult and only possible with God's grace.

The members operate as missionaries, but the pastor must be a model. From doing his or her own survey work, and from asking members for names of people who might be contacted, the pastor visits the identified families, relating to them, encouraging them, introducing them to others in the congregation who then build relationships with them.

The members usually need the pastor to model and lead the way to show them that inviting their friends is a wonderful privilege, not a burden. To make the shift to being missional in this way, the established church will need to consider changes in worship, in music, in facilities, in church structure: in almost everything. A missional church talks about God in everyday language, with illustrations from the everyday life of the community, using idioms that the people of the community can understand.

Once you identify the needs of the community, find gifts in the congregation that match those needs and develop programs to meet them. These options can be an excellent point of entry for new persons. You might offer classes in parenting, marriage enrichment, anger management, financial management, or how to buy a house. Other programs might be aerobics, divorce care, grief recovery, drug rehabilitation, HIV support groups, quilting, cooking, introduction to Spanish, English as a Second Language, introduction to computers, scrapbooking, photography, creative movement, kids' chorus, after-school care, tutoring for school children, a monthly or weekly Saturday brunch, or a men's breakfast.

Other options might be a book discussion club, feeding the homeless, offering home repairs, ALPHA or AWANA programs (discussed in chapter 9), a women's night out, a neighborhood coffee house, youth activities or sports, volunteer activities such as working at a soup kitchen. If you have a gym on your church property, the options are almost endless.

Offering these activities or programs for a short term frequently works best. Many people, especially new attendees, don't want to sign up for six months, but they may want to participate in three or four sessions. But an important word of caution here: do not take on more programs than your congregation can handle. If they become a burden, something is definitely wrong.

My experience with a childcare ministry in Lima, Ohio, was very positive. It was a wonderful way to relate to and help meet the needs of community families. Another advantage is that with a childcare ministry, you generally relate to young families. What congregation doesn't enjoy lively children? The daycare opened doors for ministering to families in the community and reaching some for Jesus.

Many Mennonite congregations have a great group of older people. With baby-boomers reaching retirement age, this could be an opportunity. Congregations might provide a senior-citizen daycare or senior clubs with activities such as socials. Senior groups can also facilitate volunteer activities, such as providing secretarial assistance for the office, assisting the church librarian, or ministering to those who are ill.

It took me a long time to learn that people from the community often respond better if you charge for services and activities rather than offer them for free. Community people are often skeptical if you offer something free; they think there must be a catch. Charging can give your project or ministry a sense of respect and legitimacy. Most people know things cost money, and they do not want to sponge off of others, especially a church and especially if they realize the church is helping people in their community.

4. *Stay here and add a worship service that is more culturally relevant to the community.* If there is a mass of teens and college-aged people, they may desire their own service. Perhaps they can meet at the same time as the existing service if your facility is adequate, or they could meet at a different time or location. While this can lead to two groups in the church, at least in the beginning both would share a common treasury, some outreach activities, plus Bible studies and other community-focused programs.

Studies show that most churches that begin a second service will reach more people. Some churches believe that the multiple services are not so much due to growth, but a cause of growth. Twenty-three percent of the American work force is working on Sunday. Who will provide a worship service and church family for them?

Launching a second service instead of launching a building expansion saves lots of money. The bottleneck of evangelism is more laborers (see Matthew 9:37 and Luke 10:2). By starting a second service instead of expanding or building a new facility, the church may be able to employ more staff with the savings. Furthermore, Americans, especially the younger generation, don't like inconvenience, and additional services give people more choices.

Sometimes the community is so culturally diverse it seems impossible to expect people to change radically enough to enjoy worshipping together. An example might be a case in which a pastor is effectively ministering to youth from a different culture than the adults in the congregation, who are mostly over sixty years old. From a biblical perspective, holding two separate worship services may be less than ideal; yet this approach is better than not reaching your neighbors at all or losing a large block of your congregation. Often those who leave a congregation are its more creative persons, whom the congregation would find helpful in being missional.

5. *Stay here and begin another congregation with the help of technology.* While this may sound far-fetched to the older generation, it is working extremely well in some places. It works like this: one pastor and a few families from your congregation who feel called by God plant a church in a new location. The pastor who stays with the home church gives the messages to both the home church and the church plant by way of technology that broadcasts the message on a screen in another location. The pastor of the church plant functions as a pastor, then, not as a preacher; the preaching is communicated from the home base. In this approach, the home-based pastor needs to be cognizant of the culture and mindset of those in the church plant and should be able to communicate well with them.

This is a much less expensive way to do church planting, especially if the pastor of the church plant is bi-vocational during the start-up phase. Many churches have had great success with this approach. For example, National Community Church, with a home base at Union Station in Washington, D.C., maintains four satellite locations. They have seventy-five small groups and many ministries. The Seacoast Church in Mount Pleasant, South Carolina, has eleven satellite churches with a total of 22,000 members.[5] Greg Groeschel's LifeChurch.tv has thirteen campuses and thousands of people in six states. Lancaster County Bible Church near Mt. Joy, Pennsylvania, has a church plant in Linglestown, thirty miles north of the home church.

For many older folks, the idea of listening to a message on the screen doesn't sound inviting. But for youth who frequently experience this in school and spend a good portion of their time in front of screens, it's not a problem. In this approach the personal relationships are experienced with the church-plant community rather than with the pastor from the home base church who they observe on the screen.

6. *Stay here but plant another congregation with the same staff.* Bill Hinton, pastor of the First Methodist Church in Houston, was in the city's downtown at a time when the local newspaper

reported that 50 percent of the Houston residents would not go to that part of the city because of safety issues. Bill challenged the congregation to be missional by planting a church in the suburbs but also keeping the church operating in the inner city. In this dual campus approach both congregations are growing with the same staff. Many are finding hope in Jesus Christ.[6]

Considerations to Moving the Church

The six possibilities discussed above allow the congregation to remain in its present location. The following four suggest moving the congregation, or part of it, to a new location. Often moving to a neutral facility like a fire hall, community center, movie theater, or college auditorium makes it easier to attract the unchurched. Church buildings often intimidate prebelievers.

7. *Move the congregation to a community of similar cultural and economic strata.* If you choose this option, you may want to rent a facility at first. Later, you can sell your building to a congregation more amenable to the immediate culture. I have worked with rural congregations that found it difficult to grow because of the economy and demographics. Jobs were scarce and the few new families moving into the community were of a different culture and economic level. If a congregation has a passion for reaching the lost, it needs to be willing to say to the Lord, "If you want us to leave this facility—where our parents carried us to church and where our grandparents and extended family members are buried in the cemetery—we are willing. We are willing to do whatever it takes to put the first thing first." Congregations willing to be that radical are rare.

When I was pastor of Cottage City Mennonite Church, the church decided to change the name it had for more than six decades to Capital Christian Fellowship. It also moved ten miles to a rented facility in a less urban area. We worshipped at Capital College for nine years until we could build our new facility in Lanham, Maryland, an urban setting a few miles from Washington, D.C. We grew to more than four hundred attendees.

8. *Make two congregations.* With this option, the church plant moves to a rented facility while the remaining group ministers to the local community at its present location. This assumes that the group staying in the community will be missional and will be able to change its style of worship and other elements to fit the local culture.

9. *Join with other congregations to plant a church.* By pooling resources with at least one other congregation, a bigger church plant with a larger vision may emerge. For example, think in terms of an auditorium of four hundred or more and plan to start a second service in a different style as soon as possible. Also, begin with the clear understanding that you will plant daughter congregations as soon as possible. A reasonable target to do this is three years. Of course, the church's leadership needs to have received this vision from the Lord. Verbalize this vision and pray before you launch the church.

It is my observation, generally speaking, that the morale of small congregations is not as healthy as that of medium-sized congregations. Smaller congregations find it difficult to support a pastor. When there are small classes of one to three children many parents feel their children are missing out on a broader range of activities that larger churches offer: clubs, choirs, community projects, and other activities throughout the week. In smaller churches, children are limited in building relationships with others of different cultures.

One could argue that it makes little sense for several small churches within a few miles of each other to struggle for survival. Youth groups are often too small to make a critical mass. Youth like to be with other youth. Some might ask if a pastor's time is being used wisely by bringing a message for twenty adults when he or she could be speaking to two or three times that number. Most Sunday school teachers would appreciate preparing a lesson for six children rather than two. A larger group could support a full-time pastor. Few congregations are missional without a supported pastor. Most pastors would rather earn their living from the congregation.

A few years ago, I had the challenge of helping to merge two older and smaller congregations that were located ten miles apart. While there were many challenges, the new, larger congregation was immediately relieved and excited to discover the newly available resources. But they continue to struggle to be missional and make disciples of the unchurched. I am convinced that unless the leadership of a congregation has a passion to reach the unchurched, congregational mergers alone will not lead to growth. It will simply delay their closing date.

Unity of Primary Importance

One of the most neglected aspects of Jesus' teaching is his passion for unity. Jesus calls us to work together instead of dividing over issues that are not central to the gospel. In John 17, Jesus clearly pours out his heart to the Father just hours before the cross, asking for his followers to be one as he and the Father and the Holy Spirit are one. The trinity is inseparable. They are intimate. When will we take this burden of our Lord seriously?

The church is more effective when we work together, and the world takes notice. Unity glorifies Jesus and expands his kingdom. In Lancaster County, Pennsylvania, there are several dozen groups all claiming to come under the Anabaptist umbrella. When the world sees this plethora of divisions, we don't need to ask why they are not running to our doors. Jesus said, "Anyone who is not against us is for us" (Mark 9:40 NLT). We can reconcile and work together even when we do not agree. I believe the Lord may need to bring times of suffering or persecution upon us before we really learn to work together. We learn obedience through the things we suffer (see Hebrews 5:8). When mission becomes our primary focus, the things that divide us become less important.

It is possible to separate in unity. Amicable family separations occur every time a man and a woman leave their own homes to begin a new life together in the covenant of marriage. Likewise, if a separation between two groups in the body of Christ occurs as a result of a peaceable agreement to take separate pathways, it can be blessed by God's Spirit. If those groups are able to continue to fellowship together and to bless and affirm each other, even though they are headed in different directions in their callings, God can honor these separations.[7]

Cell and House Church Models

10. *Start a house or cell church.* In the model of a cell church, which can also be called a house church, baptisms, offerings, and worship services take place in the cell. Some meet together once a month as a larger group, with the cells coming together in a rented facility or another church building on a Sunday afternoon/evening or on a weekday evening when most church buildings are not in use. In moving to a cell model, you may want to keep your present facility or rent it to another congregation so as to have a place for cells to meet together (perhaps monthly) for worship, fellowship, and teaching.

One barrier to becoming a healthy church is that buildings too often become our identity. We would never think of leaving our property, especially if the cemetery in which our extended family is buried is located adjacent to the church building. Too often we find our security in the building. Let's remember that we are the body of Christ. Christ dwells in us, not in a building. There were no church buildings for the first three hundred years after Christ. The church was a powerful force in the community and nation during those years.

The cell model is predominant in some countries, like China, which has millions of Christians. There is little doubt in my mind that there will be more Christians in heaven who had been nurtured in a cell model church structure than in a building model.

As someone wrote: why do we invite people to the one place we know they won't come? Try inviting people to your home. This is a place to build relationships and introduce prebelievers to our friends. In *The Emerging Church*, Dan Kimball reports that many college students are shifting away from high-tech, highly produced worship to a simpler service in smaller groupings. Some Latino churches are utilizing this model. Ministerios Fraternidad Cristiana (MFC) is a fast-growing network of cell churches in Connecticut and New York. MFC now includes a network of 140 groups organized into seven congregations that include members from all Latin American countries and the United States.

In *Back to Jerusalem*, Paul Hattaway describes the multitudes of Christians in China who have no intention of erecting buildings. Indeed, the world doesn't need another church building; it needs Jesus, and it needs to worship and grow in God's grace with other believers in their own homes, like the New Testament church (see Acts 5:42, 20:20; Romans 16:5).[8]

There may be a day when persecution comes and our buildings will be taken from us. That's what happened in Ethiopia in the 1980s, when the government forced Christians underground. At that time, the Mennonite church in Ethiopia numbered about five thousand. It emerged ten years later numbering fifty thousand. Praise God that he works through persecution and hardships. As Romans 8:28 reminds us, "We know that in all things God works for the good of those who love him, who have been called according to his purpose."

Advantages of Starting New Congregations

Helen and I planted two churches, one in Ohio and one in Florida, beginning with only two or three families in each. What's the most effective way to plant a church? Some authors present as many as nine models for church planting.[9] Helen and I started with two or three families because I didn't know better in those days. How thankful I am that God works despite our limited knowledge.

Today I can relate what I think is an effective model for planting a church. The first thing I would want is a team of intercessors. This is an absolute must. Nothing of any value will occur without the Holy Spirit, and intercessors enable God to work in his people. Next, I would want to find a few families with children and a few musicians—preferably keyboard and guitar players and a drummer—to form a core worship team. I would ask the core group for the names of friends I could contact to invite to our emerging church. It is important that they meet the church planter face-to-face. This makes it easier to accept the invitation.

I would also invite the unchurched to be part of the core group and begin to disciple them before I launched the church. It's important to utilize the gifts of those who have not yet become disciples. Think how Jesus allowed the woman at the well to bring her whole village to him. She had only talked with Jesus for a very short time. (See John 4:1-42.) Remember the demoniac who wanted to go with Jesus after being cured, but Jesus told him to go and be a witness to the Decapolis (see Mark 5:1-20). Jesus empowered people to use their gifts even though they were babes in Christ.

The advantage of using the unchurched who are coming to Christ is that these new disciples are open to your vision, which makes it much easier to move ahead in unity. Also, unchurched people tend to have natural relationships in the community; that is, new people bring new people. The longer we are Christians, the fewer unchurched friends we have, which makes it all the more difficult to reach new families. The two church plants Helen and I started grew mainly from house-to-house contacts and people inviting their friends.

Phil Stevenson writes, "The kingdom grows fastest when we start new churches because newer congregations tend to grow much faster than older ones."[10] This is true because new churches must grow in order to survive. They don't have to give energy to maintaining existing programs. Their entire focus is on being missional, on reaching the lost to make disciples, who in turn reach their friends. Older churches often lose sight of their purpose. Too often the first thing is not the first thing for an older church. Stevenson reports that the average number of converts per one hundred members decreases the older the church is. Churches that are three years old or less average ten converts per one hundred members. For churches from three to fifteen years old the average is five, and the average for churches more than fifteen years old drops to one and a half converts per one hundred members.[11]

It's also helpful to repeat that starting a second service in established churches nearly always results in an increase in attendance. Remember, in our culture, choices are important to our busy neighbors.

Finances are often an obstacle to starting a new congregation. Many churches today rent facilities to congregations of different cultures. This can be a helpful source of income for an older congregation as well as a great help for the church plant. Also, if you start a second service instead of building an addition, you can save millions of dollars and use some of those funds for additional staff to lead the church in reaching prebelievers.

For Discussion

After a time of prayer and meditation, ask yourself whether any of the ten models described in this chapter may be God's preferred future for your church. If not, to what do you believe God is calling your church?

6

Welcoming Unchurched Neighbors

Dwelling in the Word: Read 1 Corinthians 9:19-27.

Testimony

Bob's father was a minister. But Bob eventually turned his back on the Lord and the church. After living through a painful divorce, he moved in with another woman. They lived together for several years. I visited them a number of times. Bob and his girlfriend opened their hearts to Jesus and started coming regularly to church. Several months later, at their insistence, I married them in a bar because they wanted all their old friends to witness their Christian marriage. They knew many of their friends would not come to church for the wedding. Today they serve our Lord faithfully in church ministry. Bob returns to the bar, not to drink but to share Jesus with his buddies.

∼

Do we really believe the gospel is for all people? Do we accept what Scripture tells us, that God wants everyone to be saved (see 2 Peter 3:9)? If so, we need to put a passion for reaching our lost neighbors into action.

In Genesis 12:1-3, God tells Abraham that through him, all the families of the earth will be blessed. John R. W. Scott states,

> It is this expression more than any other that reveals the living God of the Bible to be a missionary God. It is this expression too that condemns all our petty parochialism and narrow nationalism, our racial pride (whether white or black), our condescending paternalism and arrogant imperialism. How dare we adopt a hostile or scornful or even indifferent attitude to any person of another color or culture if our God is the God of all the families of the earth? We need to become global Christians with a global vision, for we have a global God.[1]

Many churches expect their pastor to be available at the church study to care for the "flock." Pastors need to care for the flock, but they have to discipline themselves to spend time relating to prebelievers. Just as all members need to be missionaries, so do pastors. Churches need to free their pastor to build relationships with the unchurched.

Many Christians don't seem concerned about their neighbors' salvation. Too often our conversations are about ourselves and how to make our lives more comfortable. When we do talk about non-Christians, we often complain about the "horrible things going on in our culture." Is that what Jesus did? He was more critical of believers than of nonbelievers.

To be intentional about building friendships with prebelievers, we need to remember that Jesus is our model. In Luke 15:1 we read, "Tax collectors and other notorious sinners often came to listen to Jesus teach" (NLT).

What the Unchurched Want

Recently I went to a secular college campus to interview students. I asked them two questions: "What do you think of Jesus?" and "What do you think of the church?" Of the dozen or more students I interviewed, all were positive about Jesus except one, who claimed to be an adamant atheist. Their remarks included: "Jesus helped the poor," "He taught us self-sacrifice," "I look up to him," "He influenced history," "He was a spiritual person," "He brought hope," and "He is the Savior, the Son of God." One young woman was a committed Christian; others said they did not attend church on campus but do when they are home.

Their impressions of the church were much more negative. Responses included:

- the church has lost its purpose;
- the church has lost its focus;
- I'm not opposed, but I don't go;
- I'm not for megachurches;
- Adam and Eve and all those stories are the same as the Santa Claus story;
- the church is okay if you are working through grief;
- I don't know, I've never been to church;
- I don't need guidance, so I don't go;
- there are too many kinds of churches;
- I don't like [a particular group of Christians];
- three Jewish students saw attending synagogue as an obligation, so they don't go.

These responses show that postmodern youth are eager to talk about Jesus even though they are unenthusiastic about church.

Acceptance and Belonging

For the most part, people are looking for a community to belong to even more than a message to believe in. Evangelism is about helping people belong so that they will come to believe. Jesus befriended us before he told us what to believe (see John 3:16). We can accept people without approving of their actions. Jesus accepted the woman at the well. He accepted Levi, Zacchaeus, the woman caught in adultery, the sinful woman who anointed his feet, and others without approving of their actions.

I was taught to be sure, first of all, that people *believe*, then that they *behave*, and then that they can *belong*. With this approach people usually need two "conversions"—one to Christ and another to the church. But as my interviews with college students show, people often never take that second step.

In 1973 I participated with Christians throughout the United States in an evangelistic outreach called Key 73. Efforts were made to contact every person in the United States with the gospel. Temporary phone centers were set up for Christian workers in business establishments and in churches across the nation. Many evenings were spent in calling everyone listed in the phone book in our respective areas. Observable fruit from this effort was meager, and I suspect many people who received these calls prayed the sinners prayer of repentance but with only superficial knowledge of Jesus and what it means to invite him into your heart. We have learned that there are more effective ways to present the gospel.

It's relatively easy for people to say they believe. *Believe* in the Greek is always an action word. It's more than intellectual assent. As the Amplified Bible says, it is to trust in, cling to, and rely upon Christ with our life (see, for example, John 3:16 in an Amplified Bible).

On the other hand, sometimes I hear the statement: "Mennonites are good people." This idea may help convert people. It is often a hindrance to winning people to Christ, however, because nonbelievers have the impression they could never measure up. They don't want to fail at perceived high standards of righteousness and are therefore uncomfortable trying to be part of us. Others see hypocrisy among Mennonites, and say they don't want to identify with us for that reason.

One way to work at these misperceptions is to emphasize that as believers we, too, need God's daily cleansing. We need his grace to tear down the walls of self-righteousness that our unchurched neighbors see. Until the Holy Spirit reveals to us our own sinful nature and our need for grace, we will come across to the unchurched as self-righteous as the Pharisees. To counter this, we need to be vulnerable and transparent.

In the greater Washington, D.C., area that surrounds Capital

Christian Fellowship, we made strides in overcoming some of these misperceptions by eliminating the denominational label. Once people came and experienced warm fellowship, they were then able to appreciate the strengths of the denomination.

Belong, Believe, and Behave

As I noted earlier, traditional approaches to evangelism stressed a certain formula: new Christians should believe, behave, and then belong to the church. I find, however, that a biblical approach to salvation changes the order: first belong, then believe, and finally behave.

An unbeliever can belong, not in the sense of being a baptized member but in the sense that he or she feels acceptance and love from other believers. In belonging they are able to say, "I feel at home with these believers. They are my family. They understand and love me." After that, unbelievers come to believe in the Jesus we have come to love and worship.

In Luke 24:47-49 Jesus said, "With my authority, take this message of repentance to all nations, beginning in Jerusalem: 'There is forgiveness of sins for all who turn to me.' You are witnesses of all these things. And now I will send the Holy Spirit, just as my Father promised. But stay here in the city until the Holy Spirit comes and fills you with power from heaven" (NLT).

About this passage Robin Trebilcock writes:

> They went with the power of the Spirit of God to offer a way to exercise effective local action to people who felt powerless. They did not impose their power on the different cultures they faced as they went out in obedience to Christ. Love adapted to flourish within each new culture. Starting in Jerusalem, they first went with love and compassion to those living with Greek culture and language and overcame the liberal/conservative divide. Then love touched an Ethiopian eunuch, and they overcame the race and sexuality divide. Then they went to the Samaritans and overcame the divide of ancient prejudices. Finally, love was brought to the

Romans and the Gentiles, and the separation from the principalities and powers was overcome. Each new encounter would have been a challenge to their Jewish identity, and they wrestled with the tendency to impose that identity on others but were led by the Spirit to instead nurture an indigenous Christian identity with every culture that they met.[2]

In 1 Corinthians, we get a glimpse of how Paul welcomed the unchurched:

> I have become a servant to everyone so that I can bring them to Christ. When I am with the Jews, I become one of them so that I can bring them to Christ. When I am with those who follow the Jewish laws, I do the same, even though I am not subject to the law, so that I can bring them to Christ. When I am with the Gentiles who do not have the Jewish law, I fit in with them as much as I can. In this way, I gain their confidence and bring them to Christ. But I do not discard the law of God; I obey the law of Christ. (1 Corinthians 9:19-21 NLT)

Writing about this passage, Trebilcock says that Paul would have had an outreach program with four foci: one for slaves, one for Jews, one for Gentiles, and one for the weak.[3] But it is verse 22 that should be our life's motto and expression of our passion: "I try to find common ground with everyone so that I might bring them to Christ" (1 Corinthians 9:22 NLT).

As a church planter, Paul does all he can to fit in with the culture. In verse 21 he reminds us that he does not compromise his convictions; he follows the law of God. He becomes a servant, just as Jesus did: "The Son of Man did not come to be served, but to serve" (Matthew 20:28).

A Messy Church

Once Helen took cookies to a family hosting a summer Bible school for the neighbor children in their home. When the containers were not returned for some weeks she finally asked about them. The daughter had pawned the Tupperware to purchase drugs. In another situation, a wife who had come to church for several months told me her husband was trafficking drugs. One Saturday she called me to say the deals were taking place at a particular time out of their home. I called the police, but as far as I could tell they ignored the call. Accepting people who have little or no understanding of the Bible or what it means to be a disciple makes for a messy church.

Churches today will have a difficult time growing until the leadership and membership have a clear understanding of how they will deal with issues such as couples living together before marriage, divorce and remarriage, greed, homosexuality, their role of leadership, women in ministry, the gifts of the Spirit, and involvement with government.

The leaders need not have full agreement among themselves on these issues, but they need to be in agreement on a working position so that new people see unity among the leadership. Even though these are difficult issues, new believers need to see the church as a loving family. Jesus had a Zealot and a tax collector in his discipleship training class; that was a far more difficult pairing than Republicans and Democrats in the same congregation. Zealots and tax collectors were politically at opposite ends on many issues of the day. Jesus chose them anyway. I believe the mission of reaching the lost and making disciples was so unifying it enabled the disciples to work together and overcome their differences.

After fifty years of pastoral ministry, I have come to believe that leaders need to study the Scriptures with others, especially those who have proven by their track record that they have the gift of wisdom. Leaders need to hear from God through their brothers and sisters in God's family, and then they need to lead. Too often we get stuck in the "paralysis of analysis" by focusing on issues rather than reaching our communities for Christ. That's a trick of the devil! The church is a hospital for sinners, not a continual seminar on solving disputes. Thank God that his grace is greater than our ability to mess things up.

For example, in working with blended families I learned not to be an interrogation artist. While we need to be "wise as serpents," we don't need to find out every detail of someone's history. Past injuries and resentment must be dealt with under the blood of Christ. These are often extremely difficult and painful, but it is absolutely necessary if we are to live with a joyful and vibrant testimony. The important thing is the direction people are headed. If they are sincerely moving toward the center, which is Jesus Christ, the Holy Spirit will bring conviction and healing as we walk in obedience to the Lord.

Paul writes that "[Jesus] gave up his life for [the church] to make her holy and clean, washed by baptism and God's word. He did this to present her to himself as a glorious church without a spot or wrinkle or any other blemish. Instead, she will be holy and without fault" (Ephesians 5:25-27 NLT).

Just as Jesus presents us to the Father with the robe of righteousness covering all our sin, he covers this messy church, presenting it perfect, with his redemptive work on the cross to the Father. What a fantastic Savior we have!

Welcoming New Members

The New Testament shows at least some understanding of the idea of membership in the church. Otherwise, how could the church have excommunicated the brother who was guilty of incest (see 1 Corinthians 5:2)? Paul writes that we are to do good to all people, especially to those who belong to the family of believers (see Galatians 6:10). But what does membership in a congregation mean for us today?

Baptism

During the past twenty years of my ministry, I asked all new believers and transferring members to share their personal testimony with the congregation. If their baptism was meaningful to them, they did not need to be rebaptized.

Membership implies being "locked in" to the new church. North Americans tend to be individualistic and therefore resist membership. This is even more true for postmoderns. Therefore, we cannot make membership a big deal; rather, we should make commitment to Christ and baptism the important aspects. These spiritual commitments are more important than a commitment to membership.

Baptism should have a deeper meaning, too. Baptism identifies us with Christ. It means we have died and that he is now living his life through us (see Acts 2:38; 2 Corinthians 5:17; and Galatians 2:20). The New Testament church, at least in the book of Acts, clearly did not have long instruction classes prior to baptism. In North America, baptism is often looked upon as an acceptable ritual for those who desire it. In this context, it does not represent a radical, life-changing experience. This must change. Repentance includes not only a change of worldview but also a change of behavior. We put aside our selfish ambition and shoulder our cross each day, looking to Jesus as our example. The old life is gone and a new one has come (see Luke 9:23 and 1 Corinthians 5:17).

It is helpful if people know from the first day they enter a church what steps they need to take to become members of the church. In the church's program every week was a statement something like: "All those interested in exploring membership are invited to a class next Sunday following the morning worship service. Pastor Dave will lead the class and a light lunch will be provided."

In small congregations, classes are usually offered when one or more people express interest in membership. In the class, the pastor explains what it means to be a follower of Christ, who we are as a church, what we believe, and how we operate. It works best when mature brothers or sisters participate with the pastor in this class so they can serve as mentors for new Christians. New members then sign a covenant of membership and, if they are going to be baptized, to move ahead with it as soon as possible.

Baptism is a sign of new life. Celebrate it! I found that baptizing frequently, rather than waiting a couple months for others to join in the group, created a more victorious atmosphere in the body of Christ. Every new believer shares their testimony of God at work in their life. These testimonies enable the congregation to better understand the new believer and encourage all God's people; they can also bring conviction to those who have not yet become followers of Christ.

New Member Seminars

I have adapted Rick Warren's four short seminars in the discipling process by infusing them with Anabaptist theology.[4] Each class is a one-time session lasting three or four hours and usually held on a Sunday afternoon or Saturday morning.

Seminar 101. This first class is designed to lead people to Christ and move them toward church membership. The class concludes with candidates signing a membership covenant in which they promise to share the responsibility of the church, serve in the ministry of the church, support the testimony of the church, and protect the unity of the church. This class also examines *The Confession of Faith in a Mennonite Perspective.*

Seminar 201 helps people to grow into spiritual maturity. It focuses on the importance of the Bible, offers helpful study methods, and discusses prayer and honoring the Lord with our tithes and offerings.

Seminar 301 equips people with the skills they need for ministry. It enables each person to discover their spiritual gifts and a ministry that lines up with those gifts.

Seminar 401 gives each person an understanding of how they can best serve Christ in their daily life and witness.

When someone is baptized, it is reasonable to assume that he or she is now a member of the church. Commitment to Christ is incomplete without a commitment to Christ's body, which is the local church. People who are not connected to any congregation—what we might call "Lone Ranger" Christians—tend not to be positive witnesses with their independent spirits. In my fifty years of ministry, there have been very few situations in which someone wanted to be baptized but didn't want to become a member of the congregation. I believe, however, that to deny baptism to these persons would have hurt their spirit and caused them to stumble. My relationship with these people was more important than my position that baptism and membership are one entity.

Evangelism Training

I read conflicting data concerning churches offering training classes in evangelism. One study says that training is important for reaching the unchurched, while another says that evangelism training programs don't necessarily help.[5] Why might that be true? Evangelism is more about building relationships than about programs and methods. It is not an intellectual trip; it is lived out in life. Evangelism is not an add-on program to an already full schedule.

Evangelism needs to be our lifestyle. It needs to permeate and infiltrate our Christian lives in the workaday world as well as our church activities. It is likely that churches with training programs in evangelism also emphasize the importance of a Christian lifestyle and of being assertive in sharing faith on a daily basis.

I believe there is a place for training in techniques and approaches to help people be more comfortable and bold in their witness. Some might argue that when the Holy Spirit is moving and people are "overflowing with rivers of living water," they will not need much training. They will come together for prayer and sharing and learn from each other as they share their witnessing experiences.

If the pastor invites people to Jesus regularly during the worship service and in a very natural and non-threatening way, the members will learn much from the pastor's model. Furthermore, members will feel comfortable inviting their unchurched friends to worship, knowing both that the visitors will not be embarrassed or pressured to accept Christ *and* that the pastor will make it clear that Jesus demands we make a decision to choose him as Lord.

Too often, however, evangelism training is a little like teaching a person to swim without going into the water. Often the classroom instruction is artificial, and it is frequently focused on how to meet and overcome the objections of the unchurched. This is appropriate, but the emphasis of our witness to the unchurched needs to be on the abundant life that Jesus gives to all who accept him. The training needs to be immersed in its natural environment.

Nonbelievers won't care how much you know until they know how much you care. They will not hear you until they have been heard; only then can you start building relationships. Keeping these principles in mind will help you in your witness.

Outreach Team

As a congregation transitions from a maintenance to missional mode, the leadership may want to engage a team to assist the congregation in being sure that the great commission is the church's first thing. The assignment of this team would be to model evangelism and assist the leadership in assuring that all ministries of the church make outreach a central focus. In order for team members to be effective, they need to be granted a certain amount of authority by the church. The team would have the right to challenge each ministry to be missional, and would also be empowered to train and assist the ministries in outreach. They need tools to do this, some of which are suggested in the following pages. The team would encourage the use of these tools in making disciples and training disciples to reach prebelievers.

For this team to be effective, it must include those with gifts and passion for reaching the local community for Christ. We recognize and empower our teachers and pastors; why don't we recognize evangelists (see Ephesians 4:11)? Outreach teams in many congregations are responsible for seeing that the congregation gives programs at the local retirement home or prison and distributes Thanksgiving baskets or toys at Christmas time. While these efforts are good, they usually bear little fruit unless relationships are built. Too often the church offers handouts and then forgets about these families until next year. Relationship-building with the unchurched and sharing the Good News would be the top priority of this team. Let's recognize and empower the evangelists in our congregations to lead the church in reaching our communities for Christ.

Reaching Across Economic Divisions

An economic barrier, that is, a divide between people of different income levels, can be more difficult to cross than the racial one. In my first pastorate, some families who were poor never integrated or felt they were a vital part of the fellowship. When Helen and I left the church, so did these families. I vowed that would never happen again.

There are many challenging situations. If a group from the church decides to go bowling, or to spend a weekend at church camp, or participate in a marriage enrichment weekend, do we offer to pay the way for those who can't afford it, or would that embarrass them? Do they feel estranged because of their lack of resources? If their car is not dependable, who will take them to the church function? Who, if anyone, should approach them concerning their financial situation?

One way to work at this barrier is for a few persons in the congregation to be a bridge. These bridge persons accept people by reaching across to them with God's uncondemning love. The relationship between these parties must be at such a level that they can talk about sensitive issues with no embarrassment. When this happens, it is an illustration of agape love. This love has a way of permeating the body of Christ. It's wonderful to see God's grace transcend these humanly constructed barriers. People must become integrated into the life of the church by building friendships.

Many years ago I loaned some money to a needy person who came to church occasionally. After loaning the money, our relationship changed. I regretted my decision and told him to forget the loan, but he never returned to church. From that time forward, if I give a gift of money to someone, I have learned to say, "When you see someone in need, return the favor to him or her."

Participants are invited to be filled with all God has for them. During this retreat the whole aspect of community comes alive. We eat together, worship, view videos, share together, and play together. It's kind of a Christian boot camp where people are completely blown away by love.

After retreat we share what we experienced. Somewhere along the way people realize they have transitioned from an interested attendee to a devoted friend among their group members. This happens whether they have made a decision for Christ or not. There is something about being unconditionally loved that is intoxicating. It's obvious the Holy Spirit is at work drawing all of us to Christ, because none of us would have the energy level to keep it up. As a result, whether people made baby steps toward Christ throughout the course or dramatic leaps, they all agree they want to come back for more. With an effective ministry tool like Alpha, evangelism is no longer scary; it's an exciting team sport.

Newspapers and Fliers

Many times churches place ads once or twice in the newspaper and give up because they see little or no response. As with TV commercials, the public needs to see an ad frequently enough to associate it with your church. Some advertising experts state that you need to give the same message seven times before it gets through. Use the same logo and colors in an ad or flier so people will begin to recognize your church's identity even before they read the content.

As people from your church witness to their unchurched friends, the believers can hand out a flier or direct the pre-believer to a website or print ad. You may find that inserts in your local community newspaper work best and are more cost-effective than ads in the larger county or city paper. At CCF we frequently paid to have a flier inserted in the free local newspaper.

Bulk Mailings

I used bulk mailings to contact people in the community—

people who had some relationship with the church, often through a church member or attender. I also followed up with a phone call to ask if the person received the flier and to encourage them to come to church. If you sense there is interest, even if they don't come, don't be afraid to call again when you have a special program or start a new series of messages.

Church Mailboxes

Most small churches have mailboxes for members. How can church mailboxes become an evangelistic tool? When someone visited the church and I sensed they were interested, I would point out our church mailboxes and say, "When you come next Sunday you will find your name on the mailbox in this row." I gave them the same literature the members had received that Sunday. This communicated that we wanted the visitor to be part of our community. At times when controversial issues were covered in our church publications, I did not distribute those publications. Seekers and new Christians don't need those articles (see 1 Peter 2:2).

Website

Many people visited the church because they saw our website. As an older person I had to learn the value of this tool. An attractive website can reach the younger generation. Website visitors could listen to our music and messages and get a sense of our style of worship.[6] Members of the congregation who are adept with computers can help in developing and maintaining a clever website. You may find an upper-level high school student can do an acceptable job. If you don't have computer experts in your congregation, don't be bashful to ask for help, even from other churches (though I would recommend first checking with the other congregation's pastor). A website is an effective tool for evangelism.

Technology

Using PowerPoint or some other projection system for song lyrics, announcements, Scripture, sermon notes, and the like adds much to the learning curve of your people. They retain more information when it is projected with photos, art, or other graphics. It will also force you to produce better messages. Announcements can be shown, eliminating the need for verbal announcements during worship. Background pictures of God's creation help us focus on our awesome God.

One church I visited showed a frame before worship began that read, "Who did YOU invite to church today?" This is one more creative way to remind people to be intentional in bringing others to the banquet.

Use email for prayer requests. As the church grows, some weeks you may send prayer requests almost every day. This helps to keep people in the loop and encourages love and unity.

Blogging, I believe, is going to be one way people will be studying their Bibles from now on. Lead pastor Noah Kaye at CCF blogs every day. Reading his blog gives people insight to the heart of their pastor, and members are often informed of congregational happenings. This can be an excellent tool for making disciples for persons who are part of your congregation as well as another way to reach the unchurched.

Knocking on Doors

Evangelism is all about relationships. Building relationships with community people is a key to growth of the kingdom and our churches. I have learned through many years of ministry that if pastors of small churches simply stay in the study, their churches will never grow. The pastor needs to be a model to his or her congregation and, as Paul wrote to Timothy, "do the work of an evangelist" (2 Timothy 4:5). Larger congregations frequently have the resources to offer programs that benefit community members, who then enter the congregation through these programs.

In many small towns and rural communities, it is still appropriate to use what some say is an outdated method. Once I was in conversation with a member of a large independent Baptist church in Iowa. Their church is reaching many new families through contacting persons from the "new movers" list. A group of members meets one Saturday morning a month. In pairs they visit the homes of people new to the community and invite them to church.

The Bible describes how Jesus sent the disciples out in pairs, but in many communities where I have pastored, I often went alone to meet new members of the community. Helen was home praying, so in that sense I was not alone.

Going door-to-door is an excellent way to get to know the community. You may meet people who have a church but haven't been there for months. Your contact and words of encouragement will often help them return to their church. As you meet people, some will share their painful situations. Be free to pray with them. Prayer gives encouragement and builds warm relationships.

While studying at Eastern Mennonite Seminary in Harrisonburg, Virginia, I was student pastor at Mount Jackson Mennonite Church. This church plant came to reality when students from the college formed friendships and won the confidence of people in the community through repeated home visits. Reaching prebelievers in the community requires sacrifice, persistence, and consistency. Students often left the campus at 8:30 in the morning and did not return until 9:30 at night. They went every Wednesday and Sunday, visiting wherever there were open doors and working with people from middle-class and low-income areas, including some who were in and out of prison.

After graduating from Eastern Mennonite Seminary, Helen and I had married and moved with Helen to begin our first pastorate at Smithville, a small town in rural Ohio. Smithville Mennonite Church, with its attractive contemporary design and large auditorium with balcony, showed promise. During these years the church grew in average attendance from 150 to 200.

Almost from day one, I visited community members in their homes. I used index cards for each family to track my visits and kept the church council updated on these visits, modeling the values of koinonia and community involvement. One year I made 818 pastoral calls. Perhaps one third of these visits were to unchurched people.

At our midweek service each Wednesday evening, I handed out a list of prayer requests. It included names of unchurched persons and families in the community. If any of these persons visited the church, they were not strangers because we had been praying for them. As a result of this relationship-building, I was asked to conduct several funerals for people who had little or no connection with the congregation.

Looking back on those years, my priorities were not always where they should have been. Perhaps the hard work and long hours had as much to do with the insecurity of a young pastor trying to prove himself as with genuine love and devotion to my Lord. Our family too often took third place behind God and the church, and I thank God for a faithful wife who stood by me and poured her life and love into our children.

Offering Childcare

Lima (Ohio) Mennonite Church was the first city church I pastored. I ministered there from 1973 to 1983. Lima was an industrial city with many social problems. I immediately noted an asset that this small city church would do well to exploit: a daycare center. We invested in developing this ministry, and God blessed with capacity attendance of one hundred children. We soon had a waiting list. The daycare provided an opportunity to reach a number of community families for Jesus Christ and see them become active disciples in the church.

Two children came from the family of a school administrator. The children came home excited about the Bible stories they learned at daycare. The father, not having had religious training, didn't know the stories. He decided to come to church to hear more. The parents eventually became disciples and leaders in the church!

Sometimes when I was working with community families and learned that they might be coming to church for the first time on a particular Sunday, I came to the pulpit with two messages. If new families were present, I would use one message. But if they did not show, I would use one prepared for the established congregation. I praise God our urban church did not mind this flexibility.

We did not use the word *missional* in the 1970s and 1980s, but I believe that's what we were. Many people and families met Jesus, and lives were changed. One reason we were able to reach these families was because nearly all our daycare staff were church members and provided a direct link to the congregation. The workers discerned a sense of ownership for the church's growth, health, and development.

For congregations that offer programs in their building in the hope that program participants will begin attending the church, those programs need to be staffed by members of the congregation. In my experience, this is vital. If the program staff is excited about their church and about Jesus, they can't help but invite those who attend programs to worship or study with them. Daycare centers are one illustration of a ministry with such potential. There are many single and working mothers in our communities. What an opportunity for the church to provide support for them and care for their children.

Reaching people for Jesus often stretches us. During my years at Lima, cigarette smoking was still a visible part of the culture. We kept an ashtray in our home, because people would not come unless they could smoke. In those days, to ask smokers to go outside was not acceptable to those who smoked. After these visitors left our home, Helen and I would open the doors and windows to air out the house. I have no regrets in doing what we did, because it was a way to show love and acceptance to those caught by these enslaving habits. After thirty-five years, we still relate to one family as a result of having an ashtray in our home.

Relating to Neighbors

Children are great bridge-builders and can be influential in helping people come to church and to salvation in Christ. When children play together, parents often relate to other parents. Children frequently invite neighbors and friends to youth activities.

Helen is especially gifted in relating to our neighbors. After we lived in one particular community for some time, a neighbor told Helen how angry she had been at first that a preacher was moving in across the street. Earlier in her life, someone had knocked on her door and asked if she was a Christian; when she said no, she was told she was going to hell. This neighbor said to Helen, "You're different. No matter what I say or do, you just go on loving and accepting me." In time Jesus transformed this woman's life and the lives of her family. In celebration, the woman and her husband repeated their wedding vows in a Christian ceremony.

Showing Christian Films

During the warm summer months in Lima, we hung a huge screen on the brick church building and showed Christian movies for the community. Often someone sang or brought a short gospel message before it got dark enough to show the movie. Sadly, a neighbor complained to the police that we were making too much noise. (The man, whose marriage was disintegrating, had become upset because his wife started coming to our church with their children.) Even though we reduced the volume he did not give up, so we eventually had to terminate this ministry.

The church I attend in Lititz, Pennsylvania, hosts community nights with games and food, followed by the showing of a film. The events are quite successful.

Reverse Phone Directory

With two other families, Helen and I began a church plant in Elyria, Ohio, a city west of Cleveland. One of the first things I did was go to the library for a reverse phone directory—that is, one arranged according to addresses. I sent letters inviting people living near the church to attend our services. Many throughout the area church conference were praying, and those initial contacts were bathed in prayer. After the very first mailing, a man named George came, and he was an answer to those many prayers. Over the next couple years, George brought at least twenty-eight people to the church. George is an illustration of the "man of peace" Jesus said we need to find (see Luke 10:5-6).

Individual Name Cards

Provide attractive, generic "business" cards for the church members to hand out when inviting others to church. These cards should have the church's logo and contact information, including the website and a location map on the back. That way, the person being invited has all the information he or she needs to find both the church and your website. The card has a place for the giver's signature, which makes the invitation more personal.

Festivals

Special events can be effective in reaching communities. Many churches find that by providing a wide variety of games and free food, community festivals can be a wonderful means of exposing neighbors to Christ's love. They involve community resources by using personnel and equipment from police and fire departments, hospitals, medical organizations, and food services. Often local businesses make financial contributions or provide food or novelties for distribution.

A vital element to these events is interaction between community folks and church folks. If many people from the sponsoring congregation are shy by nature, find the church's extroverts and evangelists and turn them loose so they can engage others in conversation. If possible, don't assign them to any particular station; this frees them to give all their efforts to relating to community people. In talking to people, ask where they live and go to church. Try to get a phone number. Follow-up is crucial if there is to be a noticeable harvest.

Workers need to be trained, but when you recruit volunteers, don't minimize their role. Don't say, "All you need to do is stand here and guide the kids through this maze." This focuses on the task, while the important thing is their relationship to the parents and their children.

Friend Day

Make attractive fliers for your members to use for personally inviting their unchurched friends for a specific Sunday service. Design the service in your usual format so people get an authentic feel for your worship. Keep the service upbeat and celebrative. We have found having the children in front to sing songs with lots of motions works well. Testimonies are great to include on Friend Day; many visitors will go home talking about them.

Music that moves the heart and brings people into the presence of God is a must. A "how-to" message from the pastor on a common life issue, such as, "How to Love the People You Don't Like," or "How to Find Contentment," speaks to everyone. Sometime during the service, invite people to a new program the church may be offering, such as a marriage enrichment or parenting seminar. Provide opportunity for people to sign up during the service and drop their registration in the offering basket. The course offerings need to be short—no more than four or six sessions. Follow the worship time with lots of good food.

International Sunday

This event is the same as Friend Day but with an emphasis on inviting someone of another culture. Place flags from many nations throughout the auditorium and foyer. Feature testimonies from people from other cultures, and follow the service with international foods.

Mother's Day, Father's Day, Grandparent's Day, Children's Day

These special Sundays are natural occasions for church members to invite peers to worship. In an era when so many need help in their home lives and family relationships, congregations can capitalize on this need. With adequate planning, a church can design attractive fliers that members can use to invite their unchurched friends to these family-oriented observances.

Give members an opportunity during services on these days to share stories and testimonies of faithful parents, grandparents, or others who helped mold them. Visitors will be blessed by these stories. Do not neglect single-parent families. I have seen the testimony of a godly single mother bring encouragement, especially to other single parents. These are some of the many times when laypersons can minister effectively to the larger assembly. They can share failures and victories in managing their time and balancing family, work, social, and church responsibilities.

If you have international persons in your congregation, be sure to include them. Many of them bring experiences the congregation will find interesting and helpful. I have experienced the sharing of international persons who describe lives with very few material "blessings" but with values basic to wholesome relationships and Christian lifestyles. The pastor can highlight these values in a message.

Short-Term Mission Trips

It is appropriate to take prebelievers on a short-term missions trip where they can rub shoulders with believers 24/7. They can see the passion for ministry and experience the satisfaction it brings. They are drawn closer to the Lord as they see Christ in their friends. As people walk with us, work with us, and observe our love for others, they will be drawn to our Savior.

Prayer Walks and Street Meetings

In 2008, I attended the School of Apostles at Black Rock Retreat in Quarryville, Pennsylvania. The majority of church planters were Spanish-speaking Latinos; they have much to teach white Christians about zeal for our Lord. Street preaching and prayer walks are often effective tools. Street preaching is simply involves a Christian standing in a public place such as a street corner and presenting the Good News. Prayer walks involve groups of people, often as few as two, walking and praying over a section of a city. They lift up to the Lord the particular needs of the community, they pray for the overcoming of Satan's strongholds, such as drugs, crime, prostitution, or violence. They thank God for his presence and pray for his Spirit to bring deliverance and hope to people walking in darkness.

Helen often prays as she walks in our community. She usually begins with praise and thanksgiving and depends on the Holy Spirit to give direction to her prayers. She chats with people, listening for concerns, and prays for them. Then she checks back later to see how the Lord is answering prayer.

Music and Interpretive Dance

Music can be a way to draw youth. If you have youth with leadership skills in the congregation, they can invite others from the community, especially musicians, for a Christian music jam session. Start small in order to win the respect of these community youth before opening it up to the broader youth community. This will make it easier to keep a Christian atmosphere.

At CCF, our youth pastor is a hip hop artist. Under his leadership, CCF has held Christian hip hop concerts and basketball tournaments. Hip hop that presents Scripture is a powerful way to reach teens and young adults. CCF has been successful in ministering through hip hop music.

CCF has an interpretive dance program for young girls, teens, and adults. On occasion they present a program on Saturday evening to a full audience. Jesus is honored and people go home blessed.

Vacation Bible School

Vacation Bible school (VBS) can be a great tool to reach the community. Too often, however, children who attend VBS from unchurched homes do not become involved in the congregation's church life. To change this, someone from the church needs to contact parents of children who do not have a regular church home to try to build a relationship with the family. This calls for sacrificial service. Contacts should be made during VBS, but during the following week, someone needs to follow up with these families.

Be sure to have a good program at the end of the VBS that parents can attend and in which they can experience first-hand the warmth of the church family. Prayer and persistence along with genuine love are the keys. Remember Jesus said we are to "compel them to come in" (Luke 14:23 KJV).

Servant Evangelism

There are myriad ways to casually serve others in the community. Try giving out free water on a hot day, washing cars for free, cleaning windshields, cleaning toilets in public businesses, raking lawns, or fixing or painting mailboxes. The list is endless. One summer our youth gave out water at a traffic light, along with a note about the Water of Life and the church's address and service times. As a result, one fine young man came to church, and has been a faithful worker for several years now.

Other ways to reach your community might include hosting events such as blood-pressure checks and other health-related services, seminars on various health issues, an outdoor drama ministry for children and adults, an ice cream social for the local community, and permitting skateboarding and free parking for the neighbors in the church parking lot.[7]

Reaching Postmodern Youth

Most churches have very few youth or young adults between the ages of eighteen and thirty. Why is this? In *They Like Jesus But Not the Church*, Dan Kimball writes, "Christians are known as angry, judgmental, right-wing, finger-pointers with political agendas."[8] While we know most Christians are not like this, Kimball reminds us that as believers we are on the inside of the church, and many of us usually hang out with people over thirty. Postmodern youth see the vocal minority of right-wing evangelical leaders on the news and believe they represent all of Christianity. Most are turned off.

Building relationships is a must for reaching all ages, but it is of the highest priority if we are to reach the younger generation. They will not accept our faith until they see it lived out in our lives. They respond to a person's actions, not lectures. It will take love, time, and creative Holy Spirit-led encounters to build these relationships. Encounters need to be conversational rather than confrontational. For the most part, these encounters will need to occur outside the church walls. Loyalty is low for postmoderns, but dialogue builds trust; it needs to be earned over and over again. This will stretch the traditional church.

On the other hand, Kimball writes:

> No longer do we need to water anything down or do a bait-and-switch through an entertaining event. Evangelism in the emerging church means being bold and loving about what we believe. Not arrogant bold or know-it-all bold or pointing-fingers bold but relationally bold, sharing the good news of Jesus and of kingdom living with others. Emerging generations are craving spiritual meaning. Let's not hide Jesus anymore behind strobe lights and loud music. Show Jesus in us. Respect the intelligence of nonbelievers and be prepared to lovingly but intellectually speak about what we believe rather than just throw out a quick verse. Evangelize by making disciples.[9]

Some churches have found creative ways to foster relationships with youth and young adults, such as coffee houses or a "fifth quarter" after a football game. A church could open its fellowship hall or gym to this age group on a Friday or Saturday night. If you find the youth won't come to the church, try providing some sort of gathering at a local facility where they may feel more comfortable—a bowling alley, for example. Provide free food simply for the opportunity to invite conversation with youth. We must find creative ways to relate to them.

One church youth pastor has a great program called "catacombs," in which youth and young adults meet with him and his staff every Monday evening in the church basement. This pastor is building relationships with these postmodern youth before they become comfortable enough to attend a traditional service.

For Discussion

1. Read 1 Corinthians 9:19-27. What insights can you glean regarding Paul's methods of reaching people?

2. Does the concept of a "messy" church scare you? Do you worry that a messy church may lead your children to accept some of these evil habits? This is certainly a legitimate concern. How do we overcome it? Do you believe that Jesus will protect your children if you model a consistent lifestyle in the midst of an evil society?

3. What activities is your church doing to reach the community? What new activities might you consider as outreach tools?

7

Becoming a Missional Church

Dwelling in the Word: Read Luke 5:33-39 or Matthew 9:14-17.

Testimony

Hilda was a German woman who married a U.S. soldier during World War II. After the couple settled in the United States, her husband was promiscuous. He frequently brought women into their home and slept with them in another room. I told Hilda various times that God does not demand that she stay there; she could leave. Her response was, "Where could I go? I can't live on the street."

Hilda raised her husband's children from these relationships. Although Hilda gave her life to Christ, she continues to struggle with a smoldering temper. I prayed with her many times as she talked about murdering her husband's girlfriends. Even though she lives in this hellish situation, Hilda continues to grow in her relationship with Jesus and has had a positive influence on her family and many others. She has hosted a Bible study group in her home for many years.

~

If our churches are not reaching our communities, it is a given that change must take place. The old methods are not working. As the saying goes, "If you always do what you've always done, you'll always get what you've always got." How often churches keep doing the same thing but expect different results. We must change from ineffective practices to God's ways if we are to become missional and make disciples.

Change is difficult, but we have no alternative if we are obedient to the great commission. Tom Clegg and Warren Bird write: "Churches are going out of business because they refuse to change. Any church that doesn't shift from 'ministry as status quo' to 'ministry as mission outpost' will die or become hopelessly irrelevant."[1]

In this chapter, I will examine steps that churches can take to become missional. I'll also outline ways to ease what can be a painful transition for longtime members of the congregation.

Being Honest about Change

Let's ask ourselves: Do we really want to know those around us? Do we want them in our church? Are we willing for our church to become their church? Are we willing to go where they are and engage them on their turf? Are we willing to spend time with them, identify with them, and show genuine compassion?[2]

I expect that if we answer honestly, we will realize we have to change not just our churches but our own hearts.

Breaking with tradition can be difficult. But if an airplane sits in the hangar, it will avoid turbulence, but it doesn't get you anywhere. If the church doesn't change, members may feel safe and comfortable, but they will not be effective in reaching their community for Christ.

Without a point of crisis, it is often difficult to change. Most churches in the United States are at a point of crisis, but they are blind to that crisis. We are dying because we are not reaching our communities for Christ. Many churches, however, remain blissfully ignorant of this failure.

3:16), Jesus is the supreme and clearest revelation of God (see Hebrews 1:1-3). Since we read Scripture through the lens of Jesus, it is always appropriate to ask what Jesus would say or do. If you don't love the Word of God, ask Jesus to give you that love. A love of his word will transform your life and the life of your church (see Psalm 119:20, 97.)

4. *A fear of the future to a faith for the future.* Develop eyes of faith instead of eyes of doubt, pessimism, and cynicism. "For we walk by faith, not by sight" (2 Corinthians 5:7 KJV). We must see the possibilities in people. Use your sanctified imagination; it is a gift from the Holy Spirit. We do not depend on skills and technique. Pray, believe, and thank God for changed lives before you know who you are praying for. Take risks for Christ. "For God did not give us a spirit of timidity, but a spirit of power, of love and of self-discipline" (2 Timothy 1:7). Rather than fear the future, we must be future-focused, knowing there are better days ahead. The church will triumph (see Matthew 16:18). More people are coming to Christ now than in any time in history!

5. *A view of the pastor as chaplain to a view of the pastor as leader.* In most smaller and older congregations, the pastor is looked upon as a chaplain, a person who runs errands and who serves the people. The mentality too often is that as long as the pastor and the bills are being paid, the church is doing okay, even though new people are moving into the community and the congregation has plateaued. In order to become missional, the pastor must be a leader. He or she must cast the vision and model the vision.

6. *A culture of fear to a culture of faith.* This change is related to the two preceding points. A pastor said to me recently, "I'm so tired of living in a culture of fear." People in leadership, especially the pastor, need to be free to make small decisions without being questioned. The congregation needs to free leaders to be themselves and exercise their gifts. Seek to foster an atmosphere of trust rather than an atmosphere of constant questioning.

7. *An inward focus to outward focus.* The leadership should constantly ask the congregation, "How will this issue, program, or

activity relate to the community people we are trying to reach?" Jesus depicts his followers as salt, light, and leaven of the world. Witnessing and discipling is our focus. Maintenance is no longer acceptable!

8. *Homogeneity to diversity of people groups.* Celebrate diversity of individuals. There is unity in diversity. Just as different colors make a beautiful flower garden, so different cultures make a healthy and stronger church body.

9. *Music the congregation has always preferred to the style preferred by the people you are trying to reach.* This can be a touchy issue, and we will discuss this in more detail in chapter 10.

10. *Facilities and equipment that are out-of-date to ones that are up-to-date.* Don't expect new people to come to an outdated facility. Youth, for the most part, are now attending schools with modern equipment and technology. To make a comparison, take notice of the cars and homes of the communities around the church. Are they state-of-the-art? If so, people will expect your church to have facilities of comparable level. Are you embarrassed to bring friends to your church because the building is hopelessly outdated?

Often we update our houses before we modernize our church facilities. I am convinced that when we hear from God and seek to be obedient, he provides the resources. I've witnessed miracles concerning the finances at CCF. Funds came from places I couldn't have imagined.

Leaders need to set an example by modeling sacrificial giving for our people. As he prepared for the building of the temple, King David said:

> I am giving all of my own private treasures of gold and silver to help in the construction. This is in addition to the building materials I have already collected for his holy Temple. . . . Now then, who will follow my example? Who is willing to give offerings to the LORD today? Then the family leaders, the leaders of the tribes of Israel, the generals and captains of the army, and the king's administrative officers all gave willingly. (1 Chronicles 29:3-6 NLT)

A big vision attracts large gifts; likewise, a small vision results in small gifts. My heart's cry is for God's people to dream big visions. There are billions of people in our world who have not yet heard the name of Jesus. We have a God who is able to do far more than we can ask or imagine (see Ephesians 3:20). If our vision is lined up with God's will and we pray with faith from a humble believing heart, God will do great and mighty things.

11. *An old name to a name that communicates positive qualities.* The name of the church should be inviting. At this moment in history, denominational names can be limiting because some people have preconceived ideas of what a group stands for, and they often will not bother to investigate further. I believe theological names with words like *grace*, *faith*, *redeemer*, or *Bethel* can be limiting because they communicate a theological position that some have stereotyped. With these labels in their minds, people may eliminate those churches from consideration.

Examples of inviting names might be: Real Life Church, Life Church, Lighthouse Christian Center, Victory Christian Fellowship, or Capital Christian Fellowship. In our culture, a geographically focused name may be the least objectionable and more invitational. For example, Crossroads Christian Church, North Point, Lakewood, Willow Creek, Saddleback, Northside, and so forth.

Technical Versus Substantial Changes

Most congregations can deal rather well with what might be called technical changes. These changes usually don't threaten our personal values and are easily accepted. Some examples of a technical change include landscaping, painting, remodeling, changing class locations, changing curriculum, adding a small group, or using PowerPoint.

But technical changes are usually only Band-Aids; they may help a church be more seeker-friendly, but they usually won't open the door for a fresh breeze of God's Spirit to bring renewal. I believe that technical changes can set the stage for more substantive ones.

When giving a sermon, for example, the pastor moves from behind the large pulpit and stands on the same level as the people so he or she can communicate better. This also sends the message that he or she is not preaching or teaching down at them but reaching across to them. The following week the pastor could remove the pastor's parking sign near the entrance and designate the space for visitor parking. The pastor walking from the far end of the parking lot on Sunday morning sends a signal that the convenience of new and visiting people is more important. The pastor can begin to spend less time in the study and more time with the unchurched. These changes, especially if they occur simultaneously, are substantial. They are likely to get him or her into "hot water" with some parishioners who expect the pastor to focus on them, not the unchurched.

Missional congregations come to a place where they say, "Lord, we are willing to do whatever it takes to be salt, light, and leaven for you in this community." Passion and urgency are the energy and motivation for change. The pastor and leaders bring urgency by a continual focus on putting the first thing first.

Passion needs to be followed with strategy and implementation if we are going to be successful in making disciples. The following are suggestions for consideration to stimulate your thinking. These types of changes can help to reach the unchurched. But it's important to reiterate here that passion for the lost—the self-sacrificing love that we discussed in chapter 2—far outweighs anything on this list. In other words, this list is not the Ten Commandments!

Facilities

Most of our youth go to schools with beautiful facilities and modern equipment. By way of contrast, I was in one church where the metal chairs were forty years old. If I would go into a home of any member of that church, they would be embarrassed to offer me a chair of that quality.

If we are to reach new people just moving into our communities, nice facilities are important. Church facilities ought to be as nice as the neighborhood banks, schools, and restaurants if the church is serious about reaching these people. The buildings don't need to be lavish, opulent, or showy, but most older church buildings are not an asset to reaching the unchurched. Church buildings ought to be homey with a warm feel. Contemporary facilities, carpet, comfortable chairs, and drapes can help.

The gospel is for the affluent as well as for the down-and-out. In North American culture, you can reach across or down. It is difficult, in fact almost impossible, to reach up the economic ladder to the unchurched. The chances are slim that a congregation of low- or middle-income members will connect with the unchurched lawyer, doctor, or engineer who may have a six-figure salary. We need to face this economic reality when discussing church facilities.

Why do we find it easier to reach down? Is it because we feel we have more to offer the person who is in obvious need? Might we have emphasized 1 Corinthians 1:26-29 to the point that we feel it is more spiritual to work with those on a lower economic scale?

If we are going to impact our communities, we need to reach people at all stages of the economic ladder. If your church, or a church you are planting, is in an upscale community, it will take money to build buildings, pay staff, and make use of modern technology.

With churches, the shoe often determines the size of the body. When I was planting a church in Ohio, the new church was anxious to have its own facility. But our vision turned out to be too small, and we moved ahead too quickly. We built an auditorium with a capacity of only eighty, and the congregation now finds it very difficult to grow. Consequently, the church has plateaued and been that way for several years.

We need to search our hearts to discern where the Lord wants to direct our resources. If we learn to live sacrificially and give as God desires, he will enable us to do far more than we can ask or imagine.

Outside Appearance

Once I drove up to a church and the first thing I noticed was the chipped paint on the doors. It's curious how longtime attendees can walk past little things like that and never notice. New people notice things, and first impressions are important.

Sometimes a fresh coat of paint, a new carpet, or a good spring cleaning by the members can provide fresh excitement. As a result, members may be more willing to invite friends. Pay special attention to the rooms for youth, so they can bring their friends to a place where they say, "This is cool!"

First-time parents will demand a clean, up-to-date nursery run by friendly caring adults where children are safe. Small churches often have problems with self-esteem, but nursery facilities can help overcome this hurdle.

Try to find the things that embarrass members and upgrade them so they are proud to invite their peers. If your people are too intimidated to share their true feelings about the facility, invite a respected person in the community, maybe a real estate person with years of experience, to give their feedback concerning the appearance of your facility. It is important.

Ask if community people are drawn to the facility. Are the building's appearance and landscaping attractive? Landscaping is usually one way to improve the appearance without a great cost. Are the leaves cleared and the snow plowed? Are there ways to make your facility appear more inviting?

Church Signs and Parking

I once drove by a church with a sign in such poor condition that the person with me said it would be better if there were no sign at all. A church sign is a reflection of the total church. It should be clear, modern, and eye-catching. The lettering should be large enough to read as the motorists drive by. Be sure the sign is set perpendicular to the road so persons driving in either direction can easily read it.

Don't rule out a digital sign because of expense. The digital sign is working wonders at Capital Christian Fellowship. I had to experience the effectiveness of the digital sign to believe it was worth the money. Instead of using catchy phrases or even Scripture verses, advertise ministries the church offers, especially classes or other activities the community needs.

Avoid negative phrasing in the signage around the church. Instead of "No Parking," use "Reserved for Our Handicapped Friends." Instead of "Stay off the grass," use "Please walk on the sidewalk." Instead of "No skateboarding on the walk," say "Please skateboard only on the blacktop."

Like most of you, I drive past a number of churches every Sunday morning on my way to church. One church especially impressed me because of the fact that their early arrivers park at the far end of the lot. These early comers and church workers are modeling the principle of servanthood and humility, and this sends positive feelings to both members and visitors.

Inside

Walking into a church recently, my eyes were drawn to the literature table. There was a yearbook from a denominational publisher that was dog-eared and outdated. The paperback Bibles were anything but attractive. Any person who keeps their desk neat or their house organized would have seriously questioned relating to that church because of the appearance of the literature table. Small things are important.

The impressions created by the inside of the building are as important as those on the outside. Visitors pick up on dozens of subtle cues that make them feel welcome and comfortable in your church building.

Clearly marked doors help new people feel welcome. It's intimidating for many people to ask where the restroom is located. What I said about negative signs for the outside holds true for the inside as well. Instead of "Don't take food in the auditorium," say "Please enjoy your food and drink in the foyer." Instead of "No Running," say, "Please walk." Or instead of "No Talking," use

"Shhh! Worship in Progress." Avoid the term "old" in the names of things. If you build a new fellowship hall, don't refer to "the old hall." Instead call it "the chapel," or give it a room number.

The foyer should be large enough for fellowship. This may be an expensive change, but it is important. Foyers, food, and fellowship go together. If you are building, be sure the kitchen serving area is adjacent to the foyer. This will encourage visitors to remain after the service for a snack, and members can get to know them.

Rooms should be inviting with modern furniture. Bulletin boards need to be attractive and the white boards clean. Lighting throughout the building should be bright and trashcans should be emptied. See that the restrooms and nursery are clean, safe, and inviting.

The Importance of Numbers

Many older congregations still have an attendance and offering board in the front of the auditorium. Taking attendance is very important for the leadership; we are to keep track of our sheep. Most pastors I know would be ecstatic if 99 percent of their flock were present on Sunday; yet Jesus pictures the shepherd going after the one lost sheep. Numbers are not the vision; they are *products* of the vision. That's why I am unapologetic about numbers. Numbers represent people.

Having said that, I suggest removing the attendance and offering board if your church still uses one. It is discouraging whenever attendance and offerings are down. When attendance is up, you can always report it in the program to encourage people. When it's down, the leadership needs to discern why it's down. Attendance is important because it is one indication of discipleship. Taking accurate attendance helps you see the direction you are going.

Accountability is one aspect of discipleship. My observation is that older congregations tend to be less accountable than younger ones. For many years following worship I went home, ate lunch, and took attendance from memory. My wife and children would assist me. If a family was missing, someone on the leadership team would usually know why. We sent the weekly program to them if they missed the service. Many people would ask, "How did you know we were not here?" If they missed a Sunday or two, we would call and let them know they were missed. Because of this practice, most families learned to inform someone on the leadership team if they knew they were not going to be at church on a particular Sunday.

People will not resent this accountability if they know you have their best interests in mind, if they know you love them, and if they know you are praying for their safety as they travel. If you ask how their trip was or how their sick relative is doing, they know you have their best interests in mind. They detect your love by your tone of voice and your sincere interest.

A Program Versus a Bulletin

Refer to this tool as a *program* rather than *bulletin*. Bulletin is a church word. If you go to a concert, you receive a program, not a bulletin. Unchurched people don't use the term *bulletin*. I know from experience it will be difficult to make this minor change.

The program needs to be attractive and free of clutter. Some pastors spend endless hours in drawing up an attractive program while the surrounding community has little awareness of the Good News. The pastor needs to allow others in the congregation to use their gifts in making an attractive program.

Some churches want every detail of the worship service in the program. While it is appropriate to give prayerful thought and planning for the service, it can give the appearance of too much structure, which leaves many people cold. Many people prefer space for some spontaneity, informality, and perhaps interaction with the congregation, especially if the congregation is small. When everything is laid out in detail in the program, it gives the impression that anything not printed is seen as interference.

Most larger churches, and even some smaller ones, make their own programs. The digital age allows great flexibility. Pictures of members, youth activities, or Sunday school classes and small groups on the front cover are always eye-catchers. This makes the program more personal. Often these programs will end up on refrigerators of church families for months. Remember: don't crowd the program. Leave open space.

An interesting exercise is to check over the program and see how often you find Jesus mentioned. We seem to fill up our programs with events and often neglect to mention the focus of our events.

CCF has moved from a weekly program to an eight-page monthly magazine called "The Capital." Each Sunday the church distributes a "mini page" that reminds people of important events for the week. This seems to work well and also is cost-effective.

Offering Food

Eating with people helps to remove walls. Jesus very often related to people in places where food was involved. According to Acts 2 and 1 Corinthians 11, the New Testament churches often ate together. Weekly refreshments have become part of most growing congregations. At CCF, we offered snacks every Sunday. Keep the snacks simple and the servings small.

We found it helpful to provide small plates or containers so children would not waste as much food. It is helpful for parents to accompany their children during this time to help prevent spills. If your budget is tight, don't be afraid to place a container for donations. Have "pot-blessing" (rather than potluck) meals frequently. Compliment and thank the kitchen workers frequently and publicly. Let them know their service is a vital aspect of the church's discipleship process.

Children

Many churches would not agree with the CCF's approach to children in church. We did not encourage adults to bring neighbor children unless they were willing to be their substitute parents during church time. All children needed to be accompanied by an adult. This approach worked well for us. With our rapid growth, it was not always easy to find children's workers. This approach helped prevent burnout by those working in our children's department. Focus your outreach on the adults; they will bring the children.

Involve the children in the adult worship from time to time. Have them sing and present Bible verses from memory. The Ethiopian church I have worked closely with calls the children up front every Sunday to give memory verses and to have the pastor pray for them before they go to their class. This works well for their church of just over one hundred persons.

Contacting the Church

As I attempt to contact churches, I'm amazed to find that some do not have an answering machine. At a minimum you need to have an answering machine that gives the time of your services, directions to your facility, and the pastor's name and phone number. If the pastor feels he or she is too busy to be contacted after hours, work out a method whereby another leader or leaders can be contacted during off hours. A missional church needs to be available 24/7.

In Mark 6 the apostles returned from a tour and told Jesus all they had done. Jesus said, "Let's get away from crowds for a while and rest" (Mark 6:31 NLT). But the crowds kept coming. Jesus and the disciples barely had time to eat. A vast crowd ran ahead of them when they got out of a boat. "He had compassion on them because they were like sheep without a shepherd" (verse 34 NLT). There are many times, especially evenings, when pastors and others in leadership want to be with their families. But when there are emergencies, others come first. If there are true emergencies, I don't think it is being naïve to believe God will take care of our families as we minister to needy persons. Pastors need to delegate responsibility or they will find themselves overextended.

Nomenclature

Try to stay away from church words such as *invocation, bene-*

diction, bulletin, offertory, doxology, sanctuary, epistle, etc. Use *team* instead of *committee, auditorium* instead of *sanctuary.* Such words are user-friendly.

Use acronyms only when you are sure everyone knows what they mean. Use references to your denomination sparingly, since many young people have negative feelings concerning denominational labels.

I prefer to use the term *message* rather than *sermon. Sermon* is not a positive term to most of the younger generation. *Preach* has also come to have negative connotations. People say, "Don't preach at me." If you use terms such as *justification, sanctification, propitiation, expiation, predestination,* or other theological terms, be sure to explain them. Paraphrasing Bibles like *The Message* or the *New Living Translation* can help with this. For the most part, churches have been unsuccessful at educating members on the meaning of theological terms, so it's unlikely that visitors will understand these words.

Some persons, when they pray in public, use the older English references to God such as *thee, thou,* or *thine.* By using *you,* unchurched visitors won't feel they need to learn a new vocabulary to talk to God. Talk in your normal tone of voice when you pray. Many worship leaders have the congregation pray the Lord's Prayer in unison. I suggest you modernize it by replacing *thy* with *you* and *debts* or *trespasses* with *sins.* If possible, place the words on PowerPoint. This means the congregation will need to pray with their eyes open. (Nowhere in Scripture are we told to pray with our eyes closed.)

What about the use of titles of various people in leadership? Someone jokingly reminded me that even a toilet has a title. Paul mentioned that he was an apostle, but he did not refer to his peers as Apostle Peter or Apostle James, nor did any of the New Testament writers use Reverend Peter or Reverend James. They simply address these people by their given names. I prefer to use the title *pastor* rather than *minister,* since all Christians are to be ministers.

In some situations, it may be appropriate to introduce a speaker unknown to the congregation by mentioning his or her education or professional background, including some titles. But Scripture does not encourage the use of titles. For many of the younger generation, titles have a negative impact. Jesus emptied himself and reached across to us. We need to do the same.

It's interesting that even the more generic terms of *brother* and *sister* are not found in the Scripture except where they are used in the plural sense to refer to a group of Christians. To say that Brother John and Sister Mary are going to speak today is not user-friendly to the unchurched.

The unchurched will also gain a negative impression if they see the church maintaining aspects of organized religion. If someone wants to talk to the pastor and they have to go through a secretary to set up an appointment, it leaves the impression that people's needs are secondary to the structure. It tends to place the church in the same position as a corporation rather than a caring community. Avoid the appearance of hierarchy as much as possible.

Chairs Versus Benches

What other institutions in our society use benches? You'll find benches in most courthouses, but I'm not sure the courthouse gives a positive image. Chairs are moveable and more comfortable. They give an appearance of warmth. They give you more options; you can arrange them so people can see each other. They are also less expensive and give some people a sense of personal space. Another advantage to using chairs is that during the summer or when you know attendance is going to be lower, you can simply remove a couple rows. Usually the congregants will not even notice, and the auditorium looks more inviting. When you expect a huge crowd, as may occur for a wedding or funeral, you can usually move more chairs into the auditorium.

Someone once said that real life changes happen in circles rather than rows. We can only take people so far in their maturity process sitting in rows. Discipleship groups are usually formed in circles.

Defining a Full Church

Many churches put off building additions or starting a second service because they look at a typical worship service and say, "There is still room for more people. The whole front row is empty. There are vacant places scattered throughout the auditorium."

You will find it very, very difficult to grow beyond 80 percent capacity. This is important to recognize. A new family arriving a bit late will want to sit together. They will feel awkward unless the ushers have kept a place for them near the back where they can sit together. Unless the Holy Spirit sends a revival and a fresh wind through our communities, we are full at 80 percent, and it is time to start thinking in terms of expanding if you want to be a missional congregation.

On the other hand, when the auditorium is 50 percent or less capacity, it gives the appearance of a dying church. If possible, remove some of the seats. But the better option is to bring your neighbors and fill up the seats. Remember: they won't come unless you get to know them and invite them.

Beyond the negative appearance of a half-empty auditorium, there is a practical element of the awkwardness of receiving the offering with only a few people sitting in a row of chairs or on a bench. Unchurched people do not connect to empty benches. They relate to people! If the pastor asks people to hold hands during prayer, it is awkward if they are scattered rather than sitting together. You will also find new energy in congregational singing if you are sitting together rather than scattered throughout the auditorium. I personally find it easier to give the message to people sitting closer together rather than scattered all over the auditorium.

If you begin a second service and the auditorium is less than 50 percent full, however, I believe the "50 percent rule" does not apply. Everyone knows the auditorium is rather sparse since most people are attending the other service.

For Discussion

1. At the beginning of this chapter there is a short section entitled: "Some Painful Questions." Which of these is the more painful for you or for your church?

2. Are the eight ways to ease the pain of change helpful? Which ones might you or your group need to give the most attention?

3. The next section lists eleven changes for your consideration. Which ones speak to your need to become more missional?

4. The last part of the chapter lists a dozen or so aspects of church life, some will apply to your context. Which ones would you like to consider?

8

Church Structures and Relationships

Dwelling in the Word: Read Acts 15:1-35.

Testimony

Mary grew up in a dedicated Christian home. She accepted Jesus at a young age. During her early years, her mother was in and out of the hospital. There were times when Mary was afraid, coming home from school to an empty house. Eventually she moved with her parents to an orphanage, where she suddenly became one of thirty children. Being a daughter of the proprietors, she frequently experienced jealousy from some of the children.

In her adult years she developed a rare but severe form of arthritis and lived with continual pain. Through these difficult years, God has refined her so that many have been blessed by her vibrant testimony of God's sufficiency. Many come to bring her comfort but leave saying she has comforted and blessed them. People frequently call or send her emails to have her pray for their varied needs. Her life overflows with God's goodness even though her body suffers. Mary has brought many into the kingdom through her testimony and prayer ministry.

∼

As a young pastor, it took me several years to appreciate the importance of church leadership structures. Members need to know who is casting the vision and providing direction and leadership. For the church body to function well, leaders must respect the people and the people must respect their leaders.

Real Leadership

Too often, leaders do not really lead; they simply manage the congregation. For a church to be missional, its leadership must be composed of wise and mature members. It needs visionary people who can discern God's direction and present it to the congregation for feedback. The congregation's decisions and directions should focus on fulfilling the mission of the church: making disciples.

I believe that many pastors and congregational leaders need to be more assertive. If businesses were run as shoddily as some of our churches are, they would dissolve in short order! In smaller congregations, control is often invested in a church patriarch or matriarch rather than in the pastor or leadership team. This is unhealthy, but where it exists, the leadership needs to work with the patriarchs and matriarchs for support in order for the congregation to become missional.

In congregations of more than 150 people, decision-making power must rest with the leadership team. Otherwise, the congregation will spend endless hours trying to find consensus, and everyone will become frustrated. Communication is critical. The leadership team should keep the congregation updated on its decisions; otherwise disunity will raise its head. God gave the church the gift of leaders for a purpose, but too often leaders are afraid to lead.

When it comes to the nuts and bolts of leading, some elementary directives about meeting bear repeating. Start meetings on time. Email the agenda ahead of time. No one likes surprises; they usually make people defensive. A leader can train team members to avoid surprises by saying, "This is a new item you are bringing tonight. Since our time is limited, we will need to table it until the next time." The person who brought the item will be disappointed, but hopefully they will learn that agenda items must be given ahead of time.

Be clear in the agenda. Long-range church calendars will save time. The pastoral team should have the authority to make most scheduling decisions. I've seen groups spend inordinate amounts of time on agenda items like when to schedule communion, baptisms, parent-child dedications, vacation Bible school, or a fall festival. The calendar informs everyone when most churchwide activities are scheduled.

A good leader will anticipate conflict over agenda items or other issues. It will be helpful ahead of the meeting to contact some of those who may raise objections to see if a compromise can be worked out. If that is not possible, then the leader needs to prayerfully discern if the issue is worth the conflict. There is a community outside our four walls that does not know Jesus. For them it's a matter of life or death, so it's important not to waste time on trivial matters. Talented people are wise enough to see this waste and refuse to get involved in inefficient church structures for that reason.

If one group in the congregation makes a decision and another group overrides it, there is a structure problem. Try to avoid those situations at all cost. Persons whose ideas have been discarded will think twice before serving in the future. They will not be burned twice.

If a proposal is not acceptable, try to work out a compromise that satisfies all involved. If a proposal does not line up with the church's vision, it is necessary to point that out. But bend over backwards to stay in close relationship with the persons who brought the unacceptable proposal.

Whenever possible, the church should seek consensus among the leadership. Voting tends be divisive, but prayer works miracles in breaking down walls. Leadership should reach out to those who dissent to a decision. Statements along the following lines may be helpful:

- After prayer and counsel from many in the congregation, we believe this is the direction God is leading.

- We understand that you do not feel good about this direction. What can we do to work together on this issue?
- Will you be willing to work with us?

Church Structure

Rick Warren encourages churches to give up a certain amount of control. Congregations should allow their leaders to lead, and pastors must give up control over ministry.[1]

Most church constitutions tend to tie the hands of the leaders and allow little room for creativity and flexibility. Constitutions need to be designed so that the leadership team can cast vision, make policies, and establish procedures. Changing from a church council model to an oversight missions team can help to keep the congregation focused on making disciples. Consider moving from several boards to one vision-focused, empowering leadership team. The leaders need to be permission-givers rather than wet blankets.

Move people from committees to ministry teams. There are several differences between the two models. Ministry teams are action-oriented. They work with people and make a difference in people's lives. Do not try to motivate your members by giving them a status position on a committee; motivate them by offering opportunities for serving people. People want to make a difference in the lives of others.

Ministry teams conduct ministry, not meetings. They should not have to get approval from a committee for every new idea. As long as the ministry fits with the congregation's vision and operates within the budget, it can minister with the blessing of the congregation. Ministry teams need to check with the leadership team for activities to be placed on the church calendar, but the leadership team does not manage the actions of the ministry teams. Leadership helps the ministries succeed.

Jesus did not say, "I have come that you might have meetings." He said, "I have come that they may have life" (John 10:10). Life is not lived out in meetings at the church; it is lived out at home, at work, and at school. Some believers do not bring their lost friends to church because they don't have lost friends, and one reason they don't have such friends is because they give too much time to serving on committees at the church. That needs to change.

Church leaders need to recognize people's gifts and passions and free those people to follow their passions. Kennon Callahan says, "When a wise decision and significant results can be achieved by an individual, do not give the project to a committee. . . . Match the plays with the players."[2] Empower someone to carry out his or her passion as long as it lines up with the vision of the congregation.

The Bible's first committee was counterproductive: Moses chose twelve to spy out the land, and they came back with an evil report (see Numbers 13). Long-standing committees are usually not visionary or willing to take risks. They rarely help people mature in their Christian life.

Too much energy in most churches is spent on keeping the internal life of the congregation running smoothly while the community around them is eternally lost. The church in most communities has been marginalized. The community has no idea what the church is doing and doesn't care. When the mayor has a problem, he usually doesn't call the ministers' association. When the high school principal has a problem or the police have a problem with kids getting drunk or being violent after a football game, they don't look to the church to help solve the problem. The church has become virtually powerless in the eyes of our communities. This must change!

Keeping It Simple

Since the church's priority is to make disciples, each congregation should have a simple discipleship track, which is a process that moves new Christians to maturity in Christ. They become disciples, not simply converts.

A church with many activities and programs is "typically weak at intentionally bringing members into meaningful Christian relationships with one another," write the Rainers. "Frankly these churches are just too busy at activities to be intentional at most anything except maintaining their activities."[3]

The discipleship track should be the guide for all ministries throughout the church, from children through adults. Many churches have a plethora of programs, but members are not sure how it all meshes together to help make disciples. The leadership team needs to be empowered to develop a clear, simple disciple-making track that the congregation can enthusiastically endorse. When everyone knows this track and understands where the congregation is going, you'll begin to see the alignment and unity that results in effective ministry. A missional church is more concerned about being a united, focused congregation than about promoting events that may call attention to the church but do not contribute to making disciples.

Later in this chapter, I'll look at how the leadership team evaluates programs in relation to the discipleship track.

Eliminate Clutter

Creative, passionate people will come up with ideas that are on target to meet needs in the community. If the proposed program or activity does not fit into the disciple track, the leadership team should not endorse that program. The church can't meet all needs. Jesus did not always heal everyone in every town or meet all the needs of the poor.

Visionaries who come up with great ministry ideas that do line up with the discipleship track need to be willing to wait until resources are available. Examples of a need to wait might be a homeless shelter, a shelter for abused women, an after-school program, a TV or a radio ministry, or a Christian day school. These projects may be too large for a small congregation, but it might be possible to team up with others in the community.

Programs that are not productive drain resources and keep churches from being fruitful. They are a hindrance to our disciple-making track. Try to eliminate any activity that does not flow with the discipleship track. Don't overwork and burnout people. Allow time for the family. Most of the things you eliminate will be good things, but good things can be a hindrance to making disciples. Get rid of the non-missional programs.

People who have gone to church all their lives will not mature to the measure of the stature of Christ unless they are engaged in meaningful service. That service must have a connection to the great commission. If the focus is to keep the internal life of the church functioning, people will eventually lose their joy. They will not be excited about Jesus or his church. They will not invite their unchurched friends. If the great commission factor gets squeezed out, we become ingrown. To keep the church community healthy, we need unchurched people to be baptized and discipled. This is why we must be mission-driven. Without new Christians being born into the kingdom, workers will burn out because their life's mission of reaching the lost is not being fulfilled.

We can worship God and love other Christians, but until we serve others, especially those outside the church, we will not be growing into the stature of fullness of Christ. We become over-stuffed with biblical facts that turn people off when we try to communicate with them from a proud heart. We need to always serve from a heart of love. It's Christian service that connects us with people in the world and helps us mature in the discipleship process.

When do we meet Jesus? We meet Jesus when we feed the hungry, give a room to the homeless, stop to visit the sick, or minister to those in prison (see Matthew 25:31-46). If we are to move into maturity, we need to meet Jesus in these people.

Recruit volunteers for unpaid staff positions until the church can afford to provide to pay them. Rick Warren, who works with larger congregations, suggests the following ministry team leaders, which are somewhat different than the ones I suggest on the diagram on the next page: (1) a music director to oversee the music, (2) a membership director to oversee the care of the members and the receiving of new members, (3) a maturity director to oversee Bible study programs, (4) a ministry director to interview people

force of the congregation. There is a difference between a good idea and God's idea. God's vision unleashes the power of the church. It's a picture that produces passion!

Visions are caught more than taught. Too often our churches are like Ephraim in Psalm 78: "They forgot what he had done— the wonderful miracles he had shown them" (Psalm 78:11 NLT). We need to remember the good things and (to paraphrase Paul) forget the bad things and strain toward what is ahead, pressing on to what God has called us to achieve (see Philippians 3:13-14).

Many believers have no clue about the mission of the church. If asked, many will say the church exists primarily to worship God and for Christians to fellowship and encourage each other. They have little concept that they are sent by Jesus to be missional.

The Pastor's Role

Next to feeding the sheep, the pastor's most important responsibility is providing a vision for God's people. Without a vision, the congregation perishes (see Proverbs 29:18). It may take several decades, but it will perish. The pastor must hear from God and then listen to people, seeking their wisdom and input.

The pastor will work closely with the leadership team. Almost everything in God's creation has only one head. Is the church any different? There needs to be a team of leaders, but someone needs to be leader of the team. For a church to impact its community, for a church to be missional, it needs a vision-caster. The pastor must cast the vision.

A wise pastor knows who the spiritually mature persons are in the congregation. Even before sharing his or her vision with the leadership team, the pastor will do well to test it with a couple mature and wise persons who can bless or recommend a revision in the vision's timing or content.

Anabaptist theology holds the importance of every member, and I believe that. But I also believe that God gives some people the gifts to be pastors who can cast the vision. Michael Fletcher writes:

It has always been God's pattern to use one leader who would speak for Him in guiding the people into the vision of His destiny for them. Before Moses, there were Abraham, and Noah. After Moses came Joshua, Samuel, Gideon, and Deborah. They were followed by others: David, Daniel and Jeremiah, to name a few. Some were quick to step to the fore, while others recoiled from the prospect of solitary leadership, but all were selected by God to cast a vision for the people. Never was the formation of vision the product of a committee, and every attempt at such was met with God's displeasure.[5]

While it's true that the pastor needs to bring vision to the leadership team, that vision must be communicated clearly enough so that it can be owned by the leadership team. H. B. London Jr., writes:

> I think one of the great challenges for many of today's pastors is to exert firm leadership. Most of us come into the pastorate having tender hearts, and desire to demonstrate servantlike love and mercy. The church, however, is a spiritual battlefield and it often requires a strength of headship that is common in the secular world.[6]

If the pastor does not have a vision, the people will not have a vision. Paul Hattaway writes,

> Pastor, your primary responsibility is to give spiritual direction and leadership to the flock God has entrusted to your care. In China we believe the shepherd should be out in front of the flock, leading them through dangerous places. The willing sheep follow behind.
>
> Too many times, however, the shepherd of a church is not leading from the front but is at the back of the flock, trying to encourage the weakest and most nervous sheep to inch their way forward. This kind of leadership will never achieve anything! You will spend all your time in counseling sessions and dealing with the problems in your congregation! The devil will continually invent more problems just

to keep you tied up and away from leading your church into
the real battlefield, which is the war for souls of mankind.[7]

As the pastor prays to discern the church's vision, he or she
can focus on three helpful questions: (1) What does God want the
congregation to become? (2) What would God have the people do
to become what he wants them to become? and (3) How can we
make disciples?

In smaller congregations especially, the real leaders are often
not part of the official leadership. These undesignated leaders are
frequently the patriarchs or matriarchs of the church. I've seen this
over and over. Frequently an older member whose spouse is buried
in the church cemetery has control of the small congregation. The
pastor's hands are tied. When this is the situation, the pastor needs
to work with these unofficial leaders. This will take intentional
effort, time, and a holy boldness on the part of the pastor to
approach and confront these powerful and influential members.
Unless they are on board with the vision, it will fail. Strong leadership and teamwork must go hand-in-hand.

In *The Purpose-Driven Church*, Rick Warren reminds us
that churches can be driven by:

- Tradition: rules, regulations, rituals.
- Personality: centered around one person.
- Finances: early years driven by faith, later years driven
  by finances.
- Program: energy is on maintaining the programs.
- Buildings: too big or too small.
- Events: keep the people busy.
- Seekers: What do the unchurched want?
- Purpose: worship, fellowship, discipleship, evangelism,
  and service.[8]

Under which category does your congregation fit? I have
found that the older a congregation is, the more tradition-bound
it tends to be. We become comfortable and feel secure in our traditions. But which is more important: your comfort or your love

for the unchurched? Your traditions or your youth who may be leaving and going elsewhere? Many churches hold to their tradition as they say goodbye to their youth, who go to other churches or turn their back on the Lord altogether. Read Matthew 23 to see how Jesus reacted to the Pharisees and their dead traditions. Let's not be content to keep repeating the same ineffective activities and programs while our neighbors are on the broad way that leads to destruction.

Establishing Purpose and Strategy

I've talked a lot about a church's vision, but missional congregations need to articulate two other elements that lead the way to and result from vision: purpose and strategy. The vision statement itself should actually be quite short and should energize the congregation. It is really all the average church member needs to remember, although they should see the leadership embody this vision and live it 24/7.

In finding God's direction for a church, it is helpful for the leadership to articulate the purpose and a strategy they can use to guide their thinking.

The *purpose* of the congregation is basically the same for all churches. It is timeless and answers the question: Why did God establish the church? As I discussed in chapter 3, Jesus gave our purpose: to make disciples (see Matthew 28:18-20). The missional church should personalize the great commission and express it in a sentence or two.

Vision, then, flows from the church's purpose. It answers the question: What is God's specific call for our congregation? Vision requires faith. If one can explain every detail concerning who will carry out the vision and how, there is little need for faith. God's vision for the church is bigger than my ability to understand every future step. We must pray and exercise faith but at the same time not be presumptuous. Fruit comes at the end of the limb, not near the trunk where there is greater stability.

The Sunday immediately following New Year's Day is a logical time for a pastor to rally the congregation to the vision for the coming year. Other opportune times are at a groundbreaking or dedication of an addition or renovation, at the beginning of a Sunday school year when teachers are commissioned, upon the addition of a new staff person, on Easter Sunday, or at the conclusion of a series of messages calling the congregation to a new level of discipleship.

The vision should create excitement; it should be written to all members of the congregation. It needs to be visual: if you can't "see" it, you can't understand it or explain it to anyone else. Unless people can easily understand the statement, it will not be a driving force for the next few years.

Recall how Jesus painted pictures for his disciples. The vision statement should move people to action. Place it on a banner in a visible location, like across the front of the church. Place it in your weekly program, on your church letterhead and website, and on all communication pieces. Have the congregation repeat it aloud at least once a month.

Strategy should answer the question: How will our congregation achieve the vision? List the steps you need to take at least for the coming year. Some prefer to work with goals. These goals need to be measurable, significant, manageable, realistic, and personal. They must be owned by the leadership. They also need to be motivational: people should get excited by them. One caution about naming goals: when people achieve goals, they tend to look back too much. It is more helpful to focus on growth and maturity than on goals. Use the language of "moving to a new level" or "moving to the next level."

To achieve the strategy, you usually need to do less by cutting unproductive activities. You can be more productive and focused with activities that fulfill your vision. Ask yourself: If we were limited to doing one thing as a church, what would it be? No one can do it all; there are limited resources. Instead of asking God what to do, it might be helpful to ask what not to do and if any programs should be eliminated? As Greg Groeschel says, "When you increase your focus, you decrease your options. Good things are not necessarily God things."[9]

The Boulder Colorado Mennonite Church calls the entire congregation to an annual retreat for ministry discernment to carry out their vision. They ask: What is our ministry? Who are we? What are we about? They do this to keep the mission alive and to ensure that the vision is pressed into all the congregation's activities.[10] The retreat approach works well for a small congregation but can be adapted in larger ones.

Putting the Vision into Practice

In their book *Simple Church: Returning to God's Process for Making Disciples*, Thom Rainer and Eric Geiger list the benefits of keeping the disciple-making vision simple:

(1) Increased morale: When people expect that they'll be equipped to make disciples, rather than simply being told they need to do so, the morale of a congregation increases.

(2) Urgency: A church's sense of urgency actually grows when the emphasis shifts from merely gaining conversions to helping people grow toward spiritual maturity and ministry.

(3) Spiritual growth: People begin to take more ownership in their own spiritual growth, because the disciple-making process both shows people where they are *and* where they need to go next. As a result, people commit to Bible study, to small groups, to sharing their faith and inviting their friends.

(4) Conversions: As people invite their friends to church, more respond to Jesus and move into a life of discipleship.

(5) Stewardship: As programs that do not line up with the vision are eliminated, a church retains funds to carry out its vision. It is easier to eliminate programs after people have committed themselves to the congregation's vision.

(6) Unity. A congregation can increase its sense of unity by agreeing on the disciple-making process and working together to fulfill the vision.

Rainer and Geiger's illustration of Christ Fellowship in Miami illustrates the last point. A simple process for making disciples must jell with the church's activities and programs. The leadership team must decide which programs are best for the process. They set up weekly programs so all attendees and members can easily move through the process by moving from one program to the next. Here is how this unfolds for them.

At Christ Fellowship, the first step is to connect people to God. This is done during Sunday worship in an environment in which a growing and intimate relationship with God is stressed. The second step is to connect to others through small groups. Serious efforts are made to connect people this way. Most life changes occur in circles, not in rows. The third step is to connect to the ministry through their small groups, which are to serve as ministry teams. Everyone is encouraged to join a team engaged in a ministry they are passionate about. Groups participate in one activity outside the church walls over a two-month period. This helps connect people to the unchurched. Church members are also challenged to invite friends and families to church. Members are asked to do three things a week: come to worship, participate in a small group, and serve in a ministry. Facilitating service through the small groups greatly simplifies church life and builds disciples at the same time. These expectations are made clear to members, and potential members are told they should not join the church if they are not planning to move through this discipleship process. To facilitate everyone's movement into small groups, they are promoted in the worship services. New members are invited to test-drive a ministry without pressure to join the team. [11]

When talking about discipleship, it's important to think and speak about leading believers through the steps of maturity. The North Point Community Church in Atlanta, for example, believes that people can only go so far in their walk with Christ by sitting in rows. Real life happens in small groups, and this church has twelve thousand people in small groups that are designed to serve in some way. [12] Missional churches need to eliminate the word *program* from their vocabulary.

Hospitality

Some reports say that three out of four people do not have a close friend. Men, especially, often have few close friends. This presents our churches with a great opportunity. But many churches are not good at welcoming people.

Hospitability must be part of the DNA of the church. We need to get rid of our "insiders and outsiders" mentality, which is not scriptural: "Accept one another, then, just as Christ accepted you, in order to bring praise to God" (Romans 15:7). The Greek word translated "to accept" also means to receive, to admit to one's society and friendship. Paul writes in Romans 5:8, "God put his love on the line for us by offering his Son in sacrificial death while we were of no use whatever to him" (Msg). What a model for Jesus' followers. We are called to put our love on the line for others, even those we don't know.

Every person is created by God and a potential church member to help us win the world for Jesus. Fred Bernhard, in a seminar entitled, "Hospitality: Who Me?" gives this definition of hospitality: "Hospitality is the attitude and practice of providing the atmosphere and opportunities, however risky, in which strangers are free to become friends, thereby feeling accepted, included and loved. Their relationship thus opens up the possibility for eventual communion among the host, the stranger, and God."[13]

We often want people to be like us before they come to us, but that will not happen. A hospitable person is a lover of strangers. Are we afraid outsiders will pollute us? Are we afraid our children will be influenced by unwholesome habits? We must trust the Lord to protect our children and at the same time make wise decisions concerning their welfare.

Welcoming Visitors

First impressions are very important. Many unchurched people are convinced that the church is unfriendly and boring and that its teachings are irrelevant to life. They often form an opinion about their church experience before the first song or the message is heard. We need to intentionally welcome people the minute they drive into our parking lots. Making them feel comfortable takes a plan. Churches need greeters or hosts who intentionally welcome and connect with guests.

Welcome centers are common in growing congregations of two hundred or more. The greeter takes the first-time visitor to the center for an information packet. The host accompanies the visitors until the first-timers are comfortable.

Recruit greeters who are joyful and full of the Spirit. One greeter is not enough. Larger churches have greeters in the parking lot and another at the entrance who directs visitors to the welcome center. Greeters with programs should stand outside the auditorium, and then ushers inside the auditorium can take people to their seats.

As I said in chapter 3, it is best when the people who have no official position approach a visitor and express sincere, loving care. They are doing more to give a positive impression to first-timers than they will ever know.

In some congregations, hosts are called "advocates." They show a visitor around the facility and may sit next to them. No guest should sit alone. Hosts may explain the elements of the service, the announcements, make introductions, and invite visitors to lunch or the snack area after the service. Some churches have sponsors who help a new family "break in" and form new friendships.

Greeters need to communicate a genuine welcome to everyone but give priority to visitors.

Publicly Recognizing Visitors

Most people are introverts, so it is best not to publicly recognize visitors by name. Never call on them to stand or to speak.

At CCF, first-time visitors are recognized each Sunday. To help identify them, we invite all first-timers to briefly raise their hands. The congregation gives applause as the ushers present the first-timers with a popcorn box. This is done enthusiastically, with a sense of humor. Pastor Noah often says something like, "We don't want to be corny, but we're so glad you popped in to worship with us today. There is a yellow card in the box. You would help us by filling out the card and dropping it in the offering or giving it to an usher on the way out. We want to send you a letter expressing our appreciation for coming today." The box contains information about the church and a booklet, either *The Practice of the Presence of God* by Brother Lawrence or *How Good Is Good Enough?* by Andy Stanley. Also in the box is a small packet of unpopped popcorn. The large box readily identifies the visitors.

If you don't know whether a person is new, introduce yourself first. Be vulnerable. Don't put the visitor on trial by asking, "Who are you?" or "Are you related to somebody here?" Instead say, "I haven't met you yet. My name is . . ." Extend your hand. If they return the second or third or tenth time and you forget their name you can say, "I think we've met before. You'll have to help me. My name is Dave. Please tell me your name again." Repeating the name helps you remember it. Names are important. It's appropriate, at least in smaller congregations, for everyone to wear nametags. The nametags should all be the same so visitors do not feel unduly set apart.

You are on trial for every event at church. Therefore always have greeters, ushers, and hosts who are extroverts. God has other work for the introverts.

Follow-Up

As a church planter I told my core group that the "unpardonable sin" is to allow first-time visitors to leave without obtaining their names, addresses, and phone numbers. Of course some people don't want to give this information, and we need to respect them. But too often we are not assertive enough. You have a message of life or death; don't be bashful. Follow-up is extremely important.

Sending a letter is insufficient; follow up with a phone call thanking the visitor for coming. I often asked newcomers as they were leaving if I could visit them and answer any questions they might have. If I received an indication of openness to a visit, I tried to schedule it right away.

Dozens of families over the years said that my visit was why they came to church. If their schedule was open, I frequently visited on the Sunday evening of the day they came to church. On those visits, a prayer of blessing that mentions family members by name is always appropriate and appreciated, especially if you remember specific needs of family members. A short visit of fifteen minutes is frequently better for the unchurched than a long visit.

If first-time people do not return to church, send them a weekly program. If they do not return after two or three weeks, call again and thank them for coming. Let them know you missed them with a statement like, "Perhaps you have found a church, and if so, I don't want to be bothering you." If they haven't found a church and still don't return, call again in a month or so, depending on your sense of earlier conversations. The tone of voice often tells much.

Many people eventually came to church and found faith because of our persistence. As you and your people pray, the Holy Spirit will use your loving persistence to draw the unchurched to the Savior. I think that's what Jesus meant when he said in Luke 14:23 that we are to "compel them to come in" (KJV) to the heavenly banquet.

Let people know they are loved, wanted, and needed. Be passionate without being obnoxious. Peter reminds us that our relationship to the unchurched is to be handled with "gentleness and respect" (1 Peter 3:15).

Sunday school and vacation Bible school teachers build bridges when they call or send a card thanking their new students. Following up with children who go to VBS or summer camp makes a lasting impression on the child. Stopping by their home will be something the child will long remember. If they make a commitment to Christ, follow-up is a must. During that visit, encourage the child in the next steps in their new relationship to Christ. Taking time to show love is rare these days. The parents will appreciate your loving gesture as well.

When you have a community festival or a booth at the county fair, always remember to obtain the names, addresses, and phone numbers of persons who give any indication of interest. Follow up a week later with a phone call thanking them for stopping by your booth and talking with you. Invite them to church. If they don't show, call a month later and ask if they've found a church.

Don't Be Afraid of Youth

How old were Jesus' disciples? John was probably a teenager. The others were likely in their twenties. Many of us are afraid to call the young "thunderbolts," as Jesus nicknamed James and John, the sons of Zebedee (see Mark 3:17 CEV). Jesus was revolutionary in choosing these youth as his disciples. He did not launch his own ministry until age thirty—the age that, in Jesus' culture, one could be considered a teacher.

Jesus praises the Father that he has hidden the truths and power of the gospel "from the wise and learned, and revealed them to little children" (Luke 10:21). Little children, in this context, were the new disciples, many of whom were young.

I once urged a dying congregation to invite their college-aged youth to participate in their leadership team. That congregation has turned around. The evangelism of these youth has resulted in several young adults and families coming to church. The environment has radically changed to one of hope and life in this congregation!

Author John Drescher writes: "If youth are happy with the church, you will have happy parents. If youth are unhappy with the church, sooner or later, you will have discontented parents. If I were pastor again I would seek to involve youth in some way in every service."[14]

Why are churches across America reporting that they have so few active youth and young adults? Many of them love or at least have a good impression of Jesus, but they have a dislike for the church. Many see the church as not really interested in their ideas. They see the church as organized religion that tries to control how they think, dress, and act.

Adults must connect with and hear young people. Many of them will help us become missional if we take time to listen to them, enjoy their company, feel their passion, hear their hearts, and share their vision. Let's trust and empower them and put them to work in places of responsibility as we walk beside them. Our churches will rise to a new level of effectiveness as we utilize their dedication and energy.

Keeping New People

Some congregations are more challenged to keep new people than to welcome visitors. People may come for several months or even years and then drop out. Why is this?

The primary reason people drop out of a church is that they have not formed friendships. "People stay in a church because they are often more committed to each other, than to the mission or vision of the church," writes Michael Fletcher. "Do not kid yourself; plenty of other churches in town have great vision and wonderful ministries, but they don't have the relationships that your members have developed over the years."[15]

As we noted earlier, it's one thing to be friendly, but it's another to be a friend. One study finds that persons who do not find six friends in the first six months usually leave the church. If people get plugged into a healthy small group and build meaningful friendships, they'll participate in the life of the congregation. "New groupings or Sunday school classes have a window of about six months to gain new members. You must form new groupings or classes frequently to provide opening for potential adherents," writes Fred Bernhard.[16]

It's vital to quickly assess the interests of new members or attendees and introduce them to a ministry that lines up with their gifts. If new people learn of gatherings for fellowship or fun to which they are not invited, they soon catch on that they're not part of the "in group." If the men of a congregation get together to golf or bowl, this is an excellent opportunity to get to know the new guy. If a new person plays an instrument and the worship leader or pastor does not inquire about their talents, they may sense—rightly or wrongly—that they are not really accepted. Most churches I know can always find a spot for another instrument in their praise band. If the new attendees have not yet accepted Jesus, do not place them in leadership positions, but walk with them in loving acceptance and use their gifts where appropriate.

Years ago I attended a seminar in which the leader asked us what we can give a person who came the first Sunday to do the next time they come. While that may be too aggressive, it points to the fact that people need to know they are accepted and that one way for them to feel accepted is to invite them to participate. Ways that first-timers might serve on their next visit include helping in the kitchen, participating on ball teams, passing out programs, working as a teacher's assistant with children, helping in the church library, and many others.

People stay in your church for three reasons: faith, friends, and groups. Only a small minority leaves because of disagreements over faith or practices, such as baptizing infants, which my tradition doesn't practice. Mennonites provide a parent-child dedication service, but for a very few this may not be sufficient. Bless these people if they choose another congregation. Most people, however, leave for other reasons. Bernhard writes: "Within a year of officially joining a congregation, 62 percent of those members are less active in the church then at the time they joined. Twenty-five percent stop coming within the first year of membership."[17] We must make every effort to close the back door.

According to Bernhard, assimilation exhibits these qualities:

- Members are enthusiastic about their leaders, including pastors.
- Members are positive about the future of their church. They believe the best years are ahead.
- Members are open to innovation and new ideas.
- Members are not very attached to the facilities or location, but far more excited about Christ, the church, and sharing the Good News with others.

- There are sixty tasks for every one hundred members.
- There are seven small groups or units for every one hundred members
- One out of five groups was started in the last two years.
- A new Sunday school class was started within the last six months.
- One out of five leadership members has joined the church within the last two years.
- There is one full-time staff member for every 150 people in worship.[18]

Breaking Down a Clique

In fifty years of pastoring, I have found that the best way to keep people—especially in a small church—is for the pastor to become friends with them and get them plugged into a ministry in line with their giftedness. This gives people meaningful relationships, significance, purpose, and fulfillment.

This can be a problem, however, especially in older congregations in which cliques have developed among longtime members in particular ministries. Congregational leaders need to lead the way by enthusiastically welcoming new persons to these ministries or empowering them to create new ones. In formal and informal settings, mention the talents of new people and point out how glad you are that they're serving in this way.

Intentionally keep the focus of the church on the great commandment and the great commission. If the church's passion is to make disciples, it will get new members involved and encourage the building of friendships.

Small Groups

The key to making disciples for our churches is to involve people in healthy small groups that are involved in a community ministry. People can only go so far in their discipleship while sitting in rows. Jesus chose twelve and discipled them in his small group. For them, the church was their small group. Rainer and Geiger write: "If you can get a new believer into a small group they are five times more likely to remain in church five years later than those who were active in worship services alone."[19]

Defining a Small Group

In *The Capital*, CCF's monthly periodical, a 2007 article described our vision for small groups:

> Small groups are a safe place where people can ask tough questions, share what's on their mind and heart, and just be themselves in an environment where they will be accepted, encouraged, and involved. Such an environment makes it possible for each person in the church and eventually in the community to experience regularly and personally the caring, forgiving, and purposeful love of Jesus Christ. These groups help people grow in discipleship, and exercise their God-given gifts for the building up of the body of Christ.[20]

If our longtime members are to walk in fullness of life and in the power of the Holy Spirit, I believe they need to be active in a healthy small group. Small groups lead to relationships and accountability from which authentic ministry flows.

A challenge of small groups is that they often do not multiply. One way to work at this is to start with three or four people, not ten or twelve. The smaller group will make serious efforts to reach others. Larger groups will stay the same size and become ingrown. When new people come start a new group. From the start, have a leader and an apprentice leader in each group. Make it clear from day one that the apprentice leader will be leading a new group within six months.

Some churches decide that small groups can move the church to a new level. This often works for the short term. What happens is that the people in the groups get to know each other very well. Some are helped to walk more faithfully to Christ, and a few families who were on the periphery of the church find deep friendships, which is great. But this internal focus is too limiting to be healthy in the long haul. After awhile, the groups become stale and dissipate. They lose sight of the biblical goal, which is to make disciples.

In CCF's Basic 101 class, designed for people exploring church membership, we explained four levels of fellowship in a large congregation: (1) the Sunday morning worship, in which you are not expected to know everyone unless the church is 150 members or less; (2) the study groups of twenty to thirty people, in which you learn to know people by name; (3) the small group of four to twelve people, in which you share life together; and (4) one-on-one mentoring, in which you are accountable to another person. We worked at helping people understand that in order to grow toward maturity, you need accountability relationships in level 3 and, if possible, level 4.

Too often I hear this criticism of a megachurch: "I went there and no one talked to me." Going to a megachurch is, in some ways, like going to a football game. You don't go to meet people; you go to enjoy the game. People in megachurches go to enjoy meeting God in the worship. They experience God as the people on the platform lead them in worship. It is true that they will not likely become strong disciples if this level of fellowship is their only encounter with other Christians. However, if these believers have a meaningful daily devotional life, participate in a healthy small group, obediently living for Jesus at home, and witnessing and serving others, I can't help but believe they are faithful disciples of our Lord. To grow as Christians, it is important to develop fellowship with other believers and be involved in making disciples, whether through small groups or through a service ministry.

Informing Visitors of Small Groups

There should be some exposure of small groups to first-time visitors. An attractive display near the church entrance where visitors can't help but see it should include pictures of small groups and information about them. Provide pamphlets, even if only one page, describing the group so interested persons can take the information with them. Small groups are one of the best ways for helping people belong and move toward discipleship.

Introduce new people to the small groups by sharing how they have ministered to you. Also have sign-up Sundays throughout the year when people can join a group. I look with disfavor on closed groups. There were times when Jesus took his group away for training, but I can't picture Jesus telling people to leave because "We don't have room for you right now."

Effects

A positive aspect of small groups is that they can meet any time. This gives you a seven-day-a-week ministry. One pastor found that men are often quiet in a mixed-gender group, so his church formed men's groups that meet twice a month.

Most churches allow people to choose the type of small group that best fits their needs and interests. Rick Warren suggests four categories of small groups:

(1) Seeker groups: These are formed specifically for evangelism. They provide a non-threatening environment for the unchurched to ask questions, express doubts, and investigate the claims of Christ.

(2) Support groups: These offer support during life transition times for new parents, college students leaving home, or empty nesters. Others deal with healing specific hurts, such as loss of a mate by divorce. Still others help provide recovery from various addictions.

(3) Service groups: These groups focus on a common task such as prison ministry, feeding the homeless, children's community ministry, or foreign missionary care.

(4) Growth groups: These are dedicated to nurturing, discipleship training, and in-depth Bible study.[21]

There are times when the leadership team will request all groups to work through a particular curriculum. At CCF, we studied Rick Warren's *40 Days of Purpose* as a congregation. If the pastor has a series of messages on a particular topic, the small groups can work with the same theme for a time. This helps to promote unity and solidarity of the congregation.

Many pastors of long-established congregations may not have the influence they need to announce to the congregation that all small groups will be focusing on a particular subject these next few weeks. Pastors in these situations have a major job of restructuring ahead of them. First, they need the leadership team to agree on the benefits of the congregation-wide study. If necessary, pastors can have the small group leaders meet with the leadership team in order to somehow gain their respect so the team can lead. In many churches I work with, this is no easy task. But until the leadership team has the respect of the congregation, there is very little hope for a church to be missional. Loyalty and respect for leadership is necessary in a healthy church.

Small groups often become ingrown. For many years I used the acrostic, P-O-W-E-R, to promote small groups. Every group needs to include these five ingredients: prayer, openness to the Word, worship, encouragement, and reaching our world. We did quite well with the first four, but the "reaching out" was seldom part of the DNA of the group. Over the years I have learned that other traditions face the same challenge.

Too often we put the cart before the horse. We say we first need to love each other more, or come to greater unity before we can reach out. We think we have too many internal problems, and when we get our own house in order we will reach our neighbors. But my experience shows that churches become healthy as they quit bickering and walk in obedience to the great commission. Reaching out can and will bring healing within.

Some churches wrestle with the question of whether a Sunday school class can be a genuine small group. It is possible, but it will not happen unless the leaders are training to take the group from a primarily internally focus to an external focus.

Hiring a Church Consultant

Tom Landry, the legendary coach of the NFL's Dallas Cowboys, once said, "A coach is someone who tells you what you don't want to hear, and has you see what you don't want to see, so you can be who you have always known you can be."[22]

One of the barriers to becoming a healthy church is self-reliance. We feel we don't need others. It is often helpful to have an experienced person who can look in from the outside, someone who has led some congregations through a revitalization process. Church revitalization can be very difficult. You need the support of an experienced resource.

This consultant, or "coach," needs to be a loving but honest person who can take some of the pressure off the pastor. The coach makes it clear to the congregation that if they keep doing the same things, they will keep getting the same results. He or she will point to painful changes that need to occur for a church to become missional. The coach will help develop a clear vision and help the leadership team focus on the vision, all the while staying out of the limelight as much as possible. The consultant's objective is to help leaders to grow and succeed by enabling a church to be missional.

The church consists of great diversity but great potential for division. Jesus knew what a challenge we would have in working together; that's why he prayed for us to be one, as he and the Father are one (see John 17:11). As you give your energy to working with others so that the world may know Jesus is Lord, don't be discouraged.

For Discussion

1. Of the many topics in this chapter, which ones might you consider as action steps for your congregation? What would be the first steps to begin working on this change?

2. If you are in a small group have you found it helpful in your discipleship training?

3. Has you group reached your unchurched neighbors, if not what do you need to do to change this?

9

The Worship Service
Part 1: Structure

Dwelling in the Word: Read Acts 2:41-47.

Testimony

Elaine grew up in a Christian home. Her father was a church elder for many years. After school Elaine left home to serve the Lord. During her time of service she met Daniel, a handsome young man from another country. Friendship developed into a romance and what she thought was a Christian marriage.

Daniel participated in church activities for some time, but he was not walking with Christ. This became apparent as he returned to his roots in a different religion. Elaine has had many difficult years, but through these times she has grown in her faith. Her children see her steadfastness and have decided to follow in her footsteps. What a testimony she has been to many.

~

The weekend service is still the funnel by which most people seek God's kingdom. Worship is a vital aspect of our relationship with the Lord and is still the main entrance for the unchurched to come to Christ. So it is important to give serious consideration to it. To make our worship pleasing to God and also inviting to the unchurched, we must make every effort to be faithful to Scripture while being sensitive to the culture of the unchurched in our communities.

Defining Worship

Rick Warren writes that "worship is expressing our love to God for who he is, what he's said, and what he's doing."[1] The dictionary defines worship as expressions of reverence toward God or extravagant respect or admiration of God. I try to practice a conscious gratefulness to God as I work, drive, and live. The psalmist writes, "I'll worship in joyful fear" (Psalm 86:12 Msg).

God, not ourselves, must be the focus of our worship. Do our songs and messages focus on ourselves or on God? One of my favorite verses is Psalm 16:11: "In Your presence is fullness of joy; At Your right hand are pleasures forevermore" (NKJV). As we grow in our relationship with Christ, we grow in our love of just being with him. That is worship.

Roxanne Brant writes:

> So many people will do any amount of service rather than love. Unfortunately, we are by nature doers like Martha, instead of lovers and worshipers, like Mary (Luke 10:38-42). God is seeking those who will love Him enough to come and be with Him and worship Him. He does not seek workers but he seeks worshipers. He seeks those who will worship Him in spirit and in truth (John 4:23-24). Only after that love relationship has been rightly established and all has been centered upon Him, can He safely send us out to work with Him.[2]

God cannot use men and women who are naturally capable and self-reliant. He wants those who rely upon him for everything they do. That way, God gets the glory and not humans. All our education and training has to be put on the cross along with all our sins, so that no flesh shall be tempted to glory in itself.

Paul said the same thing about himself: "But what things were gain to me, those I counted loss for Christ. Yea doubtless, and I count all things but loss for the excellency of the knowledge of Christ Jesus my Lord . . . and do count them but dung that I may win Christ" (Philippians 3:7-8 KJV).

The gatherings in the early church were not primarily about meeting the needs of the individual but were centered on the worship of God and the strengthening of the church in its mission to reach others.

Dan Kimball writes:

> In a worship gathering, we create a place where we can express love, devotion, adoration and praise to God. . . . Worship is not something we do only once a week. Worship is a lifestyle of being in love with God and in awe of him all week long (Romans 12:1-2). Our minds, hearts, bodies, marriages, families, jobs—everything should be offered to him in worship. This includes what we think about, what we do, what we say, what we eat, and what we spend time doing—they are all acts of worship.[3]

In designing a worship service, we need to ask:

- Did we lift the name of Jesus up as the centerpiece of why we gather?
- Did we have a time in the Scriptures learning the story of God and humanity? Did we invite everyone to be part of his story today?
- Did we pray together and have enough time to slow down and quiet our hearts to hear God's voice and yield to his Spirit?
- Did we experience the joy, love, and encouragement of being together as a church?
- Did we take the Lord's Supper together as a church regularly?
- Did we somehow remind everyone of the mission of the church and why we exist?
- Did we enable people to individually contribute something as part of the body of Christ?[4]

Let's remember we are not to worship our worship. We are to worship Jesus! Sometime Christians are so convinced their worship style is the only one God appreciates that they tend to worship their worship style.

Our Personal Worship

Just as there is a relationship between personal evangelism and congregational evangelism, so there is a relationship between personal worship and corporate worship. If we are not taking time to meditate on God's Word and worship him in our personal lives, our corporate worship will be shallow. People who have not learned to let their roots go down into the soil of God's love through prayer and the Word will not stand during the times of testing. These people tend to drop out of church life. Some leave and go to other religions because their relationship to Christ is rootless. Jesus spent time with the Father. How much more must we spend time with our Father and his Son, our Savior and Lord! If your personal relationship to Jesus is not vital, earnestly ask him to draw your heart to him, to love his Word and to enjoy his presence.

Old clichés like, "I'm not getting anything out of church," or "the pastor is not feeding me," may be more of an indication of the person's immature heart than an indictment of the worship service. If we stay up late Saturday night watching TV and feeding our souls on the husks of the secular culture, we will have a very difficult time finding the Sunday worship service meaningful. But if we prepare our hearts and focus on Jesus and what he has done for us, we will go away encouraged, ready to encounter a secular world.

Worship and the Unchurched

Fear of embarrassment is one of the reasons people give for not attending church. If the unchurched simply observe the joy we experience in our worship, they may sense God's presence there and be drawn to him. We reach them primarily through their heart rather than through their head. But one reason we often do not invite our friends to church is because we think they will not be comfortable because the service is irrelevant and not seeker-friendly.

In *Future Worship*, LaMar Boschman writes:

> Just one look at Christian television and it is obvious that our attitudes, words, dress, and ideas are outdated and even dangerous. So much of the contemporary church is increasingly a museum of anthropology. It represents a crystallizing, antiquated, ineffective, even humorous display of a way of life that has not existed in years. No wonder my new neighbors politely chuckled when they heard I am a minister.
>
> Normal people may want to occasionally visit a museum; they surely do not want to live there! Seekers today want reality; they don't want to sit and stare at taxidermy of a prehistoric beast. Seekers are hungry. They want some answers, and the seeker wants God. Often all we have to offer them is a program, a song list, or best sermon of the week.[5]

By way of contrast, Dan Kimball in *The Emerging Church* gives this illustration:

> Imagine being invited by a friend to church, hearing about the meaning of Christ's sacrifice on the cross, and then seeing your friend go forward and drop to his knees. No matter how you felt about religion, you would probably think your friend must really love this God he talks about. You'd be struck by how seriously the people around you seem to take their faith. It's no wonder that in our church far more people have become believers on communion nights than on any other night. It really is a beautiful thing seeing people make decisions at a service that is probably more flat-out unapologetically spiritual than anything else we ever do.[6]

If only we'd be bold enough to share the meaning of Christ's death and come to the altar in the presence of the unchurched. Lord, hasten the day.

Technical Changes

Earlier I talked about technical versus substantive changes. Here I want to discuss technical changes that I believe can help churches become missional.

Appearance and Atmosphere of the Auditorium

A warm and inviting atmosphere is essential to draw new members, especially young adults. Modern furniture, sufficient light for reading, and well-lit hallways are a must.

In my work with declining churches, I often find the atmosphere cold. People walk by each other, especially anyone that might be new, without a greeting or smile, oblivious to those around them.

If the church is seriously focusing on reaching the unchurched, the atmosphere of the service should be celebratory and exuberant. People are attracted to a joyful fellowship. The band often plays lively worshipful music before the worship service. From the beginning there is life and vibrancy. In vibrant churches, people tend to come early and stick around after the service. In growing churches, people are talking and often laughing. They are usually difficult to gather for a meeting because they are involved in conversation.

The call to worship should be uplifting. We are coming into the presence of Almighty God who not only created the cosmos but gave his life to draw us to himself. What a dramatic expression of extravagant love!

For the call to worship, I've relied heavily on portions of the Psalms. Psalms 95–103 and 140–150 are filled with expressions of praise, thanksgiving, and prayers of gratitude, all of which help the worshipper both in private worship and in corporate worship to focus on God. We need to thank him, praise him, even lift up our voices with shouts of praises. When our children see us shouting at a ball game but standing quietly in church, they might be tempted to think sports are more important—or more fun—than worship. I believe the Lord wants us to enjoy worshipping him.

Applause has become more common in churches. Applause

can add to the celebratory atmosphere. I believe it is appropriate when the pastor makes a strong point in the message for the congregation to respond with affirmations such as saying "Amen" or to give a round of applause. People don't usually fall asleep in that kind of atmosphere, and if applied in good taste it can add to the impact of the message. Audible "amens" during prayer, if given in sincerity, let others know you are praying along with the leaders.

The gospel is Good News. There is much discouraging news in the media; we don't need more at church. People need to be confronted with sin, but grace needs to be the predominant message and praise the predominant mood. People receive renewed faith as they worship Jesus with uplifting songs and messages. At the close of the service, commission and send the congregation forth into the Lord's harvest field.

In vibrant congregations, people respond immediately when a leader or teacher in a class asks someone to read the Scripture or lead in prayer. In older traditional churches, you usually need to wait until the leader calls on someone. This tentativeness often indicates a lukewarm, lethargic attitude and is not a good indication of the vibrant and joyful life of the Christian. New Christians often are freer to lead out and enthusiastic about participating. When the group is tentative and lethargic, the leader needs to model enthusiasm by encouraging others to exercise boldness and assertiveness. New attendees can tell if we are enjoying our relationship to Jesus or if we are simply coming to church out of habit.

Positioning of Leaders

It is best when pastors and leaders sit in the first row of chairs rather than elevated on a platform facing the congregation. But if the leaders do sit on the platform, use chairs of the same type as those on the floor. This symbolizes the priesthood of all believers. The old-fashioned "throne" chairs on the platform add to the feeling that the pastor is above or separated from the people.

The smaller the congregation, the closer the pastor should be to the people. In small churches, it's helpful for the speaker to stand on the same level as the people. This facilitates communication. I picture Jesus standing close to the people as he talked with them.

If possible, remove the large pulpit and replace it with a small lectern or stand. A large pulpit can be a psychological barrier between the speaker and the congregation. In some congregations, the pulpit is "sacred," because a faithful member in the church's history donated it. If this is the case, I suggest using a lapel mike and stand to the side or stand in front of the pulpit. After witnessing this for some time, the congregation may see the pulpit as a liability rather than an asset and remove it. The principle is to avoid a stage-verses-audience feeling.

Service Times and Length

Service times need to be discerned by the culture of the people you are trying to reach. If people normally sleep in Sunday morning, a service starting at 10:30 or 11 is best. A choice of two services is even better. You many want to have the children's education during the message. The adult education can take place in the small groups throughout the week.

The length of the service also needs to be discerned according to the culture. In my experience, international people want longer services. The Ethiopian church I oversee in Baltimore has a two- to three-hour service. Most Americans want services to last about sixty to ninety minutes. Many large churches are forced into shorter services because they schedule two or three on Sunday morning. I have observed that when the Holy Spirit is moving in a powerful way, the service often will go longer and the people love it because they are being fed and their spirits are encouraged.

Flow of Service

Modern media and technology have greatly affected our culture. Many people, especially the unchurched and youth, will expect a smooth-flowing service with little down time. Some services remind me of a funeral: the songs drag and the leader lacks enthusiasm.

It is helpful if those who will be speaking sit in the front row of seats. If they need to come to the platform, they can come while the leader is still speaking. Having a person walk from the back of the auditorium while the congregation waits for him or her to reach the mike is not appropriate in our fast-moving culture. A smoothly flowing service also communicates to the people that someone took the time to plan the service.

Times of silence can be very worshipful. Most unchurched people and even many who attend regularly are uncomfortable with silence, so manage it well. The leader should explain the purpose for the silence. At Capital Christian Fellowship I have said, "Our service today is high energy. Let's take a few moments and quiet ourselves for a short time. Listen to the Holy Spirit speak to us. Tell him you love him and want to hear what he has to say. Listen with an open mind and heart." Before reading Scripture, the reader may want to inform the congregation if there is to be silence after the reading.

In *The Emerging Church*, Dan Kimball writes:

> Plan times of silence while Scripture is projected on screens. For example, after a message about our identity in Christ, we ended with eight minutes of silence while one Scripture after another appeared on the screen. No noise. No fancy moving words on the screen, either. Just slow fades of white text through a black background. While the truth of God's Word quietly worked in that room, I watched people get on their knees. Some people wept. Others simply sat and soaked in the reality of what it means to be a child of God. There were no voices, no special songs—just quiet and Scripture on the screens.
>
> Isn't silence a lost aspect in our worship today? Where else are people to learn the beauty of being quiet? Where do we allow the Spirit to speak? Where do we teach emerging generations the importance of slowing down and listening for God's voice? This is a powerful way to include an experiential element in our worship gatherings.[7]

Attire

Growing contemporary churches invite people to "come as you are." In many communities, a pastor who wears a suit and tie places an unnecessary barrier to the younger generation. The biblical principle of modesty is expected and encouraged. Our handbook at CCF urges everyone to "dress to honor the Lord. Those who serve as worship leaders, as well as all persons on the platform and anyone serving in a leadership position are to set the standard by wearing modest, comfortable clothing. Casual attire is typical."

In poorer communities, many men may not own a suit and women may not own a dress. Sometimes it is necessary to inform unchurched people to come in casual attire because the last time they were inside a church was for a wedding or funeral. Many immigrants and African-Americans "dressed up" for worship. At CCF, we decided that, as the older senior pastor, I should wear a suit and tie while associate pastors dressed casually. This seemed to work well in our international setting.

Announcements

As a missional church, your congregation should be moving from an activities-centered one to a discipleship-centered one. This means there should be fewer announcements.

Any announcements that do not involve the entire congregation tend to lose the attention of anyone not directly affected. You can direct people to announcements in their programs, or announcements can be placed on the screen before and after the service as well as during the announcement time.

Each Sunday it is appropriate to welcome visitors and offer a packet of information that includes a small gift. Almost every Sunday at CCF, we announced that anyone interested in learning more about the church was invited to the Basic 101 class.[8]

Prayer

Because Jesus is in our midst, we need to talk to him in a natural way. Talking to God in a different tone and vocabulary can make people think they have to pray the same way. I love to hear children pray. They can teach us so much (see Matthew 18:3-4). They pray just like they are talking to a person in the room.

If I were talking to you, I wouldn't say, "Now I am going to talk to you"; I would just start talking. Frequently, I do not announce that we are going to pray. I just start talking to Jesus. Jesus is there, so just talk to him. This helps people be aware that Jesus is present, listening to everything we say and seeing everything we do. He is our ever-present friend (see John 15:14). We pour out our hearts to a Father who bends over to hear our prayers (see Psalm 40:1).

Passionate and fervent prayer is important. James 5:16 speaks of fervent prayer availing much. The tone of the prayer can either communicate faith, love, and passion—or the lack of these. Jesus taught his disciples how to pray. Whoever is leading in prayer is also teaching others how to pray, and they need to model well.

When I ask an elder or layperson to lead in what traditional churches often call the pastoral prayer, I email them a list of things to thank God for, as well as needs and concerns I want the congregation to bring to the Lord. This is necessary in large and growing congregations, and it helps bring a balance between praise and intercession. To foster warmth and unity in the congregation, leaders might suggest that everyone hold hands during a prayer.

To help set a tone for the entire service, one congregation at various times begins its worship service with the following prayer:

> Lord, much as we want to worship you, this isn't something we are able to do on our own. Without the Spirit or God working in us and through us and among us, nothing of any value will take place here today. We are nothing without you. Work in us we pray, so that we can worship you![9]

Scripture

The reading of Scripture should be thoughtful and passionate. If possible, put the Scripture on PowerPoint. Young people appreciate this, and so do older persons. If you do not place the Scripture on the screen, announce the chapter and verse and be sure the congregation has time to find the passage in their Bibles. Some smaller congregations allow time for people to share a thought or question with the person beside them. Time might be given occasionally for a few persons to publicly share something that spoke to them from the passage.

Use a Bible translation that unchurched people will easily understand. This is a must for the missional church. I personally like the *New Living Translation*. I frequently quote from *The Message* Bible in my preaching ministry. *The Message* explains theological terms that the unchurched and even some of the churched do not understand.

Responsive Readings and Testimonies

If you incorporate responsive readings, put them on the PowerPoint and keep them short. Many adults are uncomfortable reading aloud, and a few might be unable to read. In one church that I pastored, I used very few responsive readings because I knew a few adults in the congregation were unable to read. Responsive reading tended to embarrass them.

The gospel is perpetuated when testimonies are incorporated into worship. Testimonies build faith. Missional churches allow time for short testimonies—three to five minutes—during worship, rather frequently. A testimony is not preaching; it is basically giving facts about how Jesus has impacted your life.

The word *testimony* makes some members uncomfortable. They may think they have to recount a highly exalted experience of a "superChristian." Members who are reluctant to give a testimony may share a "God Moment" or simply offer a time when they saw God at work during the past week.

When I was pastoring, I requested that candidates for membership email a written draft of their testimony a week before they were baptized and received as members. These drafts helped me to know they were prepared and to see that their testimony was in line with sound doctrine. It also boosted the candidates' confidence, especially if they were shy, and it encouraged them to prayerfully think through what they planned to say. Sometime people get carried away talking about their sinful past in terms that are too graphic, or they talk about their life with God in such wonderful terms that it doesn't seem real. Or they can say things that are too crass or irreverent and make others feel uncomfortable. The things that we say from the pulpit should be authentic, encouraging, and build up the body of Christ.

To help people prepare their testimony, I gave them questions that grew out of Paul's testimony in Acts 26. Where were you spiritually before receiving Jesus, and how did that affect you in your relationships? What caused you to consider Jesus as the solution to your needs? Specifically, how did you receive Christ? How did your life begin to change after you trusted Jesus? What other benefits have your experienced since becoming a Christian? Most of these questions can be answered in one sentence.

Sharing Time

Most smaller churches have a time during worship when members can share concerns or joys publicly with the congregation. This can be a difficult issue for growing churches. Personal prayer requests are best shared in small groups. In larger churches of three hundred or more, people don't expect time during the service for personal sharing and prayer requests. For small churches in which open mike time is practiced, leaders need to be sensitive to the length of the sharing but also to new people who have no idea who the person sharing is talking about.

It is helpful if the leader holds the microphone; that way he or she can more easily control the volume and help the person terminate if they are rambling or sharing unnecessary minutiae. In smaller congregations, sharing time can be an asset within appropriate guidelines.

As CCF grew from two hundred to three hundred members, it was difficult for our people to give up open mike sharing time. When we reached four hundred, it was a necessary step. We encouraged people to share in their small groups, and we provided prayer counselors at the conclusion of our worship services.

Social Issues

At CCF, a member was disturbed because I didn't speak about the evils of abortion frequently enough. Another member asked on various occasions for permission to provide literature and speaking time to urge the congregation to vote a certain way or contact politicians about various issues. This raised serious concerns with other members who had differing views.

Because of the potential divisiveness of these issues, we developed a policy for members who wanted to share these concerns with the congregation. They were to submit their concern in writing for the leadership team's discernment prior to their request to speak or offer literature. This gave us time to read their literature and to dialogue with these persons about an appropriate way to communicate their concerns, helping them see that the congregation contained different perspectives on most issues. This solution has worked well for us. We were not necessarily silent on social issues; rather, we aimed to address them in a way that would edify the whole congregation.

The Offering

Some churches use a low-key approach to receiving the offering. They have containers at the exits and members can drop in their offering. Because God loves a cheerful giver, at CCF when the offering time is announced, the congregation breaks out in applause. Other churches follow what some would say is an African tradition of making the offering the highlight of the service. They invite people to come to the front to present their offerings and prayer requests by dropping them in the containers on the front tables.

If you pass the offering container throughout the congregation, this is one place you can use a large variety of people—young and old, new attendees and longtime members. Some say that large containers help to bring large offerings. I cannot guarantee that, but it might be worth your consideration!

Avoid saying, "We will take the offering"; instead, say, "We will receive the offering." Have at least two persons count the offering to avoid any suspicions or concerns about improprieties. The church's financial records should be available for members who desire to see them. Whenever decisions involving money are made, the decisions need to be transparent so that there is no need to question anyone's integrity. Treasurers and church leaders need to bend over backward to be sure all financial matters are squeaky clean and above reproach.

Allowing people to give to specific needs will be beneficial to the overall income of the congregation. Some have found that identifying needs and listing them in the program can be helpful. If the kitchen team needs a new refrigerator, for example, or the property team needs to repair a major pipeline costing thousands of dollars, make this known in the program. Someone may feel inclined to meet specific needs because God has blessed them with a surplus. Encourage special gifts to meet specific needs.

When you have a service at which new families are present, like at Christmas, consider having an offering in which 100 percent of the money goes for meeting community needs. You may be surprised what unexpected monies your members, as well as community guests, give.

In the next chapter, I'll look at the importance of music and preaching.

For Discussion

1. Is your service one to which you feel comfortable inviting your unchurched peers? If not, what aspects would need to change before you are comfortable inviting your prebeliever friends?

2. Besides music and preaching, which are discussed in the next chapter, are there any aspects of worship you would like to see changed? Can you discuss these with the pastor and the leadership team?

10

The Worship Service
Part 2: Music and Message

Dwelling in the Word: Read 1 Corinthians 14:26-33.

Testimony

As a rebellious teen, Ken left home to hitchhike across the county. He met up with the Jesus people, and his life was transformed. Ken was baptized in the Holy Spirit, and for the first six months he says he could barely speak English. He spoke in tongues 24/7. Now, as an adult with family and children, he has a very difficult time fitting in with the organized church. His challenges and questions kept me on my toes and frequently sharpened my ministry. Ken has been both a great help and a great frustration to me, but I thank God for Ken and the way he has helped me think and move outside of the box. The church needs to include more people like Ken within its circle.

~

In this chapter, I continue our discussion of worship and focus on what are perhaps the two most visible aspects of any service: the music and the message. I also look at what postmodern prebelievers say they want in a worship service.

The Music of the Worship Service

There are more "wars" fought over music than any other aspect of church life. Multitudes move from one church to another over issues like whether hymns should be accompanied or whether a full band should play contemporary worship music.

When it comes to being missional, the music can be more important than the message because it can usually reach the heart more easily than the spoken word. In *Breaking the Missional Code*, Ed Stetzer and David Putman write:

> Scripture teaches that we are to "consider others better than yourselves" (Phil. 2:3). This includes the truth that our pref-erences should never become more important than what our church needs to be and do missionally. For that matter, the church's focus should not be the preferences of other church members either. A truly biblical church will ask, "What will it take to transform this community by the power of the gospel?" not "How many hymns do we have to sing to make everybody happy?"[1]

If our focus is on transforming the community by the power of the gospel, we will have solved the music issue and many others as well. I think God loves all kinds of music when sung from a pure heart. The question is whether it connects people with God. Does it usher them into the very presence of God? I suppose there are hundreds, if not thousands of styles of music in our world. How great it is if you have composers in your church who can capture the heart of the congregation's vision and promote it with original songs (see 1 Corinthians 14:26). Encourage this creativity.

We can broaden our love and appreciation for various styles of music, but it isn't easy. There are four options to this dilemma:

1. *Maintain the status quo.* This is fine if you are reaching the unchurched and lives are being transformed for Christ.

2. *Offer two services*, one with contemporary music more famil-iar to the unchurched and one with the traditional music.

3. *A transition model.* No one wants to be told they have to

adjust to another style of music. At CCF, when we changed from a cappella music to a worship team, we promised the congregation that we would include at least one a cappella hymn or gospel song every service. We'd begin the service with an a cappella hymn. New members began telling us they wanted their spirits lifted from the beginning. They wondered why the worship team wasn't leading all the music. Eventually we dropped a cappella singing altogether.

4. *A blended model.* Many congregations are using this approach. They provide traditional hymns and contemporary praise music. The blended model may be the best solution for most traditional churches. If the unchurched younger generation in your community feels comfortable with this approach, that is great. If not, we need to find what appeals to them so we can be missional.

As painful as it is, we need to realize that the music many of us grew up with does not connect with the younger unchurched generation. They have little appreciation for the King James language in many hymns. Changing words does not work either. I've tried this, but it was confusing and not worshipful. One concentrates on getting the words right rather than focusing on worshipping Jesus.

Singing *To* God or *About* God?

Many hymns and gospel songs talk about our relationship with God, while most contemporary praise music addresses God directly, which can be more intimate. It is more worshipful to sing "I love you, Lord," rather than "Our God is a God of love," or "You are holy" as contrasted to "Our God is holy," or "You are my rock, my salvation, my deliverer," rather than, "God is my rock, my salvation, my deliverer."

Another significant issue is that children are not taught to read music as frequently as they once were, so hymn books with notes are not as useful as in the past.

Drums

I've observed that most songs the youth appreciate are accompanied by drums. We older folks need to understand that this is the style of music our youth find worshipful, and we must be open to it for their sake and the sake of the unchurched. Most worship teams find ways to tastefully include drums, and a good worship team can make hymns upbeat and appealing to the youth.

I've often heard remarks like, "The music is too loud; the young people will ruin their ears." That may be true, but according to Scripture, in heaven there will be lots of loud music. "In a loud voice they sang: Worthy is the Lamb, who was slain, to receive power and wealth and wisdom and strength and honor and glory and praise" (Revelation 5:12).

I suggest you begin your worship services with joyful, upbeat lively music and move to slower, more meditative music. Move people from praise to encounter with the living Christ—from active worship to listening for the voice of the Holy Spirit. You don't need a professional worship band to do this. I have been in congregations where one person with a guitar consistently led five hundred people in meaningful worship. Training a worship leader is one of the most important ministries of your congregation. If your congregation does not have such a person or team, make this first on your prayer list and budget funds to send that person or team to a seminar or workshop.

The Message

Sam had a neighbor who encouraged him to come to church. "I've heard hundreds of messages," Sam said, "and I can't remember one." The neighbor asked Sam what he had for dinner last evening. Sam couldn't remember. The neighbor replied, "Then why bother to eat dinner again?" Though we don't remember the meal, we were still nourished. A good message will nourish our souls. Though most Sunday messages are forgotten by Wednesday, preaching is important.

The perspective of many of the younger generation is that a sermon is attacking them rather than sharing with them a message of good news. A young adult once said to me, "I don't want to be preached at. I like interactive messages." Jesus used an interactive style. He frequently answered people's questions, whether they were asked out loud or were in the minds of his listeners. We do well to follow his example by using various methods in preaching. Whenever Helen joined me for a dialogue message, in which we took turns in speaking or asked each other questions, the congregation always affirmed us.

Use variety in your preaching. Paint pictures in people's minds, use humor, ask questions, tell experiences, and use stories. Try not to be predictable.

Have a testimony in the middle of the message underscoring one of your points. Use visual aids. Be creative. Jesus was constantly painting pictures in the minds of his hearers. If the pastor is boring, people may think God is boring. One great pastor said, "It's a sin to be boring!"

When focusing on a particular sin, don't dwell on it for a whole message. Those who are not guilty of that sin are tempted to feel justified; those guilty of it are not in need of condemnation but of the love and grace that leads to deliverance.

The early church in the book of Acts preached more often about the resurrection than about the cross. Repentance is necessary, and it is only through the cross that we can come to live in the resurrected life. But our emphasis is on God's grace and the power we enjoy in the resurrected Christ. As people of the resurrection, we walk in newness of life. You can't be more positive than that. The unchurched need to hear this Good News. Jesus came not to condemn the world but to save it (see John 3:17). Jesus said to the woman caught in adultery, "Neither do I condemn you. . . . Go now and leave your life of sin" (John 8:11).

Still, some people like legalistic sermons that tell them exactly what to think and do. They want definitive answers so they do not need to decide for themselves what is right or wrong. Though some of these churches grow, this is unhealthy. Jesus often left people scratching their heads. He spoke in parables and figures of speech that made you think and often have multiple interpretations and applications. It's okay for a message to not have all the answers. People need to grapple with meaning and be challenged to apply the message to their lives. This approach leads to maturity.

Our son Chet, a church planter, has interviewed many unchurched people and learned that their impression about preachers is that their messages are too judgmental. Paul went to Athens where there were idols everywhere (see Acts 17). Instead of condemning the people, he presented Jesus, and the people began asking questions. He capitalized on their interest in gods. Can we find people's interests, people's needs, and then present Jesus? Let's be sure our messages exalt Jesus rather than attacking other faiths.

Preachers should be enthusiastic about their message, approaching the lectern with enthusiasm in their step and body language. This helps to communicate excitement before you begin. I have seen pastors walk to the lectern so slowly that I wondered if they were discouraged or afraid to speak.

The average person is persuaded by feelings, not facts. Of course we need facts and truth, but it is interesting that Jesus said we worship in spirit (first) and in truth (second). Passionate, spirited preaching is vital. "Speak as though God himself were speaking through you" (1 Peter 4:11 NLT). Paul asked for prayers for his own preaching, "that whenever I open my mouth, words may be given me so that I will fearlessly make known the mystery of the gospel, for which I am an ambassador in chains. Pray that I may declare it fearlessly, as I should" (Ephesians 6:19-20).

Good preaching connects the Bible to life. In *When God Builds a Church*, Bob Russell writes:

> There are three parts to good preaching and teaching: exposition of text (explaining the passage), illustration of truth, and application to life. A lot of preaching I've heard is heavy on exposition, and occasionally has some illustrations, but has no application to life. Your lessons will not be as effective in changing the hearts, minds, and lives of your hearers if you don't answer the question, *Where does that touch me?*[2]

I believe each pastor is uniquely gifted to use the methods that are the most fruitful for them. When I preach, I usually start with a story and then go to the Bible and apply it to life. If we use this approach, which is missional, we need to take special care to present solid food directly from the Scriptures. It's sad, but many churchgoers do not carry a Bible. That's why it is helpful to place the Scripture on the screen, or provide Bibles and announce the page numbers.

Jesus was the expert storyteller. People love stories. In chapter 3, I noted that many of the younger generation appreciate heart messages more than a cerebral emphasis. Jesus' method of storytelling would go well in our culture. You will get the attention of the unchurched easier by starting with a story as Jesus often did. Jesus and the apostles had a dynamic presence we need to imitate.

Don't major on controversial issues. Stimulate positive images and emotions reflecting the fruit of the Spirit: faith, trust, purpose, ambition, joy of serving, courage, and boldness. It is absolutely essential that the message exalts Jesus, who is "generous inside and out, true from start to finish" (John 1:14 Msg) and "full of grace and truth" (NIV). Is your message "full of grace and truth"? Jesus promised that if he is exalted, he will draw all people to himself (see John 12:32).

I think we need to admit that it is easier for members to invite their unchurched neighbors when messages have titles like, "When You and Your Spouse Can't Agree," or "Living Without Credit Card Debt." But freely use Scripture as the foundation material for all your teaching. Too often messages are more of a self-help manual than the powerful message of good news focused on the resurrected Christ.

The most eloquent message is powerless if the preacher cannot back it up with personal experience. People will not change their lifestyle with our words unless our words are backed up with our life. If we don't really believe what we preach, people will know. On the other hand if you believe from the bottom of your heart and preach with passion, people will be changed! They cannot remain neutral.

Issuing an Invitation

Too often people go to church out of habit and leave without being challenged or making a deeper commitment. They compliment the preacher on the message, but they have little intention of applying it to their everyday lives. With every message the preacher needs to ask what he or she wants people to do. Are they challenged to greater obedience in their commitment to Christ and the building of his kingdom in our world? Some pastors go fishing fifty-two Sundays a year but never pull in the net. No wonder the church isn't growing!

Older folks may remember invitation time as an invitation to accept Christ as Lord and Savior. But preachers today should think in broader terms. The final outcome of the message is not only decisions for Christ but disciples for Christ—changed lives with Christ living his life through us.

It's appropriate to give an invitation to accept Jesus as Lord and Savior, especially if there are first-timers coming every Sunday. I often announced at the end of the message, "If you have never accepted Jesus Christ as your Lord, you need to make that decision. Prayer counselors are here in the front following the service. They will be glad to assist you. Or you can see one of the pastors or life-group leaders in the foyer."

Accepting Christ is only the start to becoming a disciple, so the counselors lead them in a prayer of repentance and salvation if they are ready to receive Christ. But the counselors also point new believers to the next steps, such as a new members class that describes salvation, what we believe, who we are, and how the church operates.

Every message needs to help people see Jesus, his clear call to discipleship, and his indescribable grace. Especially when we preach messages that deal directly with people's conduct, we need be sure grace is presented just as clearly. Otherwise we may send people home feeling guilty and inadequate.

Invitations are always appropriate. Have a day when you encourage members to invite friends to church. On Mother's Day invite the women or on Father's Day invite the men to come to the altar for anointing to be more faithful as a model to the children. On the first Sunday of the New Year, I frequently set forth the vision, goals and strategy for the coming year. There were times when I invited the congregation to stand to indicate their willingness to join the leadership team in these goals. Other times I would invite the congregation to join hands at the conclusion of the service and pray for God to send us forth to obey a challenge presented in the message.

Other times the pastor may invite people to come forward and pray with the counselors concerning a need for overcoming a sin such as envy, jealousy, anger, laziness, pornography, drugs, or other unhealthy habits. On other Sundays the emphasis may be on the need for receiving inner healing of emotions, physical healing, assurance of salvation, or forgiveness.

One Sunday, knowing several people in the congregation were in bondage to nicotine, I gave a special appeal for anyone caught in this sin to come forward for prayer. Five men responded. For years following that incident, one man always greeted me with, "I'm still free." He was an encouragement to many! We have a God who is mighty to deliver!

Length of the Message

The first sixty seconds of the message is critical. The preacher must get the listeners' attention. But how long should the speaker go on after that? The audience may be a better indicator of how long to speak rather than the clock. If you are speaking, walk to the side of the platform and see if people's eyes follow you. It they don't, terminate as soon as possible.

In many megachurches the messages last thirty to forty minutes. At the Ethiopian church I oversee as part of my bishop responsibilities, pastors usually preach an hour or more. Revivals are not usually accompanied by short messages. One retired minister I know says that the plea for shorter sermons may be because ministers are doing a poor job of preparation and application.

Once I read that we are to preach as if it was our last opportunity to reach our listeners. One can become so overwhelmed
with that responsibility that it is difficult to live with joy. I am
still learning to depend more on the Holy Spirit. We are called to
be the Spirit's mouthpiece. Conviction is not our responsibility;
it is God's work.

The Postmodern Service

In many parts of North America, youth and young adults are for
the most part unfamiliar with the Bible and its teachings. Many
see Christians as narrow-minded and judgmental and have little
respect for the church or the Bible. Their trust in Christians is
broken and can only be restored as Christians build meaningful
relationships with them.

We older people are perhaps more influenced by facts than
youth, who are influenced more by experience. They say, "Give
me a story, or paint a picture for me." They want to experience
God, not just talk about God. They will be moved by spontaneous interaction rather than scripted messages. They want genuine, heartfelt, honest interchange, not lectures. They characterize
most traditional churches as dull and lifeless. So if we are to reach
these young people, worship services, including the message, must
be interactive. This means giving the audience the opportunity to
respond to the message with a question, observation, or even a
rebuttal. This is much easier to do in a group of less that one hundred. Many congregations now have worship first and then an
opportunity to dialogue with the pastor over coffee.

Some believe that the changes taking place in the church
today are as great as those of the Reformation and that tomorrow's
church will not be recognized by today's church. In the emerging
church, the worship leader and pastor will stand close to the congregation. Postmoderns want a highly relational church. Visuals
are important. As Dan Kimball writes, "Because our culture is
producing emerging generations who learn visually via television,

films, and the internet, we must become three-dimensional in our preaching, incorporating visual elements not as a replacement for words but in addition to words."[3]

For many postmodern youth, art, candles, and incense are meaningful in helping to create an atmosphere where they sense God's presence. Youth want to experience God's love. Objective truth isn't recognized by many youth. Personal faith testimonies and story will be more acceptable to them. One unchurched postmodern put it crassly: "I don't want someone reading from an old book telling me what to do."

For the postmodern person, the propositions of Scripture need to be interwoven with the experiences of life and truth. The Bible is the story of God and how we fit into that story. The future church must focus on relationships and helping people find their gifts, calling, and meaningful ministry. The church will encourage and empower believers to engage in direct ministry related to their gifting. They will "do" ministry in teams without having to spend hours in committees deciding the how, when, and where of ministry. The church will equip these disciples to do ministry rather than hiring more professionals to do it for them. The focus will be on sending saints in the world, not on how many saints we can gather. As one pastor said, "My goal is to empty my church by sending them into the world." Life is measured more by the lives you touch than by how many worship services you attend or how many things you acquire.

Robin Trebilcock offers four discernable "turning points" of commitment that are checked out by distrustful postmoderns. They are:

- engagement in mutually rewarding relationship (with Jesus, partner, co-workers, children, friends);
- recognition and affirmation of being held in the highest regard (by God, partner, parents, children, friends);
- change from "What's in it for me?" to "What can I do to help?"
- response with one's life to the discernment of one's life purpose (the all of God).

These four signs should be the basis for the outreach strategy to postmoderns.[4]

Worship with a Focus on Experiencing God

If youth and young adults want to experience God, then worship services need to be relational and experience-focused rather than rational or cerebral-focused. To do this, I suggest four elements for worship:

- Music that speaks *to* God rather than *about* God. I prefer singing love songs to God as compared to doctrinal platitudes about him.
- Testimonies of current experiences of the Holy Spirit's leading in our daily lives.
- Sharing of authentic hurts and needs that members are currently experiencing and immediate prayer for those needs. In large congregations, these needs are more appropriately shared in small groups.
- The pastor's message will include illustrations of encounters with God in everyday situations we all experience. Jesus scratched where people itched in everyday life.

Instead of preaching about the need for Christians to spend more time in prayer and Bible study, we can teach them by actually doing these exercises in the service. Hopefully this will extend grace to and help people to feel less guilty about not doing enough. This emphasis on experience can, I believe, take hold in small groups, where people know and can disciple one another. The message is no longer the focal point of the service; rather, it's the experience of the gathering.

Postmodern theology sees evangelism as a conversation, a process that occurs through relationships, trust, and example. Evangelism is an initiation into the kingdom of God instead of spelled-out ways to get to heaven. It's less of an invitation to an event and more of an invitation to enter into community.[5]

Rick Warren sums it up:

In our affluent culture, in which so many needs are already met and comfort is maximized, heaven is not as interesting as it is for those in pain and poverty. What most people (both believers and unbelievers) are looking for today is meaning: What is my purpose? What on earth am I here for? That is life's fundamental question, and the answer is found in the kingdom of God, not through self-help books.[6]

A frequent challenge is fitting postmoderns into an established congregation. Some churches may want to start a new congregation using a postmodern worship style. Perhaps this is what Jesus meant when he said we can't pour new wine into old wine skins.

Dan Kimball writes:

> We in church leadership typically agree that 80 percent of true discipleship and spiritual growth occurs from mentoring, smaller group gatherings, relationships, serving, etc. I also bet (if we are brutally honest) that probably only 20 percent of discipleship really is a result of our weekend gatherings. So it is rather ironic that in most churches we pour 80 percent of our energy and resources into something that produces only 20 percent of long-term spiritual growth.[7]

He also gives this helpful contrast:

The Church Isn't:	The Church Is:
A place or a building you go to. The weekend meeting where a sermon is delivered and some songs are sung.	Disciples of Jesus wherever they are. Groups of disciples meeting in homes or smaller settings through the week and who may gather in larger meetings to worship on Sunday.
Christians who go to a weekend meeting to get their religious goods and services.	Worshippers of a local body on a mission together.
Christians who go to "church" on weekends to get their inspiration and feeding for the week.	The people of God who are passionately dependent upon God in worship and prayer all week long.

The Church Isn't:	The Church Is:
Christians who ask, "What does this church have to offer me?"	Disciples who ask, "How can I serve and contribute to this local body in its mission?"
A place where Christians go to have the pastors do "spiritual" things for them.	A community where the pastors and leaders equip the people for the mission and to serve one another.
A place to bring children & youth for their spiritual lessons while you receive your sermon and sing a few songs.	A community where leaders help train you to teach the children the ways of God and incorporate children into community so they aren't isolated.

If we are to be missional, members as well as the unchurched who visit must sense God's presence as they walk toward our churches. Sensing God's presence they will be drawn to our Lord, and their lives will be changed as they become disciples going forth in the power of the Holy Spirit to transform their world.

For Discussion

1. Picture yourself going to a Buddhist or Hindu temple. Are you apprehensive? Many unchurched people feel the same about coming to worship in our churches. Discuss how we can understand this apprehension and show understanding and love. Where do you think the apprehension comes from?

2. What specific changes do you think might help to make worship more meaningful for you and for the unchurched in your community?

3. This chapter has described some postmodern expectations for worship. What aspects of this view of Christianity and worship do you appreciate? What concerns do you have?

11

Setting People Free to Use Their Gifts

Dwelling in the Word: Read Romans 12:3-8.

Testimony

Lisa and her family lived in a communist country. She had not been to church except for the few times that her grandmother took her secretly to an Orthodox service. Lisa came to the United States and began working at a preschool. George, one of our members, kept inviting Lisa to church. She said, "I don't have clothes for church." "Come as you are," he said. "This is how I dress when I go to church." After several years she finally came with her children. She accepted Jesus and continues to grow in God's love and grace. The joy of the Lord is clearly seen in her life. Her husband is beginning to participate in church too. They plan to return to their native country and share the Good News of Jesus.

～

George used his spiritual gift of evangelism. Spiritual gifts are special abilities given by God to all Christians, either potentially at birth or bestowed at the time of conversion, for ministry. You have a spiritual gift, and you likely have several. Of the nearly seven billion people in the world, you are unique. Not only are you unique as an individual, your congregation is unique compared to any of the hundreds of thousands in North America. God has gifted it in special ways for being missional. Understanding this giftedness can make a congregation more effective in ministry, more healthy, and more missional.

A healthy church frees people to use their spiritual gifts. We grow not only through learning and fellowship but also by using our gifts in ministry to others. Usually a person's passion lines up with their giftedness. Someone once said, "One person with passion is a critical mass." If that person has a good character and passion that line up with the vision of the church, do all you can to empower him or her to exercise their gift. If they have a vision but are not a leader, find persons who are gifted in leadership to team up with their passion.

Raising Up Leaders

A highlight of our church plants and pastorates was that several young men felt the call to pastoral ministry. One became pastor of Peace Mennonite Church, a church plant in the Cleveland area, and he is still ministering there after nearly two decades. As founding pastor I was greatly blessed to speak at this church's twenty-fifth anniversary celebration and see the fruit of my ministry. Praise God for raising up pastoral leaders.

If you're a church leader, ask the Lord to open your eyes to see persons with gifts to serve. Tap them on the shoulder. Encourage them by talking with them, praying for them, and mentoring them. Nudge or prod them to consider a ministry in the leadership of the church. Give them opportunities to serve as you walk with them. We need more pastors and church workers (Luke 10:1-2).

Retired Persons

Some churches have a large number of older members. In *Taking Back the Good Book*, Andrew Kroll writes:

> Seniors feel the church has been stolen from them. All that

was familiar to them has been taken away. We force them to stand for long periods of time as we repeatedly sing praise choruses with which they are unfamiliar. When the church does provide a program for its seniors, the program is often condescending, designed to keep them busy but denying them vital ministry. They feel like they've been shoved aside and so they simply drop out of church.[1]

We have not used the gifts of older members in our congregations. Several years ago I observed another pastor bring on staff a man in his early fifties who had just retired with a sizeable pension. He willingly served the church with token financial remuneration. His gift of service to the church was an important factor in growing the church from ten to one thousand members.

Be creative in developing valid kingdom-extending missional activities that use the gifts of our retired sisters and brothers. As baby boomers retire, we have more members available with talents and resources. Our denominational mission organizations are developing programs for seniors to minister in many ways, often at a distance from home. Let's develop meaningful programs in our local congregations.

Retired people often have extensive time for ministry. Those with the gift of evangelism should be empowered to use that gift to the fullest possible extent. If you find a retired person with the gift of organization and administration, he or she could organize and operate a seniors' program for the church and the community. They can coordinate meals and visits for those returning from the hospital. Find persons with the gift of mercy and encourage them to visit the shut-ins. Those with the gift of service may do the legwork for bulk mailings or serve on the kitchen team. They may enjoy cleaning the church facility and serving as custodians. Those with teaching gifts need to be given opportunities.

Don't be afraid to honor these persons. From time to time, their ministries should be noted, recognizing how necessary it is for the health of the body of Christ. Occasionally all workers should be encouraged with a banquet or a trip to a dinner theater.

Gift and Consecration Theology

Paul writes in Romans 12:1-2:

> I plead with you to give your bodies to God. Let them be
> a living and holy sacrifice—the kind he will accept. When
> you think of what he has done for you, is this too much to
> ask? Don't copy the behavior and customs of this world,
> but let God transform you into a new person by changing
> the way you think. Then you will know what God wants
> you to do, and you will know how good and pleasing and
> perfect his will really is. (NLT)

How do I discover God's will? Part of the answer is to discover
your spiritual gifts, as Paul goes on to describe in verses 3-8:

> As God's messenger, I give each of you this warning: Be hon-
> est in your estimate of yourselves, measuring your value by
> how much faith God has given you. Just as our bodies have
> many parts and each part has a special function, so it is with
> Christ's body. We are all parts of his one body, and each of
> us has different work to do. And since we are all one body in
> Christ, we belong to each other, and each of us needs all the
> others.
>
> God has given each of us the ability to do certain things
> well. So if God has given you the ability to prophesy, speak
> out when you have faith that God is speaking through you.
> If your gift is that of serving others, serve them well. If you are
> a teacher, do a good job of teaching. If your gift is to encour-
> age others, do it! If you have money, share it generously. If
> God has given you leadership ability, take the responsibility
> seriously. And if you have a gift for showing kindness to oth-
> ers, do it gladly. (Romans 12:3-8 NLT)

"Gift theology" is probably more helpful for knowing God's
will than "consecration theology." Consecration theology means
consecrating or committing ourselves to the Lord. To do the "good
and pleasing and perfect will of God," you must think soberly of
yourself. To think soberly, you must be realistic about the measure

of faith God has given you. Discern which of the gifts described in verses 3-8 God has given you. Discover how this fits your personality and passion.

We should know our spiritual gifts. We will be accountable to God to develop each of our gifts to the peak of their potential. Pastors should know the gifts of church leaders and members of the congregation. If we don't, we will constantly be trying to find workers because people burn out quickly when they are not serving within their giftedness.

The aim of spiritual gifts is to build up the body of Christ. Ultimately, the gifts are in the church rather than in the individual (see 1 Corinthians 14:12). Peter gives the same message as Paul, "Each one should use whatever gift he has received to serve others, faithfully administering God's grace in its varied forms. . . . so that in all things God may be glorified through Jesus Christ" (1 Peter 4:10-11).

Our missional ministry is accomplished through the gifts of individuals. Perhaps even more importantly, the congregation's ministry is expressed through the corporate gifts found in the congregation. Often churches expend extravagant quantities of time and energy in ministries that do not line up with the gifting of the congregation. Then leaders beg for workers and wonder why they don't show. Frequently congregations hear of another church with a fruitful ministry in a particular area, so they pour emotional and physical energy into a similar project, only to fail. I was part of a church in my youth in which we distributed Christian literature; no effort was made, however, to build relationships with the people. There was no obvious fruit.

Leaders need to be aware of the unused potential and make the best use of the abilities God has given to their congregations. Many churches have settled for far less than God intends because resources within congregations have remained undiscovered.

Of course there are times of emergency needs in our communities, and these may not line up with our giftedness. When a neighbor is ill, we show love and care in whatever way we can even if mercy is not our predominate gift. We pray even though we may not have the gift of intercession. In emergency situations, God provides the grace to minister in areas not in our giftedness.

Discovering Gifts

Many congregations use questionnaires that help members discover their spiritual gifts.[2] These processes help people look at their passions, abilities, personality, experience, and talents. But I also believe we find our gift by experimenting with different ministries. God made us all different, and therefore standardized inventories have limited usefulness.

I found the following relatively simple exercise to be helpful in discerning people's spiritual gifts. I have used it with hundred of persons over the years. Simply ask them the following questions:

- Since you have sincerely committed your life to the Lord Jesus and are walking as his faithful disciple, assume you are given unlimited finances and unlimited time and energy: what would you like to do with your life?
- What energizes you?
- What excites you?
- What really turns you on?
- What is your passion?

The answers give clear indication of areas where people will find fulfillment. But churches can do basically the same exercise as individuals. When you ask the pastor and the leaders in your church what they really want to see this church become, you discover the church's predominant gifts.

Many believe the seven gifts listed in Romans 12:3-8 are really motivational gifts and that every Christian operates from one or more of these seven. This approach posits that the more than twenty other gifts mentioned throughout Scripture operate through one of these seven motivations.

Some examples of these other gifts that operate under the

umbrella of the seven motivations are gifts such as: helps, hospitality, pastoring, shepherding, evangelism, intercession, faith, discernment of spirits, music, writing, knowledge, wisdom, craftsmanship, speaking in tongues, interpretation of tongues, miracles, and healings.

To illustrate further, let's take the gift of evangelism and observe how it expresses itself through all seven motivational gifts. If the evangelist's motivation is service, he or she will focus on a practical gospel and ask, "What is humanity's greatest need?" If the motivational gift is exhortation, the evangelist will focus on the best way to overcome a problem. He or she might ask, "Would you like to hear how I dealt with this problem?" If the motivational gift is administration, the evangelist will ask questions like, "Why do you think God created us?" or "What is the main message of the Bible?" If his or her motivational gift is mercy, the evangelist will work at the level of feelings; logic leaves them cold. He or she will ask, "How do you feel God wants you to treat others?" If the evangelist's motivational gift is teaching, he or she may ask, "Why do you think God sent Jesus? Look at these verses." If the evangelist's motivational gift is prophecy, the evangelist will ask questions about right and wrong, or good verses evil. They will ask why is there so much evil in the world and in individuals.

Often a church becomes known by the primary gift of the pastor or the gifting of those in leadership positions. And if a congregation is focusing on ministries that do not line up with its predominant gifts, it is not a healthy congregation. It's like a person trying to sing without the gift of a musical ear.

To focus on the seven motivational gifts, complete the questionnaire below. After each gift, there are five questions that will help you discern if that gift is predominant in your congregation. Place a "0" before the statement if it does not describe your church. Place a "5" before the statement if the statement seems to fit perfectly. Add up the total following each gift. Those with the highest scores describe your church's predominant spiritual gifts.

Mercy

If your church's primary motivational gift is mercy, the church will be known for meeting the needs of hurting people, especially emotionally hurting people. You will find strong programs of ministry for the emotionally and physically challenged. You will minister in nursing homes and hospitals. Churches with mercy as their predominant gift will often provide after-school programs for community children, assist with homes for abused mothers, minister to the homeless, and provide transportation for persons in wheelchairs. You will seriously consider starting support groups for those with an issue like overcoming depression, grief recovery, divorce recovery, HIV recovery, and drug addiction.

Questions to consider concerning the gift of mercy:

_____1. Our church ministers to many persons society would call mentally, physically, or socially challenged.

_____2. Our church is known for its love, especially to those who are marginalized or are on the fringes of society.

_____3. Our church finds it easy to find volunteers to visit people in hospitals and/or prisons.

_____4. Our church was one of the first to offer handicapped facilities.

_____5. Our church is known as one that cares for physical and emotional needs of the poor.

Teaching

The teaching gift is mentioned more often than any other spiritual gift in the Bible. If teaching is the predominant gift in your church, it will offer in-depth Bible studies, classes for both believers and prebelievers in Bible topics and in areas like divorce care, marriage enrichment, financial management, parenting, home ownership, sewing, quilting, cooking, introduction to Spanish, introduction to computers, understanding Islam, and an endless variety of other subjects for the congregation and the community.

The missional focus of this congregation will encourage it to offer classes in various locations throughout the community, because it will recognize that unchurched people, especially the younger generation, are more comfortable in a neutral place.

The teaching gift focuses on the "what" questions. For example, when someone is ill, a person with the teaching gift will ask, "What can be learned from suffering?" When mistakes are made, the teacher will ask what new insights can be gained from the errors. This congregation will likely have a detailed doctrinal statement and will appeal to people with intellectual questions about the major problems of the world.

Questions to consider concerning the gift of teaching:

_____1. Our church strongly emphasizes Bible teaching. People carry their Bibles to church and open them during the message. They are biblically literate.

_____2. Our church emphasizes truth and Bible doctrine. Our people know what they believe.

_____3. We have very little trouble finding teachers for our classes.

_____4. Our church emphasizes training other believers for ministry.

_____5. Our church offers classes on a wide variety of subjects.

Giving

In one church I pastored, two previous pastors had the gift of giving, and this had a positive effect on the congregation. Their example and testimony inspired the congregation to meet tangible needs. There were very few budget hassles. This generous spirit spilled over into nearly every church program, including staff remuneration. The generous spirit of the congregation made it easy to provide basic necessities such as food and clothing for community people in need. Offerings were freely given for emergency needs of local people as well as foreign missions. When missional projects were proposed, seldom did anyone say, "We can't do that because we don't have the money." It was a blessing to pastor this generous congregation.

Money is often a major hurdle when it comes to church expansion. I pray daily for God to bless a particular businessman so he will help a congregation that needs a better facility to reach their surrounding community of upper-income people. We should pray for God to bless our committed businesspeople just as we pray for God to bless our pastor or Sunday school teachers.

Questions to consider concerning the gift of giving:

_____1. Our church always meets its budget without begging for funds.

_____2. When our church gives a gift, we are careful to give the best quality.

_____3. In our church, one of the highlights of the worship is the offering time.

_____4. Our church undertakes many projects, and we always seem to have enough money to meet the challenges.

_____5. When there is a need for funds, our pastor announces the need and people give spontaneously without complaint.

Serving

Every pastor loves to have members with the gift of serving who can provide practical assistance to those in need. Servers step up to the plate when there is a need. It is usually easy to spot them. They will offer to help clean up after a potluck dinner—actually, they'll jump in and help without asking. They will often offer to help in areas even where they are not particularly gifted. If there is a need for tenor singers they may say, "I can't sing well, but I'll try."

Congregations with serving as their predominant gift will find it natural to offer programs like home repair, meals on wheels, ministering to the homeless, or Saturday morning brunch for community people. If single parents need car repairs, this congregation will step up to assist. You would expect to see people from this congregation serving in the volunteer fire company or helping with local charities.

Questions to consider concerning the gift of service:

_____1. Our church facility looks immaculate at all times.

_____2. When someone has a tangible need, our pastor announces it and people respond freely.

_____3. Our church finds it easier to find people for a work day around the church or for a mission project than it does to find Sunday school teachers.

_____4. We have many parties and socials at church and in the homes of our members.

_____5. Our people love to help the pastor and church leaders so we can be more effective in ministry.

Prophecy

Since the motivation of the prophet is to correct, these churches seek to issue bold statements on matters that concern their members. They also speak clearly to social issues in the community. Their voice will be heard at town meetings; some members may occupy key positions in the local government. Being missional for these congregations means making public statements about injustice.

Questions to consider concerning the gift of prophecy:

_____1. Our church is known for taking a clear stand on controversial issues. We don't hesitate to give messages of warning or judgment when people refuse to change their ways.

_____2. Our church proclaims God's truth in a way that at times strikes hard at traditional Christianity.

_____3. Our church seems to have no problem relating the Bible to social issues of our day.

_____4. When situations are not the way they should be in the community and nation, our church speaks up publicly and tries to correct them.

_____5. Our leaders receive some criticism for their stand on controversial issues, but they don't seem to mind.

Administration

We can expect these congregations to organize programs both within the congregation and with other churches to meet social, physical, and spiritual needs. They will take the initiative to organize sports leagues and community youth programs. These congregations will pull churches together to help a family whose house burned down.

Questions to consider concerning the gift of leadership:

_____1. Our church is often the first one in the community to provide help with community projects.

_____2. When our church starts a project, we move ahead judiciously until it is finished.

_____3. Our church is nearly always working on a major project, either on our campus or with foreign missions.

_____4. Our church has clear and detailed reports for all members. We are kept up to date on activities throughout the congregation. Our leaders receive some criticism for their stand on controversial issues, but they don't seem to mind.

_____5. Our church is well-organized, and everyone knows who to go to when they have a need. Meetings have clear agendas and begin on time.

Exhortation

If a church's predominant gift is exhortation, it is motivated by the need to correct the future. This church will take steps and offer programs to help people mature. Paul's entire life was focused on helping people mature in Christlikeness. This congregation will find it natural to offer counseling for members and individuals in the community. The exhorter's focus is on the practical step-by-step solutions for people, breaking unhealthy habits so they can move on to maturity. These churches offer programs like marriage enrichment, divorce recovery, Christian parenting, financial management, anger management, drug, alcohol, and HIV rehab. Grief counseling, freedom from pornography, and tutoring for school children are other programs they would be delighted to provide.

Questions to consider concerning the gift of exhortation:

_____1. Our church strongly desires to see people grow in their Christian life and offers a strong discipleship training process.

_____2. Our pastor's messages and Bible classes frequently offer step-by-step formulas to move people to maturity.

_____3. Our church programs offer free counseling for a variety of needs.

_____4. Our church has a strong emphasis concerning the importance of unity in the body of Christ.

_____5. People in our church are transparent concerning their weakness and sins.

Add up the scores of these seven gifts to determine which of the seven in your congregation is strongest.

For Discussion

1. Which of the seven motivational gifts is predominant?

2. Do you agree with the finding of this exercise?

3. Perhaps you feel more than one gift predominates in your church.

4. What things would you name as the primary strengths of your congregation?

5. How might the Holy Spirit have you build on these strengths to become more missional?

12

Dealing with the 'E' Word: Evangelism

Dwelling in the Word: Read Acts 17:16-34.

Testimony

Esther was from Africa, and she knew what persecution was. She had no green card to be in the United States, and it seemed to me the best word to describe the position she was now living in was "slave." She cooked the meals, did the laundry, and took care of several children 24/7 with barely a toothbrush to call her own. A neighbor brought Esther to church, and over a period of several years the family she cared for started coming to church. Esther has been a great influence on relatives and friends from her native county as well as many in our church.

~

Many Christians would rather get a root canal than be involved in evangelism. The word is a negative for many Christians and the unchurched. Christians often feel guilty because they believe they are not doing a good job sharing the Good News. The churched and the unchurched have been turned off by hellfire approaches and by Mormons or Jehovah Witnesses who go door-to-door and interrupt their schedules.

But the apostles were so excited about being with Jesus that they couldn't help but share their faith and the Good News (see Acts 4:20). Evangelism was their lifestyle, and it must be ours as well.

Longtime African missionary Don Jacobs writes:

> Many of my African friends were more open that I was about their witness. Their eagerness to share tended to put off some of us missionaries. One missionary sister could restrain herself no longer. "Why," she demanded, "do you have to talk about salvation so much?" One of the Africans reached down and embraced one of her little children and asked, "When this one was born, weren't you excited when you heard that first cry? You would have been concerned if the baby had not cried. We are simply announcing that we are born again."[1]

Contrast this description by Robin Trebilcock of the situation in Australia:

> Books on church growth sometimes urge Christians to invite friends, neighbors, fellow workers, and family members to church. In Australia, even dedicated Christians will not risk the potential damage such asking could do to important relationships.[2]

Note that our Australian brothers and sisters are talking about church and not about Jesus. We dare never be ashamed of Jesus, but there are times when I am ashamed of the church and would not invite people because of the quality of the fellowship (see 1 Corinthians 11:17). Many in North America are still open to at least listening to the Christian worldview, though I expect the culture is moving toward the hostility Christians find in Australia. May we be prepared to live a life of faithfulness so the world will respect us enough to hear the gospel.

In Acts 4:18, the authorities ordered Peter and John not to speak about Jesus. Is this the hostile culture we are moving toward in North America? Certainly we all are aware that in many places around the world, Christians suffer and even risk their lives to share the Good News.

While this book is about making missional congregations, there is a clear relationship between church growth and the need for individuals to utilize their gifts in reaching their neighbors for Jesus. In *Road Signs for the Journey*, Conrad Kanagy informs us that while members in Mennonite churches believe evangelism should have high priority in the denomination, they are lax in being evangelistic. A third of us have never invited a non-Christian to attend a service or activity at our church, and only 13 percent do so as frequently as once a month. No wonder our churches are not growing.

"Evangelism efforts appear to have declined over three decades," Kanagy writes. "In 1972, 16 percent of members had never invited a non-Christian to church compared to 33 percent in 2006. Seventy-seven percent had tried to lead someone to faith in Christ in 1972 compared to 58 percent in 2006."[3]

Christians should always be praying for at least one other person whom they are seeking to lead to Christ or nurture in discipleship.

Called by God

Various studies have indicated that 10 percent of Christians have the gift of evangelism. Does that leave 90 percent with no responsibility to share Christ? If you don't have the gift of teaching, does that mean you never teach? If you don't have the gift of intercession, does that mean you don't pray? Of course not! Where there is a need to use a particular gift, God will supply the ability for that occasion. God's call to witness is not for a select few. Isn't it interesting that not one of the seventy-two Jesus sent out in Luke 10 said to him, "I can't go; I don't have the gift of evangelism"?

Jesus told us three times in Matthew 10:23-33 to not be afraid to witness (verses 26, 28, and 30). There will be persecution, but what he whispers in our ear we proclaim from the roof, and what he tells us in the night we speak in the day. Then he adds a blessing: if we acknowledge him, he will acknowledge us before the Father, but if we deny him, he will disown us. Someone once told me there are 365 "fear nots" in the Bible, one for each day.

Perhaps one reason many Anabaptists are timid is because we emphasize peace as a central aspect of the gospel. It's difficult for us to speak boldly when we know that the gospel often brings a sword instead of peace. But Oswald Chambers challenges us:

> God did not direct his call to Isaiah—Isaiah overheard God saying . . . "Who will go for us?" Whether I hear God's call or not depends on the condition of my ears, and exactly what I hear depends upon my spiritual attitude. "Many are called but few are chosen," Matthew 22:14. That is, few prove that they are the chosen ones. The chosen ones are those who have come into a relationship with God through Jesus Christ and have had their spiritual condition changed and their ears opened. Then they hear "the voice of the Lord" continually asking, "Who will go for us?" However, God doesn't single out someone and say, "Now, you go." He did not force His will on Isaiah. Isaiah was in the presence of God, and he overheard the call. His response, performed in complete freedom, could only be to say, "Here am I! Send me."

> Remove the thought from your mind of expecting God to come to force you or to plead with you. When our Lord called His disciples, He did it without irresistible pressure from the outside. The quiet, yet passionate, insistence of His "Follow Me" was spoken to men whose every sense was receptive, Matthew 4:19. If we will allow the Holy Spirit to bring us face to face with God, we too will hear what Isaiah heard—"the voice of the Lord." In perfect freedom we will say, "Here am I! Send me."[4]

If we took Chambers' words seriously, our lives and the lives of our fellow members would be revolutionized. Years ago I heard a speaker say, "The need is the call." We don't need a "special" call. Others appropriately remind us that if we focus on the need rather than on the Lord, we will burn out. Only obedience to Jesus, his call, and his enablement will enable us to persist in faithful and fruitful ministry.

Jesus' Approach

All of Jesus' words are important, but I suggest that his final words recorded in Matthew 28:18-20 and Acts 1:4-8 are especially important. In the great commission, Jesus gives us the authority to make disciples, and in Acts 1:4-8, he gives us the power to witness. We need both the authority and the power to be effective. The early Christians in Acts recognized that both had been granted to them, and they turned the world upside down with boldness given them by the Holy Spirit.

Brian McLaren writes:

> The way conservative Christians talk about "personal salva-tion" seems to me to try to persuade by exclusion. In other words, the arguments says, "You, the unsaved, are on the outside and I'm on the inside. I'll tell you how to get inside if you want." I think we would be more in line with the spirit of the gospel if we invite by inclusion saying, "God loves you, God accepts you. Are you ready to accept your acceptance and live in reconciliation with God?[5]

Jesus spent the majority of his life as a carpenter, not as a preacher. Of his public appearances recorded in Scripture, all but ten were in a marketplace. Forty-five of the fifty-two parables are set in a work environment.

"The gospels record that Jesus had forty-seven contacts with various individuals. He never forced himself on anyone," writes Jim Montgomery.[6] "There are twenty-four incidents recorded in the life of Christ in which he engaged in a conversation with an individual but in which he did not perform a miracle. In thirteen of these, people came to Christ with a question or comment."[7]

If there ever was a time in Jesus' life when "cold-turkey" evan-gelism was called for, surely it was while he was on the cross between two criminals; it was now or never. Yet Jesus did not open a conversation about their eternal destiny. He responded to the one who acknowledged him but said nothing to the other. This was his pattern. It appears that he did not take a "cold-turkey" approach except with his disciples.

Jesus responds to people who showed interest in spiritual matters. He could discern who was open to receiving the Good News. People flocked to Jesus, and he was the talk of the town. Today Christians are often ignored.

Perhaps Jesus had an advantage because he performed miracles. Roland Allen writes: "One day we shall perhaps recover the early faith in miracles. Meanwhile, we cannot say that the absence of miracles puts an impassable gulf between the first century and today, or renders the apostolic method inapplicable to our mission."[8]

But until we recover that "early faith in miracles," we are not to sit passively until somebody rings the doorbell and asks for spiritual advice. Neither are we to make the boldfaced, frontal attack that has crept into our concept of witnessing and that we so eagerly shy away from. Neither seekers nor mature Christians appreciate loud street preaching in our towns and cities.

The pattern of Jesus is what Jim Montgomery called the "AA" approach. First, we *arouse curiosity* by our words and actions. Then we *answer questions*. In modern sales terminology, we could say we create a demand for what we have to offer. This is done not with gimmicks and deceptions, but by our speech.[9]

Jesus was strategic. He started wherever people were. To farmers he talked about sowing seed and harvesting; to fishermen he talked about catching fish; to the thirsty and hungry he talked about living water and eating his body. He didn't use the same method twice. In John 3 he says to Nicodemus, "You must be born again." In John 4 he says to the woman at the well, "I give you living water." To Zacchaeus who was lonely and needed fellowship he said, "I'll come to your house." To the rich young ruler he promised treasure in heaven. To the woman who anointed his feet Jesus said, "Your faith has saved you; go in peace" (Luke 7:50). To the woman caught in adultery he said, "Go now and leave your life of sin" (John 8:11). To all he used different methods for the same message: repent and believe.

Jesus went out of his way to witness to those who were not accepted by his peers. He deliberately broke numerous barriers in talking with the woman at the well: (1) he went through Samaria, a region Jews avoided, (2) he talked with a woman, which was unacceptable especially for a teacher, and (3) the woman was promiscuous, which was all the more reason to avoid her.

Do we go out of our way to meet people on the margins of our society? The disciples were surprised by Jesus' actions, and we need to be prepared for the same negative reaction when we cross boundaries.

Jesus was a foreigner in Samaria. We are now foreigners in a post-Christian culture. We must think and act like missionaries. Missionaries listen, study, and learn the beliefs and values of the culture. We too must understand the culture without embracing it. Then with respect we can build bridges from that culture to Jesus.

While Jesus did not buttonhole people, he had great compassion that came through to people. May we learn from our Master.

Peter's and Paul's Approach

Following Jesus' ascension and the outpouring of the Holy Spirit, there was a new boldness among Jesus' disciples. Peter boldly proclaimed that Jesus is Lord (Acts 2:36), and he and Paul exercised bold assertiveness throughout their ministry. I believe we need to do the same.

In Acts 1:8, the Greek word that we translate as "witnesses" can also mean "martyrs." The apostles were willing to die for the cause of Christ. We are called to do no less. Jesus said in Luke 9:23 that we must take up our cross daily. This cross is not simply an ornament hung around our necks as jewelry; it is an instrument of torture, and one that reminds us that we must be willing to suffer for Christ.

Acts 8:4 says, "Those who had been scattered preached the word wherever they went." They were scattered because of persecution, but wherever they traveled they preached. Preaching in the New Testament was an activity focused toward the unchurched. What our pastors do on Sunday morning is not preaching in the New Testament sense; it is teaching the saints. We are all called to be preachers of the Word to the unchurched. But since preaching carries negative overtones in our culture, let us say we are simply sharing, presenting, or giving the Good News.

In 1 Peter 3:15, the apostle writes that we need to be ready to give an answer to anyone who inquires about our faith. "Be ready to speak up and tell anyone who asks why you're living the way you are, and always with the utmost courtesy" (1 Peter 3:15 Msg). We must do this with gentleness and respect. Do people ask you about your faith? Arouse curiosity by your lifestyle and by your words.

Evangelism: A Process or an Event?

Usually we don't fall in love all at once. People seldom fall in love with Jesus the first time they encounter him. Evangelism is both a process and an event. Prayers of repentance are very important, but we must not pressure persons to pray the prayer of repentance and salvation unless the Holy Spirit is making it clear to us they are ready to become a disciple of our Lord. It can be detrimental when a person is pressured to pray a prayer of repentance before he or she is ready. Often there is a huge gap from the prayer of repentance to a life of discipleship nurtured by the body of Christ. In many citywide evangelistic crusades, few of those who come forward to pray a prayer of salvation are in church a year later. In using this approach people nearly always needed "two conversions"—one to Christ and then a later one to the church.

Coming to Christ is often a process of many smaller steps. But everyone, when they are ready, needs to pray a prayer of repentance and salvation inviting Jesus into their life. If we understand this, we will find it much easier to share our faith without feeling the undue pressure of getting people to pray a prayer of salvation.

The discipling process usually begins before conversion, as we build a relationship with the unchurched. Out of that relationship the unchurched person begins to feel at home with you and your church friends. They experience God's love and grace through you and your friends. They may begin to like what they see.

Building Relationships

As I've said throughout this book, relationship-building is the key to evangelism. Jim Montgomery gives six stages of relationship that people go through in the process: contacts, acquaintances, responders, seekers, converts, and disciples. Contacts are people we meet. We need to work at turning these contacts into acquaintances and then into responders—that is, people who begin to connect with us. These relationships then lead to some becoming seekers. Seekers are persons who are beginning to ask questions about our faith and about Jesus and the meaning of Christianity. From seekers we find that some will become converts. These are the babes in the faith who are ready to begin to walk with Christ and grow to maturity. Finally they become disciples.[10]

The North American church is usually inwardly focused, hiding our light under a bushel, inside the four walls of our church buildings. Too often we are isolated from the unchurched. We need to let our light shine like a city on a hill—in our communities, schools, and workplaces. We must let it shine for our neighbors.

Those who are open to Christ's peace (see Luke 10:5-6) are the ones receptive to Jesus' love. We need to pray to find these persons of peace. They are known by their relatives and by others in their community. They have influence on others. They may be good or bad, but once they receive Jesus, they are assertive in inviting others to him. We need to empower these people to reach their neighbors. This was evident in our church plants. New people brought new people, starting with their families and then their work peers.

Jesus and the apostles found men and women of peace. People in the early church brought their households. That is happening today. When someone accepts Jesus, or even before they become Christians, we need to encourage and train them to bring their families. As we work with them, the Holy Spirit will give them courage to invite their unsaved family and friends. We need to tell them when they are baptized to send special invitations so their friends and family can hear dynamic testimonies.

Confrontational styles such as Evangelism Explosion or the Four Spiritual Laws tend not to recognize people's pain or needs. They are focused on getting the person to say a prayer with little understanding of its meaning. In years past these approaches were much more effective because most people understood that to be a Christian, they needed to repent. But this is seldom true in post-modern culture. The canned approach too often turned salvation into easy steps without real repentance. Nevertheless I have used these approaches and experienced some positive results.

Prebelievers may ask challenging questions, such as: If God is God, why is there so much suffering in our world? Why all the poverty? Why the HIV epidemic? Why famines, tornadoes, earthquakes, and tsunamis? You can politely ask them: What would our world be like if people obeyed the Ten Commandments? There would be no more murder, no more lying, cheating, stealing, and no more broken homes. Children would honor and obey their parents. Remind them that we bring most of the suffering on ourselves. We reap what we sow.

There are many types of unchurched people. We need to listen to their stories. Listening is showing love. But often we do not listen; we take turns talking.

As you begin to witness more, you will notice different types of unchurched people:

- Those who grew up in church but are now turned off for any number of reasons. You need to discover those reasons and listen to their pain.
- Those who are burned out. They feel they've given more than their share, and that it's time for others to step up to the plate. These people need to be challenged to not bury their talents.
- Those who say they believe but never really became a disciple of our Lord. They need to understand that many will say on the day of accountability they did this or that, but Jesus will say he never knew them (see Matthew 7:21-23; Luke 14:26-27).

- Those living for pleasure with no time for God. They need to be reminded that they will give an account of how they used their time and resources (see Luke 16:19-31).
- Those who do not feel welcome in the church. To these persons we must bend over backwards to extend a loving welcome. Perhaps we will need to invite them to our home and have them meet other truly genuine welcoming Christians.
- Those who are anti-church, offended by the organization and its self-preservation. To these we listen and, when appropriate, share that perhaps their criticism is true. Then hopefully we can point out many illustrations where the church is caring for the poor and meeting genuine needs of people as Jesus outlines in Matthew 25:31-46.
- Those who are offended by all the divisions and fighting in the church. To these we must confess our lack of love and show by personal example that we and our congregations are on a journey to becoming a more forgiving people who work together with many others.
- Those who see only hypocrites in the church. Admit that we all are hypocrites at times. No one is perfect. We all need to confess our sins and show loving acceptance as Jesus did. Invite them to experience a group of humble, vulnerable, Christians.
- Finally, there are the true unbelievers. We first listen to them, and then we share Jesus and explain how he died for our sins. If these individuals are open and ready, we invite them to receive our Lord as their personal savior. This is followed by witnessing to what the cross of Christ means in our daily life.

As we listen to people in all these groups and love them, we show them acts of kindness—which, Scripture tells us, are acts done to Jesus. We share how Jesus gives us meaning and purpose for everyday living. And when we sense the Holy Spirit's leading, we lovingly invite them to consider the resurrected life that Jesus offers them. When they respond in faith, they are born into God's eternal kingdom.

For those ready to receive Jesus, it is helpful to use what some call the "Roman road." This begins with (1) Romans 3:10, "There is no one righteous, not even one." (2) Romans 6:23, "For the wages of sins is death, but the gift of God is eternal life in Christ Jesus our Lord. This is followed with (3) Romans 10:9-10, "If you confess with your mouth, 'Jesus is Lord' and believe in your heart that God raised him from the dead, you will be saved. For it is with your heart that you believe and are justified, and it is with your mouth that you confess and are saved."

If they sincerely confess their sin and believe Jesus was raised from the dead, they are saved. But if we stop there, it is like a woman who gives birth to a baby then leaves the baby on the street when she leaves the hospital. When we nurture the new believer, we "make disciples," as Jesus commanded.

My prayer is for our churches to become communities of love and faith—little villages of Christlike disciples where people connect with, care for, and love each other, and where we help people belong so they can come to believe. Let's become seeker-sensitive in our work and in our worship. Our heart attitude is what counts.

Practical Ideas

When you invite people to church, they may respond with a flat-out no. But if they do not, always try to keep the door open. By that I mean you interpret a non-committal answer as an open door to return. Read their body language and hear their tone of voice. Give open-ended responses, such as, "Perhaps if you can't come this week, maybe some other time," or "Give some thought to what we discussed; I'll check back with you later." Very, very few will come the first time you approach them.

Family and friends may be more receptive to the gospel than others. You already have a relationship with them, so invite them. The New Testament has many examples of family members coming to Christ. In several situations, whole households came as a group to know Jesus (see Mark 1:16-20, Acts 16:15, 33). This occurred several times in my ministry when people brought their peers and relatives to church.

Visitors who come to your church without a personal invitation may be few, but when they do come, follow-up is extremely important. Some people have needs that you can meet. Pray for wisdom to spot those needs and build bridges to those people.

Unchurched people are more responsive to the gospel during periods of transition, such as when they move to a new community, the death of loved one, a marriage, divorce or separation, the birth of a child, personal injury or illness, a loss or change of a job, graduation or retirement, a major financial loss, a child leaving home, or trouble with the law. These times of disruption and transition are great opportunities for ministering to people in need.

When you see a U-Haul in your neighborhood, introduce yourself and welcome the family to your community. A plate of cookies is always a winner. Ask if there is any way you can help, and be ready to follow through. If they have moved from a distance away, they may appreciate help with finding phone numbers for utilities or finding stores. Invite them to church. If they have children, tell them about classes and activities for children. Become a helping friend. You will not build a friendship with one initial visit, so follow-up is a must.

Reaching Lower-Income Families

If the new family is of a different nationality or economic status, they will not come unless they are sure your invitation is sincere. You won't convince them of your sincerity with only one contact. It will likely take several contacts before they feel acceptance. If you can spot a special talent or hobby in the person, you may win acceptance by inviting them to share that gift. When they are contributing, they feel love and acceptance.

If you are a middle-class or upper-middle class congregation, marginalized people will not come to your church. To reach them, you need to find ways to meet them in the places and routines of their life. You will need to build bridges, which means meeting them on their turf. It will mean sacrificing time as you intentionally build authentic relationships. Go out into the community and organize and put on a program for them. Do random acts of kindness and hospitality. Help them move; help them find jobs or medical assistance. Capital Christian Fellowship helped many families move. Even small gestures may give surprising results when given with genuine love. One church gives out chewing gum at football games with the sticker, "God loves you and we do too!" The name of the church is printed on the stickers. Give out lollipops for younger children. Pray for guidance and practice your hospitality outside your faith community.

There are lots of activities churches can use to draw people to the Lord. Find items to give away that somehow advertise the church's name, address, and phone number. Offer a free light bulb to the homes you want to reach with a sticker that says, "Jesus is the Light of the World" and the church information. As I described earlier, our youth gave out water on a hot summer day at a traffic light near the church and as a result, one young man showed up at church and has been a faithful worker for several years. On another occasion the youth gave out church fliers, and another family came and became true disciples. Of course, these activities are only fruitful if they are bathed in prayer.

Open your church doors for community groups to meet there. Once people are in your facility, it is easier for them to return.

Styles of Reaching People

Many postmodern youth and young adults are turned off by the church. But if they seem open to Jesus, it's appropriate to ask questions. Ask them what they think of Jesus, who they think Jesus is, how they feel about him, and what contribution they believe Jesus makes to our world.

With older people, you may want to break the ice by asking

them three questions: What do they worry about? What makes them happy? Where might God fit into any of this? You can also invite them to church more easily since they may not have the hang-ups about church that postmodern youth have.

Bring God into your conversations. When you leave the check-out person at the grocery store, the teller at the bank, or the tele-marketer on the phone, learn to say, "God bless you. Have a great day." God's creation is so wonderful that I find it natural to make comments like: "Isn't the sky fantastic? God simply does himself in!" Or, "When I see this beauty I can't imagine what heaven must be like." Or, "Those flowers are absolutely gorgeous. God and his beauty are beyond me." Or, "This is a beautiful day. I can't get done thanking God for all his beautiful creation. He simply blesses the socks off me." Or "This rain is just what we needed; God is good."

Once we had an ice storm, and I said to a number of neigh-bors, "I can't understand how God keeps this stuff up in the clouds. This one shovel of ice must weigh 50 pounds." I once asked someone who understands nuclear energy why we don't drop our biggest bombs in the center of a hurricane and blow it apart. The answer was that our most powerful bomb wouldn't even phase the hurricane. God is a powerful God, and there is value to giving recognition to our Creator.

People like to complain about the government and about how bad things are in the world. During these conversations, it may be appropriate to mention that we can't be sure for whom to vote, but we can trust God to put in the leadership we deserve. We are part of a kingdom whose King is perfect.

We each have our own unique way of sharing our faith and carrying out the great commission. We can expect fruitfulness and freedom in witnessing when using our God-ordained style. In *Becoming a Contagious Christian*, Bill Hybels and Mark Mittelberg list six approaches to evangelism.[11]

1. *Invitational—Come and see.* Befriending and then inviting unchurched people works. I believe Jesus built a relationship with his disciples before he called them. They heard about him and

observed him before he called them. More than half the people who come to church in the United States come through an invitation style. I have certainly found this to be true from my personal experience.

You will find this style especially effective with youth. First, build a relationship; second, talk about faith and introduce Jesus; finally, invite them to church. For those over thirty, I have found it more fruitful to invite them to church and let them find Jesus in the context of Christ's body.

Our friends know us and accept us. Jesus said, "Anyone who accepts your message is also accepting me. And anyone who rejects you is rejecting me" (Luke 10:16 NLT). This teaching indicates that we need to win people to ourselves so they receive Jesus' message of Good News. That is not being proud; it is being expedient. If we are always conscious of Jesus living in us, I believe most people will like us and be drawn to him who lives his life through us (see Galatians 2:20).

For the invitational approach to bear fruit, churches need to have services at which the unchurched feel comfortable and the gospel is presented in a way they can understand it. Unchurched friends should not sense that they will be put on the spot or in some way embarrassed.

Gentle persistence in a loving manner communicates to the unchurched that we care. When Elwood, a new believer, went to a church conference, someone asked him why he started coming to church. He said, "Because Pastor Dave kept inviting me. He wouldn't give up." I had gone to Elwood's home and visited with him and his family many times. I called occasionally and prompted others in the church to do the same. This is how we "compel" them to come (see Luke 14:23 KJV).

2. *Serving—How can I help?* Traditional Mennonites are usually comfortable serving others. We are known for relief efforts like Mennonite Disaster Service and Mennonite Central Committee. But too often we have not shared the gospel with those we serve.

Some Christians feel like second-class citizens because "all they can do" is serve others. But serving with joy from a heart of compassion leads people to thank you for your act of kindness. Respond by saying, "God has been so good to me that I can't help but passing on his goodness to others." You may want to add, "He changed me and made my life complete. Now I enjoy helping others. I want you to know you matter to God too." You will plant seeds that others can water and the Holy Spirit can bring to fruition. Many unbelievers need someone like you to soften their hearts through your acts of service. Be that person for them.

3. *Relational Evangelism—Live it out.* This is sometimes referred to as *friendship evangelism.* When Jesus called Levi, he left everything and followed Jesus. Levi held a banquet for Jesus at his house, and a large crowd of tax collectors and friends came. What a way to introduce people to Jesus! (See Luke 5:28-29.)

After Jesus cured a man with an unclean spirit, the man was so overjoyed that he begged to be allowed to follow Jesus. But Jesus said, "Go home to your family and tell them how much the Lord has done for you. . . . So the man went away and began to tell in the Decapolis how much Jesus had done for him. And all the people were amazed" (Mark 5:18-20). This man became a relational evangelist, sharing his faith with those he already knew. Anne, a beauty salon stylist, shares with her clients how Jesus is transforming her life. She has invited many to church and some have come. Anne is a relational evangelist.

4. *Testimonial—How he changed my life.* When Jesus healed a blind beggar, the Pharisees questioned the godliness of someone who would heal on the Sabbath. They asked the blind man what he thought of the man who healed him. His answer was simple: "One thing I do know. I was blind but now I see!" (John 9:25). This approach applies not only to physical blindness but to spiritual blindness. Former nonbelievers too can say, "I was blind, but now I see. Jesus Christ changed my life, and he can change yours." Testimonial evangelists are usually not people who become Christians as children and follow a steady path of spiritual growth. Often they will say they thought they were Christians because they went to

church occasionally and tried to live a moral life. Then they found out what it really means to be a Christian and began to trust Jesus as their personal Savior. "It was the best decision I ever made," they'll say. "It revolutionized my life! If you are interested, I'd be happy to tell you more."

You have a testimony! Many seekers don't need to hear a sermon; they just need a Christian like you to share with them how Jesus made a difference in your life. Your testimony will be one more step the Holy Spirit uses to bring them closer to the kingdom.

5. *Intellectual—Think it through.* If you like to struggle with intellectual questions, you may find it natural to use this style to witness. In this approach, you study with seekers. You refer them to books and other resources.

We need to recognize that we never have all the answers, but we need to make a commitment before we have everything figured out. If we had everything answered, we would be God. We can invite people to follow Jesus in spite of their doubts and questions. Questions are welcome when they are asked in humility, which is one of the steps we all must take to come to God. As we walk with Christ in faith, the questions are either answered or become less important to us. "Central to the Christian experience is the art of questioning God," writes Rob Bell. "Not belligerent, arrogant questions that have no respect for our maker, but naked, honest, vulnerable, raw questions, arising out of the awe that comes from engaging the living God."[12]

Acts 19:9 records that Paul went to the lecture hall of Tyranus and debated daily for two years. In Acts 17:3, he reasoned with the Jews and God-fearing Greeks, "explaining and proving" Christ's resurrection. He conversed with the intelligentsia and debated with the philosophers of Athens. In his sermon on Mars Hill, he ingeniously used the Athenians' altar to an unknown god as an introduction to his presentation of the true God.

Lee Strobel, once a skeptical journalist, freely recognizes the difficult questions and exposes them, revealing that faith in Christ is an answer very much worth considering. Josh McDowell, known worldwide for his ministry to university students, uses this approach very effectively. My friend Mike relates to Jehovah Witnesses and goes on the Internet and debates with those of other faiths. He uses his gift of intellect to invite people to encounter Jesus.

In using this approach, always remember that we are not called to win an argument but to show God's love with gentleness and respect.

6. *Confrontational—You crucified the wrong man!* Some people must be confronted if they are to respond to Christ. God has equipped certain believers with the personality and drive that makes it natural for them to confront others. Billy Graham uses this approach. He often says, "You must be born again!" Charles Stanley and Bill Hybels use this approach effectively too. Charles Stanley says, "Listen, listen!" many times during his presentations.

On the day of Pentecost, Peter said in his first sermon to the Jews in Jerusalem, "Let all Israel be assured of this: God has made this Jesus, whom you crucified, both Lord and Christ" (Acts 2:36). Peter in essence is saying. "You crucified the wrong man. You killed the Son of God." Pierced to the heart, they asked Peter, "What shall we do?" "Repent and be baptized," he replied. "Save yourselves from this corrupt generation." He laid it on the line, and three thousand responded (verses 37-41)!

I once knew a believer named Joe, who sold security systems. When he entered a home as a salesman, he confronted people about their relationship to Jesus. His boldness, at times, made me uncomfortable. If there was a dog in the house he would ask if their dog was saved, which led him to then ask the homeowners if they knew Jesus! But at his funeral, I was amazed to hear one person after another testify to how Joe helped them come to Jesus. These testimonies were so powerful I didn't feel the need to bring a funeral message. Joe lived out Proverbs 28:1: "The righteous are as bold as a lion."

Think and Pray Big Prayers

Some have said that the late Bill Bright has been influential in leading more people to Christ than any other human being in history. Bill wrote,

> It is my strong conviction that it is impossible to ask God for too much if our hearts and motives are pure and if we pray according to the Word and will of God. Remember, it is a basic spiritual principle that whatever we vividly envision, ardently desire, sincerely believe and enthusiastically act upon will come to pass assuming, of course, that there is scriptural authority for it. It is this principle that is the foundation of praying supernaturally.[13]

Do you believe God can use you in the way that best fits your personality and your giftedness? Jesus told us, "Whatever you ask for in prayer, believe that you have received it, and it will be yours" (Mark 11:24). When we invite people to church and to faith in Christ, do we "see" them coming to Christ? Do we see them taking practical steps toward faith, worshipping in our church, or being baptized and giving their testimony? If we can't imagine them moving toward Christ, then we need to question our faith. Ask God to give you more faith, remembering that even a "mustard seed" faith is honored.

I believe it is usually appropriate to share with people that, as you pray for them, you see them moving toward Jesus and becoming a person God will use to encourage many others. With the Holy Spirit's direction, offer positive statements like, "I can picture you someday standing in front of the congregation giving your testimony." Or, "I can see you being baptized, with your spouse and children and everyone rejoicing with you as you declare your faith." Or, "You will bless me and be an encouragement to everyone." These statements presented in faith will have a positive and encouraging effect on the pre-believer.

Be Sure to Listen

If you can identify the kind of person the seeker is, it will help you determine which approach will work best for building a relationship with them. Is he or she asking intellectual questions? If so you need some reasonable answers. Is he or she an emotional seeker needing acceptance? Many, many people are in this category. They have been rejected and are hurting; some have quite specific spiritual needs, like those caught in a cult, false beliefs, or addictions. Love and listen to them all.

Pray for opportunities to relate to people and invite them to church. Let God do his job. Jesus drew the seeker to himself. Seekers need to like you; if they don't like you, they will have a difficult time loving your Savior.

There are many influences and conversations that precede a person's decision to come to Jesus. Some plant, some water, and some harvest, but God gives the increase (see 1 Corinthians 3:5-9).

Persevere, pray, evangelize. How wonderful it is that God has chosen to use us in this great task of bringing others to a life of discipleship in Jesus Christ our Lord. Are you inviting people to Jesus?

For Discussion

1. Find your style and use it. Paul wrote, "To the weak I become weak, to win the weak. I have become all things to all men so that by all possible means I might save some" (1 Corinthians 9:22). Have you learned to identify with people as Paul did?

2. Can you verbalize your faith? Pray for the Lord to help you develop a plan of action to share your faith with others. Remember that God "is able to do immeasurably more than all we ask or imagine, according to his power that is at work within us" (Ephesians 3:20).

13

Effective Missional Leadership

Dwelling in the Word: Read Ephesians 4:14-21.

Testimony

Greg was a "PK"—a preacher's kid. He gave his life to the Lord when he was eleven. His dad served in a mission church with several established Mennonite churches in the surrounding rural community. Greg's dad told him to expect the most difficult temptations from the other church kids, rather than from the kids who didn't attend church. That had been his dad's experience. The kids of the world didn't expect Greg to smoke or do drugs; they knew where he stood and respected his position. But some of the church kids would say, "Come on Greg, have a smoke; give it a try."

Greg was faithful to the Lord. A mother of one of Greg's friends thanked his mother for allowing him to be her son's friend. She said that since Greg was associating with her son, she saw a big difference in him. Her son had become more respectful, and his grades had improved. Greg is now serving the Lord as a church planter and has won many to the Savior.

～

Much of my training as a pastor placed little emphasis on leadership. We were taught to be enablers rather than leaders. Elmer Towns, a seminary professor and author of many books about reaching the unchurched, believes that a leader "should be authoritative without being authoritarian. When the pastor realizes he is an under shepherd, receiving authority from the Word of God, he gives an authoritative leadership to his church. When the pastor localizes power in his personality, he gives authoritarian leadership to the church."[1]

I have stressed in this book the importance of pastors being leaders. Every team needs a captain. For the church to grow, it needs strong turnaround leaders. They come with different temperaments, personalities, gifts, and ages. Turnaround leaders believe that Jesus can change people. They are confident, not arrogant. They know where they stand. They have clear convictions and a clear sense of what God wants to do through his people.

Proud people don't demonstrate a dependence on God. Self-confident people are usually aware of their weaknesses, but they have experienced God's power and blessing in their ministry. They know their limitations and have learned to trust God to use them in spite of their weaknesses. They know the more they give away to others, the more God will give wisdom to them. They are open and transparent. They are free to encourage others, and they know how to celebrate.

Bill Hybels makes a compelling case for pastors to be leaders:

> Most often there is a faithful core of sincere believers who would love to help their church have greater impact, if they just knew what to do. But they don't. So they sit in their comfortable pews, frustrated as they watch a long line of pastors pass through the revolving doors, each devoted to God and willing to study and preach, but none, apparently, challenged or trained (or perhaps gifted) to exercise leadership.
>
> These good people . . . have never been led. They've been preached to and taught. They've been fellowshipped and Bible-studied. They've taken courses on prayer and evange-

lism. But with no one to inspire them, to mobilize them, and to coordinate their efforts, their desire to make a difference for Christ has been completely frustrated.

I believe that the great tragedy of the church in our time has been its failure to recognize the importance of the spiritual gift of leadership. It appears to me that only a fraction of pastors worldwide are exercising the spiritual gift of leadership, organizing the church around it, and deploying church members through it. The results, in terms of church growth and worldwide spiritual impact, are staggering. . . . Other gifts languish, the church becomes inwardly focused and impotent, and unbelievers end up with a one-way, nonstop ticket to the abyss.[2]

George Barna echoes the same theme. In his 1997 book *Leaders on Leadership*, he recounts a long list of Bible doctrines, then writes:

I believe all this and much more. I also believe that in America today, fewer and fewer people will embrace these things unless the Church can raise up strong servant-leaders who will commit their lives to using their natural abilities, marketplace experiences, education, training and spiritual gifts to maximize their call to lead God's people forward.[3]

My observation is that pastors who hear God's call to the pastorate while they are in the business world and then enter the pastorate are just as effective as those who have been trained in Bible college and seminary. How can this be? So much of the effectiveness of leadership has to do with passion and skills. If one is called by God and committed to kingdom building, he or she will study the Word and feed the flock. This is not to discredit education; I am glad for mine, including my doctor of ministry degree. But I have observed many effective pastors called from the business world whom God is using in a powerful ministry. God doesn't seem to call the equipped; rather, he equips the called.

I would choose a person with passion and a servant heart over persons who look at their pastor position as merely a profession.

God is more interested in availability than in ability or education. Always choose character over skills and talents. You can develop skills, but you cannot develop character in another person.

Turnaround leaders are people of faith, vision, and strategy. They know the church will never be strong until it can raise up indigenous leadership. They pray for, seek out, and disciple leaders, just as Jesus did.

Mentor Future Leaders

Few of our congregations are producing pastoral leaders. I believe one of the top priorities of the pastor is to mentor others for leadership. Take time to talk with potential leaders, both youth and adults, and mentor them for ministry. As someone once said, "Success without a successor is failure."

A healthy church will not have a shortage of workers. Jesus admonished us to pray for workers because the harvest is great and the need is urgent; the harvest is now (not four months from now) and it is ripe (see John 4:35). Pastors and their congregations should be prepared to help the potential leaders financially to receive some training.

Leadership transitions can be a difficult time for a congregation. It's helpful if a pastor can mentor a successor, though church polity may limit this. If the pastor has done a good mentoring job, the congregation should recognize gifted people who are ready to step into the pastoral position. The transition may be less traumatic, and the congregation can move ahead smoothly.

Pastoral Authority

Earlier I wrote that Jesus bestowed to all Christians both the position and the power to witness (see Matthew 28:18-20 and Acts 1:8). Many churches have given pastors the position but not the authority to carry out their ministry. Pastors need both to lead effectively. There is a lost world to reach with the Good News. Pastors shouldn't be sitting in endless planning meetings in which committee members fight over who is in charge.

When we place someone in a position of responsibility, they need the power to carry out that responsibility. Without this, we create an impossible situation for them. In chapter 8, I wrote that the pastor is the vision-caster and, along with the leadership team, devises a strategy to implement that vision.

Leading by Example

The apostle Peter writes:

> And now, a word to you who are elders in the churches. I, too, am an elder and a witness to the sufferings of Christ. And I, too, will share his glory and his honor when he returns. As a fellow elder, this is my appeal to you: Care for the flock of God entrusted to you. Watch over it willingly, not grudgingly—not for what you will get out of it, but because you are eager to serve God. Don't lord it over the people assigned to your care, but lead them by your own good example. And when the head Shepherd comes, your reward will be a never-ending share in his glory and honor. (1 Peter 5:1-4 NLT)

We are to lead and care for God's church willingly, eagerly desiring to serve God. We don't dominate people, but we lead them by our example. Peter reminds us that if we do this, our reward will be great.

Jesus tells Peter to prove his love by feeding the sheep (see John 21:15). In Luke 15:3-6, Jesus says the shepherd is to leave the ninety-nine in the fold and search for the one lost sheep. These verses give us a balance between feeding the flock and reaching the lost.

Once the vision of the church is set, leaders walk with the people, encouraging them to use their gifts to carry out that vision. They don't dominate others by insisting only on their own strategies. Turnaround leaders empower people and allow them the freedom to develop strategy according to their giftedness. They are committed to making people's lives more productive. As I've noted several times, God is more concerned about our growth than about our comfort. Leaders are called to make disciples, not to be comforters.

The Pastor's Character and Spouse

Without a strong foundation, a building will fall. Many leadership failures are failures of character. Character is who we are when we think no one is looking. In *Overcoming Barriers to Growth*, Michael Fletcher writes, "Look for people who are FAT—faithful, available, and teachable. Do not be deceived by talent, giftedness and ability. . . . People don't do what you expect; they do what you inspect." Accountability is a must. "Without accountability and further training, even the best leaders will tend to slip backward."[4]

When I was pastoring, I was exceedingly blessed to have a spouse who helped build the church through her gifts of intercession, encouragement, and exhortation. In this way we were a team. When new families entered the congregation, it was a great asset to have a spouse who welcomed them with open arms. I know of churches in which the pastor's spouse has never taken the initiative to greet new members or attendees. No wonder that church has a difficult time growing. The spouse needs to model openness and hospitality for the congregation.

Do the Work of an Evangelist

While you may not have the gift of evangelism, Paul reminds us to do the work of an evangelist (see 2 Timothy 4:5). Even if you are not gifted as an evangelist, ask the Lord to give you opportunities to share your faith. God will open the door if we pray for opportunities. I guarantee that if you pray in the morning for God to bring someone with whom you can share God's love, he will answer that prayer.

Preachers should enable others to share their faith with illustrations from everyday life. For example: "Yesterday while I was waiting in the long checkout line at the grocery store, the person in front of me looked discouraged. I started a conversation with him and found out that his wife and children were ill. I expressed concern and told him I would be praying for his family. I could tell he appreciated this expression of caring. I invited him and his family to church, and he gave me his phone number. Join me in prayer as I keep in touch with this family."

Try to find other models that show the congregation how they can share God's love with people in their daily lives.

The churches in Ethiopia appoint evangelists before they choose pastors. Do you know who the evangelists in your congregation are? Studies indicate that 10 percent of Christians have the gift of evangelism. Identify them, encourage them, and empower them for ministry.

It took me years to have the courage to tell my worship leaders as they met for prayer just before the worship service that I believe it is best for me to meet the people as they enter the church, especially new families. I have all week to pray. Many attendees come to church carrying burdens they will share with the pastor if he or she is available. Sometimes these burdens may be of such a nature that you can include them in the pastoral prayer. Other times, praises for answered prayer might be appropriate to share with the congregation. Sometimes people will share things relevant to the message. Sharing these with the congregation, if the person gives permission, helps make the worship relevant and alive.

Choosing Staff

Create or call staff persons ahead of the actual need for staff. For example, if you believe God is calling your church to reach youth, don't wait until you have thirty youth to bring on a youth leader. Do so when you still have a dozen or fifteen and allow the staff person to grow with the ministry. This person may be a volunteer or paid.

Some questions that you will do well to ask about potential staff persons are: Are people attracted to this candidate? Do people naturally gravitate to him or her, especially before or after the worship service? Can they enlist volunteers easily? Do others seem to follow the candidate? If the answer to any of these questions is no, it is probably best to continue to mentor and develop the candidate.

Someone very wisely said the best time to fire a person is before you hire them. If you find that a staff person just cannot live up to the demands of a position, move them to a position where they can use their gifts in building up the body of Christ. This way people know this is a safe place to serve the Lord.

Values, Convictions, and Passion

A pastor once said, "If you are not crying or broken every day for the lost people in your community, you are not where God wants you." If a leader doesn't bring conviction and passion to the table, the congregation will not move forward. Although others in the congregation may have these qualities, unless they have the authority and platform, their gifts usually remain buried. These people often leave for another church. In order for effective outreach to occur, the pastor needs to model the gift of evangelism and empower believers for this ministry.

I have observed situations in which the lead pastor is maintenance-oriented. When the associate pastors come with passion for reaching the community, the maintenance lead pastor stifles this vision. When this happens, the associate either resigns or judicially waits until he or she is called to the lead pastor position. It's extremely difficult for a congregation to be missional without clear vision from the leadership.

We all have values, but missional leaders need more than that; they need convictions. Note the difference between values and convictions that Gene Wood and Daniel Harkavy point out in *Leading Turnaround Teams*:

As a person of conviction and passion, Jesus worked with the slow-learning disciples. We need to hold our convictions humbly and realize that we may not have all the light on any given situation.

Values	Convictions
Will commit to...	Will sacrifice for...
Will contemplate the cost of...	No cost is too great...
Are negotiable...	Non-negotiable...
Ask others to subscribe...	Expect/demand others to subscribe...
Decided by the group...	Decided by the individual...
For a season...	For a lifetime...
Can be changed by vote...	Cannot be changed...
External compliance acceptable...	Internal ownership essential...
Can be political...	Never political...
Can remain if changed...	Cannot remain if changed...[5]

Equip the Saints, Mobilize the Laity

Paul writes that Jesus gave the gifts of apostles, prophets, evangelists, pastors, and teachers to build up the church (see Ephesians 4:11-12). Jesus says in Luke 10:2 and Matthew 9:37-38 that we are to pray for workers so the Lord can send them to the harvest, which is great. Pastors must pray to find a group of men and women who can be trained, discipled, and empowered for ministry.

One of my greatest mistakes in my younger years as pastor was not tapping people on the shoulder, encouraging and empowering them to use their spiritual gifts in ministry. I am convinced that the necessary spiritual gifts are usually present in the body of Christ to move the congregation forward. Pastors and leaders need to search them out and release them for operation in the body of Christ.

Effective leaders understand the necessity of getting things done through others. Pastors must operate from their strengths and find others to supply the gifts they lack. Leaders need to pray for the Holy Spirit to enlighten their eyes to see the gifts of others, then pray for courage to challenge those Christians to step out and use their gifts.

Working with Those Who Disagree

If the pastor and the leadership team have prayed and agreed on a specific direction and some in the congregation do not agree with it, then the leaders need to talk with those in disagreement. More importantly, perhaps, leaders need to *listen* to those who disagree. After you understand their concerns, repeat their concerns back to them in your own words and ask if you have understood them correctly. If possible, offer a compromise, as in Acts 15. If this is not an option, ask if they will cooperate even though they don't agree. Often the gesture of listening and understanding helps dissenters become more open to working along with you. A person who feels understood feels loved.

There are times when it may be best to postpone a decision for the sake of unity. If you feel time is of the essence, move ahead while praying for God's grace and making every effort to maintain the unity of the body.

Paul told Titus, "Avoid foolish controversies and genealogies and arguments and quarrels about the law, because these are unprofitable and useless. Warn a divisive person once, and then warn him a second time. After that, have nothing to do with him" (Titus 3:9-10). A divisive person is someone who, more than just disagreeing, threatens the unity of the church. This person must be confronted, and if he or she does not repent, needs to be warned twice. Then, as Paul says, he or she needs to distance themselves from the body.

Difficult persons, sometimes referred to as "EGR" persons ("extra grace required"), gravitate toward smaller congregations. In small congregations it's easier for EGR persons to gain a platform. EGR persons disrupt the church more easily than in a larger congregation. In larger congregations it's usually easier for the leadership team to listen, offer love, then gently but firmly say, "We understand your concern, but we have decided to move in this direction."

One helpful way to foster unity in the congregation is to see that everyone is serving where they are gifted. When the disciples were fighting about who would be greatest in the coming kingdom, Jesus taught them that the one who serves is greatest (see John 13). When people think about others and serve them, they don't have time for criticism.

In *Leading Turnaround Churches*, Gene Wood writes, "What is required for any size church is a leader with a fire in his gut for redemption of lost souls. This passion will likely be what sustains him in the heat of the spiritual battle. There is no turnaround without pain. The godly leader, therefore, accepts the role of a surgeon. The body of Christ must be made well."[6]

Power struggles can also affect church unity. These are different than conflicts that arise with EGR people. Most struggling churches have at least one bully in the congregation. Bullies get some of their self-worth by keeping the church intimidated. Often the leadership sees clearly who this person is but is not willing to confront them.

Too often we let a few people insist on keeping the status quo, which stymies the entire church. A leader needs to have the courage to deal with such persons in love but not let them control the church or hinder the vision.

Paul frequently warned the churches he planted against disunity:

> And now I make one more appeal, my dear brothers and sisters. Watch out for people who cause divisions and upset people's faith by teaching things that are contrary to what you have been taught. Stay away from them. Such people are not serving Christ our Lord; they are serving their own personal interests. By smooth talk and glowing words they deceive innocent people. (Romans 16:17-18 NLT)

Putting up with divisive individuals is like needing surgery: painful as it is, you must operate so the church can be healthy. Paul cautions, "Take note of those who refuse to obey. . . . Stay away from them so they will be ashamed. Don't think of them as enemies, but speak to them as you would to a Christian who needs to be warned" (2 Thessalonians 3:14-15 NLT).

Burnout

Burnout comes not from overwork but from work with little or no results. It's remarkable how much work you can do when you see results and know you are doing God's will. At the same time, it is necessary to live a balanced life. Are you disciplined? Do you take time to pray and feed your spirit to hear from God? Do you have an accountability partner? What about your body? Are you exercising? Is your spouse your best friend?

Burnout is one reason pastors move to another church. They often move to get a fresh start. I know that was true for me. But unless we are able to change our style of leadership and empower others, we will find ourselves just as overworked as in the previous church.

Author Bob Russell describes it well:

> When our church was small, I visited every member who was in the hospital. I loved to hear people say to me, "Bob, you were really good to me when I was in the hospital. I'll never forget it." Now I seldom go to the hospital. When I do, it's usually because a staff member or church leader is ill. . . . The only time I visit other members is when they are near death's door. I joke with our members, "You don't want to see me coming when you're in the hospital. That's not usually good news."
>
> Now when I see people in the hall, they'll say, "Hey, I was in the hospital recently for about a week." I'll cringe, afraid they're going to criticize me for not coming to visit them. But then they'll say, "The church was really good to me." Which is better—for a member to say, "Bob, you were really good to me," or "Bob, the church was really good to me"?[7]

Meetings

I have been amazed at the shoddiness of many leadership meetings. Here are some elementary principles that are so often broken:

- Begin on time, even if everyone is not there.
- Agendas are powerful tools. Give considerable thought to the agenda and email it ahead of time so team members can give prayer and thought to it before the meeting.
- Agendas need to give highest priority and greatest time to mission issues. Routine issues are relegated to the last part of the meeting.
- Dwell in the Word. God's Word is our authority. We need to apply it to our context. See chapter 1 for an explanation of "Dwelling in the Word."
- Pray for guidance. Don't use only bookend prayers that open and close the meeting. Pray throughout the meeting as items come to the floor. When it is obvious that God has led the team to a clear decision, stop and thank God for the wisdom and unity he gave you. When you are stymied, stop and ask

the Holy Spirit for wisdom. This sounds so simple, but you may find it hard to break old habits, especially if you have people on your team who do not understand the power of praise and prayer.

- Encourage diversity of ideas, but discourage the clash of personalities. If a discussion is heated, cool it by asking a neutral person about his or her feelings on the issue.
- Allow digression but control the length. The restlessness of the group members is a good indicator that you need to get back to the agenda.
- After each item, restate the decision. This helps the group feel they have accomplished something.
- Deal with a negative person by agreeing that they may have pointed out a problem and ask for possible solutions. If someone is clearly angry, find something in what he or she says that you can agree with. You may want to ask why he or she feels so strongly about the issue and if they see a solution to this situation. Tell them you appreciate their willingness to share, and then move back to the agenda.
- As much as possible, do not read reports. They should have been emailed with the agenda so they can be read ahead of time.
- Conclude by pointing out one or two things that were accomplished.
- Have the secretary email the minutes as soon as possible; within 24 hours is best. This helps to prevent future discussion about whether an item was recorded accurately.
- The secretary or pastor communicates via phone, email, or in person to anyone whose ministry was affected by a decision.
- Minutes are placed at a designated place where everyone can read them.

Use of Time

One of my biggest mistakes as a young pastor was not delegating more responsibility so I could have more time relating to the unchurched. As pastor I felt it was my responsibility to do much of the work in the gathered community, which is what they were paying me for. But this is neither biblical nor practical. Churches cannot grow this way. Pastors are to equip the saints for the work of ministry in the world as well as in the gathered body (see Ephesians 4:11-12).

Pastors and many church leadership teams often spend much of their time with negative people, who are most strongly motivated to make their feelings known. The leadership team agenda is nothing more than responding to these problems. On the opposite end of the spectrum are people who are gifted in spiritual wisdom and expertise, but they are too busy to come forward. Go to them for their insightful and helpful counsel. One of the secrets of time management is making a list of the things you do *not* need to do. Pastors need to delegate and empower.

Empowering People

It's important to trust in people's desire to please and serve the Lord. Give them opportunities in which they can experiment, but walk with them so they do not hurt themselves or others. If they don't do well, it doesn't reflect on the leadership. But take some risks.

In larger missional congregations, the role of the lead pastor should be to lead the church to all God has called it to be. Therefore, associate pastors should handle duties such as hospital visitation, counseling, weddings, and funerals. The senior pastor empowers the associates and elders for their leadership ministry. The leaders then empower and release the congregation for ministry.

We err by not empowering our people. If we examine our hearts about this, we may see that we want to maintain control. Let's pray for the Lord to open our eyes to see the laborers among us and for wisdom to discern the passion of our members and send them forth in ministry.

When there is a need for workers, congregational leaders often place an announcement in the program stating the need. This is not usually the best approach, because someone without the ability to serve in the announced capacity may volunteer; then it will be difficult to explain why we need to say no to him or her. When that happens, try to find another area of ministry in which this volunteer can serve effectively.

It usually takes more than an announcement to find qualified volunteers. Pastors know their sheep. Elders need to give pastors some freedom to invite persons to ministry positions. This is one way we affirm people—by believing in others more than they believe in themselves.

Recruit people to a dream, not just a job. Ask people to lay down their lives for the task of making planet earth a better place. Challenge them to give up their convenience and time to invest in the great commission.

Dan Kimball writes about churches that help clean city streets, parks, and graffiti walls. Others went to a local public school and helped wherever they could. One teacher said, "If that is Christianity, tell me how to be part of it." The time has come when people won't ask what denomination the church is part of; rather they will ask what you are doing for the poor and marginalized. We will become known for what we are for rather than what we are against.[8]

The best recruiting is done individually, face to face or on the phone, but always heart to heart. Try not to start with positions that need to be filled, forcing people into pigeonholes. Start with the person, and see where God would have them serve. Know their spiritual gifts, offer them options, and challenge them to help build God's kingdom. And allow them to say no if they believe it is not the right time.

The congregation does the work of ministry. Pastors need to spend time leading and building relationships with unchurched families. When the congregation observes the passion of the pastor, it is encouraged by the joy in sharing Christ with the unchurched.

Commissioning

An integral aspect of the gospel is the joy of being sent. As I wrote earlier, I believe the church of the future will focus on *sending* rather than *gathering* saints. The word *sent* appears two hundred times in the New Testament. Jesus was very conscious of being sent by the Father, and we need to be conscious that Jesus sends us.

Most churches commission people going into long-term missions work, but those going for short terms should be commissioned too. Commission those called to help plant a church even if it belongs to another denomination. During the commissioning service, call these persons to the front and lay hands on them. Point out that missional churches minister beyond themselves because we are all sent and commissioned by God to serve him.

The Effects of Congregational Size

In *One Size Doesn't Fit All*, Gary McIntosh compares small (15-200), medium (201-400), and large churches (401 or more). He finds that major changes occur when the size of the congregation changes.

The pastor in a small church is an "errand runner," in a medium church an administrator, but in a large church a leader. Most pastors are strong relational persons, but they are often bogged down in administrative and organizational tasks and meeting with one committee after another. There are others in the congregation, if we find them, who can do many of these things better than the pastor.

Leadership in small churches resides in key families, usually longtime members of the church. For the pastor to become the leader, he or she needs to earn the respect of the patriarchs and matriarchs of the church. In medium-sized churches leadership resides in committees, and in large churches it resides in select leaders or staff. In small churches you look for volunteers and train them; in medium and larger churches you look for leaders. These leaders are mentored as they carry out the church's vision. But the elders need to release their pastor to lead alongside them, as a team.

Change in the small churches comes from the bottom up, through key people. In medium-sized churches, it comes through key committees, and in large churches through key leaders. One of the miracles in moving Cottage City Mennonite Church to Laurel, a town ten miles away, was that there was a unanimous vote to make this move. It was nothing less than a miracle for this congregation of seventy years. One reason it happened is because I went to each family and personally sought their opinion. I knew this would assure a positive outcome. Of course, in medium and large churches, it would be difficult and perhaps impossible to visit with each family. Those decisions are made in committee or staff meetings.

Growth comes through relationships in small churches. In medium churches, it often comes through programs and ministries. But in large churches, it often comes through proclamation. Once I was working with a small church in which a few members went and cleaned the yard for a woman whose husband died. The following Sunday she showed up at the church, and now members are relating to her. I believe it is easier for this new widow to relate to this smaller body of hospitable believers than to a larger congregation of several hundred members. If the larger congregation had small care groups, however, she'd be welcomed and cared for just as well.

Decisions in small churches are made by the congregation and driven by history. In medium churches they are made by committees and driven by need. In large churches decisions are made by staff and driven by vision.[9]

Dedication of Leadership Team

Often leadership teams of smaller congregations meet monthly. I am convinced a church cannot be missional with its leadership meeting so infrequently. If the church is to move from lukewarm to hot, from maintenance to missional, its leadership needs to be crying out to God for a spiritual breakthrough to reach the community. When this breakthrough comes, situations needing attention often arise daily, even in smaller missional congregations. Issues come up that can't wait for two, three, or four weeks before action is taken. But even if the pastor is empowered to make decisions, he or she will need to counsel with the leadership team if only for the sake of communicating the needs so they can join the pastor in prayer.

One important reason that Capital Christian Fellowship grew from forty-five to more than four hundred is because we had a dedicated leadership team that began meeting every two weeks. After several months, the agenda was so full we met every Friday morning at 6:30 for more than two hours, time that was possible because people had flextime at work. As pastor I usually sent the agenda via email so the team knew what was coming. We prayed together, ate together, and discussed church life in general. The agenda usually listed the new families who came the previous Sunday, making the leadership team acquainted with their names. Attendance figures and offerings were included, and if either were down we sought to discern the reason.

In these weekly leadership meetings we frequently discussed a chapter of a church growth book like Rick Warren's, *The Purpose-Driven Church*, Bob Russell's *When God Builds a Church*, or Wayne Schmidt's *Ministry Momentum*. We were continually trying to apply these to our context. I often left those meetings thanking God for a core of dedicated leaders to help carry the responsibility of pastoring. The revitalization of Cottage City Mennonite Church would not have happened without their dedication.

Sometimes a leader may feel the pressures of work or other obligations more than their commitment to a leadership position. Bill Hybels describes what he does in such situations. He says something like: "I'm sorry things are so tense at work. Let's pray right now about the challenges you're facing. But don't forget that thousands of Willow Creekers need you to show up tonight, fresh, prayed up, and ready to give your best energy and creativity to the challenges that affect the future of the church."[10] Church members need to be challenged to remember that kingdom work must be given high priority.

Pastoral Relations

Churches do not grow when pastors stay for short terms of two or four years. It usually takes several years before the congregation trusts a pastor who has not grown up in that congregation. Especially in smaller congregations, a pastor needs an extended time of earning trust before leading the congregation into permanent growth.

A church will not have an impact until it is recognized as a vital part of the community. I have seen groups of dedicated Christians serve sacrificially for many years but with little success because they never really become integrated into the local culture. When leadership indigenous to the culture has been called, the pastor can expand the staff or move on to plant another church or serve another pastorate.

When a pastor resigns, it is best if he or she moves on and allows the new pastor to lead. Lyle Schaller writes, "Of all the leadership transition mistakes, two occur most frequently: (1) leaders tend to stay too long in a position rather than not long enough. (2) Leaders who stay too long do much more damage than those who don't stay long enough."[11]

Many congregations choose a pastoral relations team of three to five mature people, including one youth, to relate to the pastor and his or her family. This team meets with the pastor and their spouse usually three times a year to discern the health level of the family and to work through any questions or problems. If there is dissatisfaction, the team will try to face it realistically and work toward remedies.

For Discussion

1. Many pastors leave the pastorate because they can't meet the demands of the congregation and become discouraged. What can you do individually or as a church to help remedy such situations?

2. Do you pray regularly for your pastoral leaders and the leadership team? How can you foster prayer and loving support for them?

3. Every pastor needs a team of leaders to help set the vision and model it for the congregation. Discuss how you can encourage the leadership to empower people for ministry and encourage members to accept responsibility for ministry.

14

Conclusion

Dwelling in the Word: Read Acts 8:1b, 4-8.

Testimony

Andy came from a very poor family. As a child he went to a conservative Mennonite church, but he complained about it a lot. I asked him why he continued to attend. "They were the only people who loved me," he said. Andy went off to war in Vietnam and experienced indescribable horrors. Upon returning he was a leader in the Hell's Angels motorcycle gang. I spent hours with Andy, and he often repented on his knees for things he had done. He was married to a beautiful woman, but because of his intense jealousy and frequent fits of rage, she finally left him. Andy was incensed and employed a "hitman" to kill his wife. Ironically the hitman turned him in to the police, and Andy has been behind bars for many years now. I have not seen him since we moved from that area, but I feel Andy is crying out to God for mercy. I have to leave people like Andy in God's hands. He is the final judge.

～

In Ezra 3, the Israelites are returning from exile to their homeland. They learned that God would not protect them unless they obeyed him. Upon their return to Jerusalem, the first thing they did was build an altar and offer daily sacrifices to the Lord, as Moses had instructed them. The people sought God's guidance, rededicating themselves to living as he commanded and asking him to forgive their sins. They realized the importance of obeying God not merely out of habit but from the heart.

Notice that they built the temple first before rebuilding the city wall, a major project undertaken by the returned exiles. They knew that without God, the strongest wall would not protect them. They knew their spiritual lives were a higher priority than national defense. For a church to turn around, we too must first "build the altar" and dedicate ourselves daily to the Lord. Just as it took time for the returned exiles to lay plans for rebuilding the temple, another major project, we must take time, perhaps many months, to seek the Lord's vision and discern strategy for a church's revitalization.

After the exiles made their plans, young and old worked together (verses 8-9). We likewise need to own the vision and work together. If young and old do not work together, the church will be greatly hindered; many such congregations will eventually die.

When the foundation of the temple was laid, there was celebration with shouts of joy and sounds of weeping. Why weeping and rejoicing at the same time? The younger people were celebrating, and the older ones were weeping. Both were appropriate. The older people who had seen Solomon's temple fifty years before remembered how beautiful it was compared to this temple. Today the older people remember when their church was full and the congregation was growing with lots of children. For them, the new life in the church may not yet measure up to this former glory.

In verse 10, when the foundation was finished, the priests wore spotless vestments; trumpets blared while the Levites were clanging cymbals. They took their places to praise the Lord, as prescribed by King David. "With praise and thanksgiving they sang to the Lord: 'He is good; his love to Israel endures forever'" (Ezra 3:11). There was unity as they praised God together.

Is your congregation ready to work together? Encourage older members to empower youth who are committed to the Father even though they may do things quite differently. God will bring renewal to a dying church if we work together and celebrate the steps we are taking to bring new life.

A Word to Lay Leaders

You may be saying, "I want to follow some of the principles set forth in this book, but I'm not the lead pastor. What can I do?" Take the principles of this book and apply them to the area of ministry in which you are already involved. Whether you're a Sunday school teacher, a small group leader, a worship team leader, or a youth worker, pray for wisdom to take creative steps in moving your ministry from an internal focus to one that ministers to the unchurched.

If you lead a small group, model what it means to build friendship with those who don't know Christ. Lead your group not only in regular Bible study, but also come together at least once every month or two for ministry outside the church walls. Spend time relating to a lonely person, helping a single mother, or getting to know those at a youth correction facility, prison, hospital, or nursing home. If someone in the group has an unchurched friend who likes to bowl, or golf, or play volleyball, schedule an evening for these activities.

Use your influence to move people from church work to the work of the church. Move them into ministry. They will be energized. Pray for your ministry to be a model for other ministries in the congregation. I have seen a youth group become the driving force of a congregation. Pray for and communicate with the senior pastor and the leadership team so they feel part of what is happening and hopefully catch the vision God has given you.

Prayer

John Wesley said, "God will do nothing but in answer to prayer." Prayer is the work, and everything we do after that is simply gathering in the results. But let's be honest: we don't really believe in prayer. If we did, our prayer times would be crowded with participants. While God is self-sufficient, he has chosen to limit his work according to our faith. It is often hard to believe that God is at work now. But faith begins when the Holy Spirit brings possibilities to our minds that are expressed in our prayers. These prayers must be followed by actions as we walk in obedience to God's will. To be missional, we must put shoe leather to our prayers and take Holy Spirit-directed risks.

Prayer is a two-way street, not the monologue that is characteristic of prayer in our worship services. We pray and expect God to listen. We must learn to hear his voice in personal time with God. In John 10:3 Jesus said his sheep recognize his voice. This implies *intimacy*: "in-to-him-you-see."

We have been taught that the Bible is the only word of God. The Bible doesn't always give us answers for the situations we encounter each day. Therefore we need to hear his still, small voice in our spirits. Of course, this voice will never contradict the written Word of God. Jesus said the Spirit "will guide you into all truth" (John 16:13). But we are often wary of trusting the Spirit because of persons who have abused its gifts. This caution cuts off the power supply for effective ministry.

The church will not be missional unless people have a passion to pray for its mission. Intercessors must stand in the gap. Pastors need to discern those in the congregation who have this gift and utilize it. John Dawson writes,

> When we minister in a given city we . . . are hindered by the spirits oppressing the people, until we discern the nature of the enemy's deception and "bind the strong man" by acting in the opposite. To overcome the enemy we must resist temptation then continue in united, travailing prayer until we sense that we have gained authority and that God has broken through.[1]

I know of one man who for twenty years has come to his church once a week at six o'clock in the morning to pray for revival. God will not overlook those prayers. Pray for workers and the unchurched using people's names and bringing their needs to our Father. Pray in the morning for God to give you eyes to see and ears to hear the hurting people you will meet today, as well as the courage to reach out to them with the love of Jesus. He will answer! To pray without believing that God is already at work is to pray in vain. To pray with the eye of faith is to see the possibilities of each person as God sees them.

God hears our instant prayers, the ones we say on the run. Often those prayers are self-focused and seldom grow out of the heart of God. Prayers that grow from the heart of God usually grow out of meditation. Jesus often spent extensive times of prayer. Likewise, we will not find God's will for our lives or our churches without seasons of prayer.

A church's pastors and the leadership team must give priority to prayer, which unleashes the awesome power of the limitless resources of heaven's unstoppable forces. George Hunsberger describes one congregation:

> Sometimes as many as one hundred [members] gather and in smaller clusters walk the streets of the urban strip a few blocks away, or the neighborhood bungalows, or the newer monster homes, praying as they go. They pray for shopkeepers, for civic officials, for corporations, for older residents on fixed income, for young families starting out, for wealthy new Asian immigrants, for whomever comes to their attention as they walk and watch and listen.[2]

Walter Hobbs writes of a congregation that has adopted Brother Charles' prayer of abandonment as its "prayer of surrender":

> Father, I abandon myself into your hands; do with me what you will. Whatever you may do, I thank you; I am ready for all, I accept all. Let only your will be done in me and in all your creatures. I wish no more than this, O Lord. Into your hands I commend my soul; I offer it to you with all the love of my heart, for I love you, Lord, and so need to give myself, to surrender myself into your hands, without, reserve and with boundless confidence, for you are my Father.[3]

Peter Wagner writes:

> Christian leaders need the spiritual protection that comes
> through specific, intentional prayer for them as individuals.
> Nothing threatens the devil more than effective prayer. . . . As
> soon as aggressive Christian leaders move into action prayer,
> teaching and modeling the rules of prayer and installing intense,
> systematic prayer ministries in their churches . . . the world of
> darkness takes note. Satanic attacks of all kinds that may not have
> been noticed at all in the past may begin in earnest. Demonic
> forces may issue what amounts to a declaration of war![4]

The body of Christ must wage warfare against these principalities and powers if we are to be overcomers. How often I have
thanked the Lord for a praying church. May God help us to be
people of fervent prayer!

Fasting

My experience with fasting has been limited, so I have so much
to learn. Scripture mentions fasting scores of times. Jesus fasted (see
Matthew 4), the apostles, prophets and teachers in Antioch fasted
(see Acts 13:2-3), and Daniel fasted (see Daniel 9:30).

Jesus said, "*When* you fast . . ." (Matthew 6:1), not "*if* you
fast." From accounts of persons and churches that practice this discipline on a regular basis I have no question that God blesses those
who seek him earnestly with times of fasting.

Peter Wagner writes:

> What did Daniel's prayer and fasting set in motion? In
> response, God sent Daniel His answer: heavenly hosts to the
> rescue. The angel said he had been dispatched the minute
> the prayer had started. You might say that Daniel started the
> battle by praying, pleading with God.
>
> The Lord sent an answer, and then Satan countered by
> sending an opposing force to interfere with God's plan. For
> 21 days the battle raged, out of Daniel's sight. So the battle
> against the evil forces, in this case the prince of Persia, was
> obviously not Daniel's.[5]

Dake's Study Bible gives an interesting comment here: "All wars lost or won on earth are results of wars that are won or lost by the heavenly army. The battles are fought in the heavenlies, between Satan's angels and God's angels, not down here."[6]

It appears that there is a clear relationship between fasting and breaking the power of demonic forces against the church.

Our Greatest Enemies

I believe there are strongholds that can bind churches. The first is the gospel of good works.

Did you ever notice that Paul complimented every church, including the very carnal Corinthians (see 1 Corinthians 1:4-9), but he never complimented the Galatians? I believe it's because he was exasperated with the Galatian church. Christians there were replacing faith in Jesus with faith in good works, and this was more serious than the sinful carnality and wickedness in the Corinthian church. Let's be aware of the stronghold of a *gospel of works*, which is a false gospel. In Galatia, some believers set aside the work of Christ on the cross with their insistence of obedience of obeying the law to be saved. "You who are trying to be justified by law have been alienated from Christ; you have fallen away from grace" (Galatians 5:4; see also 3:11-12; 4:9-11).

A second prevalent stronghold is *cultural religiosity*—the unwillingness to give up cultural traditions in order to reach our unchurched neighbors. Older congregations especially, but not exclusively, are subject to living on the memory of the church's good old days. Throughout the Bible and especially in the book of Acts, the Holy Spirit was creative. He was characterized by Jesus as wind, which we cannot guide or control. Because we are more comfortable with whatever we can explain and control, we tend to be uncomfortable with the creative working of the Holy Spirit. We lock into our traditions, interpretations, preferences, and viewpoints. And the longer we live with them, the more sure we are in the rightness of our perspective. When others come with different interpretations or viewpoints, we resist them and label them as unorthodox.

All of us need to search our hearts, confess our sins, and continually guard against this spirit of religious pride. It cannot bring Jesus into the hearts of people. No church can be healthy with it.

Another stronghold on the church is *lack of unity* within the body of Christ. Just before he gave his life on the cross, Jesus prayed for the unity of his church (see John 17). Satan loves it when we squabble and quarrel. We are more comfortable with our internal conflicts than we are being obedient to our mission in the world. May the Holy Spirit help us to make that mission our first thing. Then most of our differences will be drowned in God's love for reaching a lost world.

A fourth enemy is the *anti-Christian culture* in which we all live. Jesus sends us into the culture as lambs among wolves. Perhaps we will understand better what that means in the near future. As the culture moves away from Christian values, we will be persecuted for our values, like upholding heterosexual marriage, or maintaining that homosexual relationships, premarital sex, witchcraft, idolatry, fits of rage, selfish ambition, drunkenness, and the like are all sinful activities (see Galatians 5:19-21). Every Christian must become a missionary if our nation is to turn from darkness to light.

A fifth stronghold is that of the *social gospel*, which places emphasis on material needs and neglects the spiritual. It's a century-old movement of Christians who give priority to solving social problems such as poverty and injustice over traditional evangelism's focus on salvation of the soul. It is easier for us to work on these social efforts independent of God than to engage in spiritual warfare (see Ephesians 6:10-18). Watchman Nee, who has been a powerful influence in my life, wrote that while the church in Acts carried out relief efforts for the poor in Jerusalem and elsewhere, they were temporary. As K. P. Yohannan writes:

> The trouble with the *social gospel* . . . is that it seeks to fight what is basically a spiritual warfare with weapons of the flesh. Our battle is not against flesh and blood or symptoms of sin like poverty and sickness. It is against Lucifer and countless demons who struggle day and night to take human souls into a Christ-

less eternity. . . . If we intend to answer man's greatest problem . . . with rice handouts, then we are throwing a drowning man a board instead of helping him out of the water.

A spiritual battle fought with spiritual weapons will produce eternal victories. This is why we insist upon restoring a right balance to Gospel outreach. The accent must first and always be on evangelism and discipleship.[7]

Humanitarian efforts are of little eternal value unless they are energized by God's Holy Spirit and keep pointing people to Jesus as the primary focus.

You *Can* Be Missional

God has a preferred future for each individual congregation. Your future is unique to your church. Because the Holy Spirit is creative, you might not follow any of the options presented in this book. Or you might end up with a composite of ideas from several places so no one person can be credited for the congregation's missional process. Then you can truly say "It seemed good to the Holy Spirit and to us" (Acts 15:28).

As I stated at the beginning of this book, church revitalization is often painful, but it is the most rewarding investment you will ever make. After fifty years of pastoring growing congregations, I am more optimistic than ever that the unchurched "are ripe for harvest" (John 4:35) and that "the harvest is plentiful" (Luke 10:2). These promises of Jesus must motivate us to be workers in the harvest fields.

Through prayer and fasting, God will give us a passion and a strategy to do what it takes to reach our communities. This means we will study the culture of the communities around our churches, and by God's grace and the Holy Spirit's power we will build bridges to those communities. The question is whether we're willing to sacrifice to make it happen. Jesus promised that if we lift him up, he will draw all people to himself (see John 12:32). Now go forward: stay focused on Jesus, step out in faith, and take risks in obedience to the great commission.

God put more in you than you will ever realize. All authority is yours. Cry out to God for his blessing so that you can bless others for eternity!

For Discussion

1. Imagine you are a Pharisee a few years after Jesus' resurrection. You hear the gospel and accept God's plan of salvation. What are some steps you would take? Where would you go from that point? Would you stay with the synagogue or would you leave? Imagine that several families in your synagogue found new life in Jesus Christ. What should your synagogue do? Can you work together in unity to bring new life to your congregation?

2. What have you learned during this study, and what are you going to do with what you learned?

3. Did any of the ten options presented in chapter 5 seem workable for your congregation? Which ones?

4. What direction would you like to see your congregation take to become more missional? What should your congregation do next?

Appendix

This tool can facilitate discussion about congregational perspective and focus. Each item below has two statements about attitudes in the congregation. Circle the number you feel best describes your congregation's perspective. A 1 indicates total agreement with the statement on the left, and a 5 indicates total agreement with the statement on the right.[1]

Unhealthy	Healthy
1. Cares mostly for those in the church	Cares for both insiders and outsiders

    1   2   3   4   5

2. Visitors are strangers   Visitors are guests of God

    1   2   3   4   5

3. Keeps things the same   Flexible

    1   2   3   4   5

4. Insiders versus outsiders   We are for the outsider

    1   2   3   4   5

5. Church facility is for us   Church facility for others too

    1   2   3   4   5

6. Prayer mostly for ourselves   Prayer for ourselves and the unchurched

    1   2   3   4   5

7. Occasional mission projects   Everyone is a missionary

    1   2   3   4   5

8. Emphasize getting it right   Try, evaluate, learn from mistakes

    1   2   3   4   5

9. Long-standing committees   Flexible teams

    1   2   3   4   5

10. Budget dictates ministry   Ministry first, funds follow

    1   2   3   4   5

11. Identified by our heritage   Identified by beliefs and values

    1   2   3   4   5

12. One big, happy family   A community of Christ's people

             1   2   3   4   5

13. Being a member   Being a disciple

             1   2   3   4   5

14. Goal: more members   Goal: Christ-like transformation

             1   2   3   4   5

15. Saving for a rainy day   Now is the time

             1   2   3   4   5

16. Fundraising attitude: we have little   Fundraising attitude: God has given much

             1   2   3   4   5

17. Missions: something we give to   Missions: everything we are and do

             1   2   3   4   5

18. Missions: somewhere out there   Missions: at our doorstep and around the world

             1   2   3   4   5

19. Missions: one of many programs   Missions: the central organizing purpose

             1   2   3   4   5

20. More than 50 percent of money, energy, leadership, attention, programs, and prayers are spent on current members   More than 50 percent of money, energy, leadership, attention, programs, and prayers for those not represented or underrepresented in the church

             1   2   3   4   5

Notes

Preface
1. Chad Hall, "How to Help Your Church Look Upward, Inward, and Outward," www.BuildingChurchLeaders.com.

Introduction
1. Hybels, *Holy Discontent*, 23.

2. Church Innovations' terminology and approach to Scripture is formational rather than informational. Formational reading approaches Scripture humbly with an openness to hear, receive, and respond to the words of God. We read the text aware of God's presence rather than reading the text quickly and unconsciously. We desire to be shaped by the text rather than attempt to control the text based on our desires, wants, or needs. We are a servant of the text rather than master of the text.

Chapter 1:
The Mission Field is Here
1. Billheimer, *Destined for the Throne*, 95.

2. To investigate this method, call New Movers Evangelism at 1-800-856-8614 or go to www.newmovers.org.

Chapter 2:
The First Thing: A Passion for Souls
1. Clegg and Bird, *Lost in America*, 26-29.

2. Clegg and Bird, *Lost in America*, 25.

3. Stetzer and Putman, *Breaking the Missional Code*, 8.

4. Wood, *Leading Turnaround Churches*, 151.

5. Silvoso, *That None Should Perish*, 91-92.

6. Chambers, *My Utmost for His Highest*, October 26.

7. Hattaway, *Back to Jerusalem*, 96.

8. Kimball, *The Emerging Church*, 205.

9. Personal email correspondence on Feb. 14, 2007.

10. Kanagy, *Road Signs for the Journey*, 55-56.

11. Fletcher, *Overcoming Barriers to Growth*, 55.

12. Miller and Schaller, *The Parish Paper* (August 2003), 2.

13. Yohannan, *Revolution in World Missions*, 95-96.

14. Kanagy, *Road Signs for the Journey*, 55-56, 72.

15. Wood, *Leading Turnaround Churches*, 152.

16. Hattaway, *Back to Jerusalem*, 68.

17. Ibid., 128.

Chapter 3:
The Other First Thing: The Great Commandment

1. Warren, *The Purpose-Driven Church*, 208.

2. Miller, *Blue Like Jazz*, 220-21.

3. Kimball, *The Emerging Church*, 69.

4. Richards, *Unlocking Our Inheritance*, 109-10.

5. Clegg and Bird, *Lost in America*, 35.

6. Kanagy, *Road Signs for the Journey*, 106.

7. Longhurst, "What the Church Visitor Saw."

8. Finzel, *The Top Ten Mistakes Leaders Make*, 45.

Chapter 4:
We are Wounded Healers

1. Seamans, *Healing for Damaged Emotions*, 25-35.

2. Barnhart, Elita L. "My Theological Position." Unpublished paper, May 2007.

3. Barclay, *The Daily Study Bible: The Gospel of Luke*, 76.

4. Wright, *How to Get Along with Almost Anybody*, 21.

Chapter 5:
Knowing Our Context

1. Kanagy, *Road Signs for the Journey*, 56.

2. Groeschel, *It: How Churches and Leaders Can Get It and Keep It*, 31.

3. Warren, *The Purpose-Driven Church*, 190-91.

4. Ibid., 179-80.

5. Websites for these two churches are www.theaterchurch.com and www.seacoast.org.

6. Clegg and Bird, *Lost in America*, 19-20.

7. Richards, *Unlocking Our Inheritance*, 217.

8. Hattaway, *Back to Jerusalem*, 108.

9. See, for example, Stevenson, *The Ripple Church*.

10. Stevenson, 11.

11. Ibid., 46.

Chapter 6:
Welcoming Unchurched Neighbors

1. Scott, "The Living God is a Missionary God." Quoted in Crossman, *Perspectives Exposure*, 14.

2. Trebilcock, *The Small Church at Large*, 35.

3. Ibid., 120.

4. Warren, *The Purpose-Driven Church*, 130.

5. Lee, *Theology of Administration*, 5.

6. CCF's website is www.capitalchristian.org.

7. Two books that focus on specific ideas for reaching our community are: Steve Sjogren's *101 Ways to Reach Your Community* from Nav Press and Diana Davis' book *Fresh Ideas: 1000 ways to Grow a Thriving and Energetic Church*, B&H Publishing Group.

8. Kimball, *They Like Jesus But Not The Church*, 32.

9. Kimball, *The Emerging Church*, 207-8.

Chapter 7:
Becoming a Missional Church

1. Clegg and Bird, *Lost in America*, 14.

2. Ibid., 139.

3. Trebilcock, *The Small Church at Large*, 96.

4. Warren, *The Purpose-Driven Church*, 15.

5. Yohannan, *Revolution in World Missions*, 89-90.

Chapter 8:
Church Structures and Relationships

1. Warren, *The Purpose-Driven Church*, 378.

2. Callahan, *Effective Church Leadership*, 218.

3. Rainer, *Essential Church*, 147.

4. Warren, *The Purpose-Driven Church*, 147.

5. Fletcher, *Overcoming Barriers to Growth*, 26.

6. Quoted in Barna, *Leaders on Leadership*, 118.

7. Hattaway, *Back to Jerusalem*, 127-28.

8. Warren, *The Purpose-Driven Church*, 77-80.

9. Groeschel, *It: How Churches and Leaders Can Get It and Keep It*, 64.

10. Barrett, *Treasurers in Clay Jars*, 55.

11. Rainer and Geiger, *Simple Church*, 94-96.

12. www.northpoint.org

13. Bernhard, Fred, Seminar booklet: *Hospitality: Who Me?* Presented at Stumptown Mennonite Church, Oct. 6, 2007, 4.

14. Drescher, "What I Am Learning."

15. Fletcher, *Overcoming Barriers to Growth*, 135.

16. Bernhard, *Hospitality: Who, Me?* 10.

17. Ibid., 16.

18. Ibid., 16.

19. Rainer and Geiger, 157.

20. *The Capital*, April 2007, 6.

21. Warren, *The Purpose-Driven Church*, 146.

22. Wood and Harkavy, *Leading Turnaround Teams*. 14.

Chapter 9:
The Worship Service Part 1: Structure

1. Warren, *The Purpose-Driven Church*, 240.

2. Brant, *Ministering to the Lord*, 19.

3. Kimball, *Emerging Worship*, 4.

4. Ibid., 10.

5. LaMar Boschman, *Future Worship*, 29.

6. Kimball, *The Emerging Church*, 164.

7. Ibid., 164.

8. See *Simple Church* for why fewer announcements are needed if your discipleship track is the focus of your church life.

9. Barrett, *Treasure in Clay Jars*, 124.

Chapter 10:
The Worship Service Part 2: Music and Message
1. Stetzer and Putman, *Breaking the Missional Code*, 51.
2. Russell, *When God Builds a Church*, 31.
3. Kimball, *The Emerging Church*, 284.
4. Trebilcock, *The Small Church at Large*, 61-62.
5. Kimball, *The Emerging Church*, 284.
6. Warren, quoted in *Kimball*, 29.
7. Kimball, *Emerging Worship*, 29.

Chapter 11:
Setting People Free to Use Their Gifts
1. Kroll, *Taking Back the Good Book*, 90.
2. I suggest you go the Peter Wagner Gifts Inventory or the Wesleyan Spiritual Gifts Inventory. See www.fuller.edu. I also recommend Rick Warren's Basic 301 class questionnaire.

Chapter 12:
Dealing with the 'E' Word: Evangelism
1. Jacobs, *Consider Jesus*, 42.
2. Trebilcock, *The Small Church at Large*, 47.
3. Kanagy, *Road Signs for the Journey*, 72.
4. Chambers, Oswald, *My Utmost for His Highest*, entry for January 14.
5. McLaren, *A New Kind of Christian*, 109.
6. Montgomery, *I'm Gonna Let it Shine!*, 91.
7. Ibid., 102.
8. Allen, *Missionary Methods: St. Paul's or Ours*, 48.
9. Montgomery, 77.
10. Ibid., p. 87.
11. Hybels and Mittelberg, *Becoming a Contagious Christian*, 20-25. I am indebted to Hybels and Mittelberg for the material in this section.
12. Bell, *Velvet Elvis*, 31.
13. Quoted in Montgomery, *I'm Gonna Let it Shine!*, 147.

Chapter 13:
Effective Missional Leadership
1. Quoted in Wagner, *Leading Your Church to Growth*, 115-16.

2. Hybels, *Courageous Leadership*, 67-68.

3. Barna, *Leaders on Leadership*, 19-20.

4. Fletcher, *Overcoming Barriers to Growth*, 111.

5. Wood and Harkavy, *Leading Turnaround Teams*, 28.

6. Wood, *Leading Turnaround Churches*, 24.

7. Russell, *When God Builds A Church*, 176-77.

8. Kimball, *They Like Jesus But Not the Church*, 110-11.

9. McIntosh, *One Size Doesn't Fit All*, 143-44. For a similar comparison, see Michael Fletcher, *Overcoming Barriers to Growth*, 48.

10. Hybels, *Courageous Leadership*, 167.

11. Quoted in Finzel, *The Top Ten Mistakes Leaders Make*, 159.

Chapter 14:
Conclusion

1. Dawson, *Taking Our Cities for God*, 20-21.

2. Hunsberger, "Discerning Missional Vocation," in Barrett, *Treasure in Clay Jars*, 54.

3. Hobbs, "Dependence on the Holy Spirit," in Barrett, 125.

4. Wagner, "The Importance of Prayer in Leading People," in Barna, *Leaders on Leadership*, 292-93.

5. Wagner, *Engaging the Enemy*, 79.

6. Ibid., 79.

7. Yohannan, *Revolution in World Missions*, 108-9.

Appendix

1. In *Breakout Churches*, Thom Rainer includes a Church Readiness Inventory to help congregations determine if they are ready to become missional (241-44). A twenty-question readiness tool in *Advanced Strategic Planning* by Aubrey Malphurs may also help your congregation discern if it is ready to move ahead with revitalization (270-78). I encourage you to work through one of these exercises.

Bibliography

Alford, Deann. "What's Next?" *Christianity Today*, October 2006, 82.

Allen, Roland. *Missionary Methods: St. Paul's or Ours?* Grand Rapids, MI: Eerdmans, 1962.

Augsburger, Myron. "Evangelism in a Multireligious Society," *The Mennonite*, April 15, 2008, 8-9.

Baker, Jonny, and Doug Gay. *Alternative Worship: Resources from and for the Emerging Church*. Grand Rapids, MI: Baker Books, 2004.

Barclay, William. *The Gospel of Luke*. Edinburgh: Saint Andrew Press, 1958.

Barna, George, ed. *Leaders on Leadership: Wisdom, Advice, and Encouragement on the Art of Leading God's People*. Ventura, CA: Regal Books, 1997.

———. *Turn-Around Churches: How to Overcome Barriers to Growth and Bring New Life to an Established Church*. Ventura, CA: Regal Books, 1993.

Barrett, Lois Y., ed. *Treasure in Clay Jars: Patterns in Missional Faithfulness*. Grand Rapids, MI: Eerdmans, 2004.

Bast, Robert L. *Attracting New Members*. New York: Reformed Church in America and Church Growth Inc., 1988.

Bell, Rob. *Velvet Elvis: Repainting the Christian Faith*. Grand Rapids, MI: Zondervan, 2006.

Bernhard, Fred. "Hospitality: Who, Me?" Seminar at Stumptown Mennonite Church, Bird in Hand, PA, October 6, 2007.

Billheimer, Paul E. *Destined for the Throne: A New Look at the Bride of Christ*. Christian Fort Washington, PA: Christian Literature Crusade, 1976.

Boschman, LaMar. *Future Worship: How a Changing World Can Enter God's Presence in the New Millennium*. Ventura, CA: Renew Books, 1999.

Brant, Roxanne. *Ministering to the Lord*. New Kensington, PA: Whitaker House, 2000.

Callahan, Kennon L. *Effective Church Leadership: Building on the Twelve Keys*. San Francisco: Jossey-Bass, 1997.

Carmichael, Ralph. *New Church Hymnal*. Waco, TX: Lexicon Music, 1976.

Chambers, Oswald, 1992. *My Utmost for His Highest: An Updated Edition for Today's Language*. Grand Rapids, MI: Discovery House Publishers, 1992.

Clegg, Tom, and Warren Bird. *Lost in America: How You and Your Church Can Impact the World Next Door*. Loveland, CO: Group Publishing, 2001.

Crossman, Meg. *Perspectives Exposure: Discovering God's Heart for All Nations and Our Part in His Plan*. Seattle: YWAM Publishing, 2003.

Davis, Diana. *Fresh Ideas: 1,000 Ways to Grow a Thriving and Energetic Church*. Nashville, TN: B&H Publishing Group, 2007.

Davis, O. James. "32 Quotes on Effective Preaching," www.SermonCentral.com, accessed December 2007.

Dawson, John. *Taking Our Cities for God: How to Break Spiritual Strongholds*. Lake Mary, FL: Creation House, 1971.

Drescher, John, "What I Am Learning." Unpublished paper March 2006.

Eshleman, J. David. "Discovering and Utilizing Spiritual Gifts for Church Planting." DMin diss., Ashland Theological Seminary, Ashland, OH, 1984.

Finzel, Hans. *The Top Ten Mistakes Leaders Make*. Colorado Springs: Communications Ministries, 2000.

Fletcher, Michael. *Overcoming Barriers to Growth: Proven Strategies for Taking Your Church to the Next Level.* Minneapolis: Bethany House, 2006.

Groeschel, Craig. *It: How Churches and Leaders Can Get It and Keep It.* Grand Rapids, MI: Zondervan, 2008.

Guyon, Jeanne. *Experiencing the Depths of Jesus Christ.* Beaumont, TX: The Seed Sowers, 1975.

Haggard, Ted. *Primary Purpose: Making It Hard for People to Go to Hell from Your City.* Orlando, FL: Creation House, 1995.

Hall, Chad. "How to Help Your Church Look Upward, Inward, and Outward." Building Church Leaders website, Christianity Today International, www.buildingchurchleaders.com.

Hattaway, Paul. *Back to Jerusalem: Called to Complete the Great Commission.* Waynesboro, GA: Gabriel Publishing, 2003.

Hession, Roy. *The Calvary Road.* Fort Washington, PA: Christian Literature Crusade, 1974.

Higgs, Liz Curtis. *Slightly Bad Girls of the Bible: Flawed Women Loved by a Flawless God.* Colorado Springs: WaterBrook Press, 2007.

Hybels, Bill. *Courageous Leadership.* Grand Rapids, MI: Zondervan, 2002.

————. *Holy Discontent: Fueling the Fire That Ignites Personal Vision.* Grand Rapids, MI: Zondervan, 2007.

Jackson, Wayne T. *Miracles Do Happen: The Power and Place of Miracles as a Sign to the World.* Shippensburg, PA: Destiny Image Publishers, 2005.

Jacobs, Donald. *Consider Jesus: Daily Reflections on the Book of Hebrews.* Scottdale, PA: Herald Press, 2006.

John, J. "Evangelistic Preaching," www.SermonCentral.com, accessed March 17, 2008.

Johnson, Gregg T. *The Character of Leadership: Six Pillars of a Leader's Character.* Kearney, NV: Morris Publishing, 2003.

Kanagy, Conrad L. *Road Signs for the Journey: A Profile of Mennonite Church USA.* Scottdale, PA: Herald Press, 2007.

Kimball, Dan. *The Emerging Church: Vintage Christianity for New Generations.* Grand Rapids, MI: Zondervan, 2003

————. *Emerging Worship: Creating Worship Gatherings for New Generations*. Grand Rapids, MI: Zondervan, 2004.

————. *They Like Jesus But Not the Church: Insights from Emerging Generations*. Grand Rapids, MI: Zondervan, 2007.

Kotter, John P. *Leading Change*. Boston: Howard Business School Press, 1996.

Kraybill, J. Nelson. "Jesus' Family Values," *Mennonite Weekly Review*, February 26, 2007.

Kuhne, Gary. *The Dynamics of Personal Follow-Up*. Grand Rapids, MI: Zondervan, 1976.

Lawrence, Brother. *The Practice of the Presence of God*. New Kensington, PA: Whitaker House, 1982.

Leadership and Authority in the Church. Scottdale, PA: Mennonite Publishing House, 1981.

Lee, Harris. *Theology of Administration: A Biblical Basis for Organizing the Congregation*. Minneapolis: Augsburg Fortress, 1981.

Longhurst, John. "What the Church Visitor Saw," *OurFaith Digest*, Spring 2007, 19.

Malphurs, Aubrey. *Advanced Strategic Planning: A New Model for Church and Ministry Leaders*. Grand Rapids, MI: Baker, 2005.

Mann, Alice. *The In-Between Church: Navigating Size Transitions in Congregations*. Bethesda, MD: Alban Institute, 1998.

McLaren, Brian D. *A New Kind of Christian: A Tale of Two Friends on a Spiritual Journey*. San Francisco: Jossey-Bass, 2001.

————. *The Last Word and the Word after That: A Tale of Faith, Doubt, and a New Kind of Christianity*. San Francisco: Jossey-Bass, 2005.

McIntosh, Gary L. *One Size Doesn't Fit All; Bringing Out the Best in Any Size Church*. Grand Rapids, MI: Revell, 1999.

Miller, Donald. *Blue Like Jazz: Nonreligious Thoughts on Christian Spirituality*. Nashville: Thomas Nelson, 2003.

Miller, Herb and Lyle E. Schaller. "Resisting Growth Resistance," *The Parish Paper* newsletter, August 2003.

————. "Ministry Teams Are Not Committees." *The Parish Paper*, newsletter, October 2002.

Mittelberg, Mark, and Bill Hybels. *Becoming A Contagious Christian*. Grand Rapids, MI: Zondervan, 1995.

Montgomery, Jim. *I'm Gonna Let it Shine!* Colorado Springs: Dawn Ministries, 2001.

Osborne, Larry. "Sticky Preaching to a Diverse and Moving Target," www.SermonCentral.com,/article.asp?article=a-L_Osborne_06_23_08&ac=true, accessed June 23, 2008.

Rainer, Thom S. *Breakout Churches: Discover How to Make the Leap*. Grand Rapids, MI: Zondervan, 2005.

Rainer, Thom S., and Eric Geiger. *Simple Church: Returning to God's Process for Making Disciples*. Nashville: B&H Publishing Group, 2006.

Rainer, Thom and Sam Rainer III. *Essential Church: Reclaiming a Generation of Dropouts*. Nashville: B&H Publishing Group, 2008.

Richards, Janet Keller. *Unlocking Our Inheritance: Spiritual Keys to Recovering the Treasures of Anabaptism*. Morgantown, PA: Masthof Press, 2005.

Rusaw, Rick and Eric Swanson. *The Externally Focused Church*, Group, Loveland, CO: 2004.

Russell, Bob. *When God Builds A Church: 10 Principles for Growing a Dynamic Church*. West Monroe, LA: Howard Publishing, 2000.

Schmidt, Wayne. *Ministry Momentum: How to Get It, Keep It, and Use It in Your Church*. Indianapolis: Wesleyan Publishing House, 2004.

Seamands, David A. *Healing Damaged Emotions*. Colorado Springs: David C. Cook, 2002.

Silvoso, Ed. *That None Should Perish: How to Reach Entire Cities for Christ through Prayer Evangelism*. Ventura, CA: Regal Books, 1994.

Sjogren, Steve. *101 Ways to Reach Your Community*. Colorado Springs: Nav Press, 2001.

Stetzer, Ed, and David Putman. *Breaking the Missional Code: Your Church Can Become a Missionary in Your Community*. Nashville: Broadman and Holman Publishers, 2006.

Stevenson, Phil. *The Ripple Church*. Indianapolis: Wesleyan Publishing House, 2004.

Stutzman, Ervin R. *Welcome! A Biblical and Practical Guide to Receiving New Members*. Scottdale, PA: Herald Press, 1990.

Sullivan, Bill M. *Ten Steps to Breaking the 200 Barrier*. Kansas City, MO: Beacon Hill Press, 1988.

Towns, Elmer. *How to Reach Your Friends for Christ*. Lynchburg, VA: Church Growth Institute, 1990.

Trebilcock, Robin J. *The Small Church at Large: Thinking Local in a Global Context*. Nashville: Abingdon Press, 2003.

Warren, Rick. *The Purpose-Driven Church: Growth Without Compromising Your Message & Mission*. Grand Rapids, MI: Zondervan, 1995.

Wagner, C. Peter. *Engaging the Enemy: How to Fight and Defeat Territorial Spirits*. Ventura, CA: Regal Books, 1991.

———. *Leading Your Church to Growth*. Ventura, CA: Regal Books, 1984.

Willard, Dallas. *The Divine Conspiracy: Rediscovering Our Hidden Life in God*. New York: HarperOne, 1998.

Witmer, Dave. *Inspirit Revolution*. Fairfax, VA: Xulon Press, 2006.

Wood, Gene. *Leading Turnaround Churches*. St. Charles, IL: Churchsmart Resources, 2001.

Wood, Gene and Daniel Harkavy. *Leading Turnaround Teams*. St. Charles, IL: Churchsmart Resources, 2004.

Wright, H. Norman. *How to Get Along with Almost Anyone*. Dallas: Word Publishing, 1989.

Yancey, Philip. *What's So Amazing About Grace?* Grand Rapids, MI: Zondervan, 2002.

Yohannan, K. P. *Revolution in World Missions*. Carrollton, TX: GFA Books, 2003.

Young, David S. *Servant Leadership for Church Renewal: Shepherds by the Living Springs*. Scottdale, PA: Herald Press, 1999.

The Author

J. David Eshleman served as a pastor and church planter for fifty years at numerous Mennonite churches in the United States. He helped Capital Christian Fellowship near Washington, D.C., grow from forty-five attendees to more than four hundred. He served as bishop in Lancaster Mennonite Conference from 2006 to 2008 and as a member of the conference's revitalization team. He has served as a church  planter in Ohio and Florida. Dave began work as a church consultant in 2007. He is an adjunct instructor for Eastern Mennonite Seminary at the Lancaster, Pennsylvania campus. Dave holds a degree from Eastern Mennonite Seminary and a doctorate from Ashland Theological Seminary. He lives in Manheim, Pennsylvania.